Tara Croser

Kate Kyriacou has been a journalist since 2001. She has written for newspapers around the country, including the *Sunday Herald-Sun*, the Adelaide *Advertiser* and *Sunday Mail*, and Brisbane's *Courier-Mail* and *Sunday Mail*.

She has been the *Courier-Mail*'s chief crime reporter since 2012 and has won awards, at both a state and national level, for her work as a crime writer.

THE STING

THE UNDERCOVER OPERATION THAT CAUGHT
DANIEL MORCOMBE'S KILLER

KATE KYRIACOU

echo

Echo Publishing
An imprint of Bonnier Books UK
4th Floor, Victoria House, Bloomsbury Square
London WC1B 4DA
www.echopublishing.com.au
www.bonnierbooks.co.uk

Copyright © Kate Kyriacou 2015

Echo Publishing acknowledges the traditional custodians of country throughout
Australia. We recognise their continuing connection to land, sea and waters.
We pay our respects to elders past and present.

First published 2015
This edition published 2018
Reprinted 2022

Printed and bound in Australia by Pegasus Media and Logistics

MIX
Paper from
responsible sources
FSC® C008194

The paper in this book is FSC® certified.
FSC® promotes environmentally responsible,
socially beneficial and economically viable
management of the world's forests.

Edited by Linda Funnell
Cover design by Luke Causby / Blue Cork
Page design and typesetting by Shaun Jury
Internal photographs courtesy of Queensland Police Service unless otherwise credited
Every attempt has been made to trace and acknowledge copyright. Where an attempt
has been unsuccessful, the publisher would be pleased to hear from the copyright
holder so any omission or error can be rectified.

NATIONAL
LIBRARY
OF AUSTRALIA

A catalogue entry for this book is available from the National Library of Australia

ISBN: 9781760681036 (paperback)
ISBN: 9781760067441 (ebook)
ISBN: 9781760067458 (mobi)

🐦 echo_publishing
📷 echo_publishing
f echopublishingaustralia

Contents

*For the 'Joes' and the 'Fitzys', whose faces will never
be shown and whose names will never be known.*

Author's note: Some names have been changed in this account to protect privacy and for legal reasons.

Preface

On Sunday, 7 December 2003, 13-year-old Daniel Morcombe vanished from a bus stop on Queensland's Sunshine Coast. His disappearance sparked the largest police investigation in Queensland's history, and eight years later, on 13 August 2011, resulted in the arrest of pedophile Brett Cowan for abduction and murder. Cowan was eventually sentenced on 14 March 2014 to life in jail with a non-parole period of 20 years.

This is the story of how the police set a trap to catch a child-killer.

PROLOGUE
THE MEETING

SEVEN HOURS OF LONG-BAKED bitumen stretches out between Perth and Kalgoorlie. The sleep-inducing drive from Australia's fourth-largest city to a middle-of-nowhere mining town is one of long open roads where kangaroos dodge road trains with mixed success and fields of wheat eventually make way for desert.

It was Tuesday, 9 August 2011. Paul 'Fitzy' Fitzsimmons and Brett Peter Cowan were an hour down when the shrill of a mobile phone cut across the car's radio.

'It's the boss,' Fitzy told his mate. 'Jeff, how ya going? What's up?'

Brett sat quietly as Fitzy nodded along to instructions.

'Forget about it?' he repeated, his voice rising in surprise. 'Fuck.' He listened some more. 'Oh, rightio. So not even worry about it?' Fitzy pulled the car off the Great Eastern and turned them back to Perth. The job was off. The big boss was in town.

'All right, I'm on my way,' he told Jeff and rang off. He turned to Brett.

'Fucken hell. Arnold wants to have a chat to ya. I didn't even know he was over here,' he said.

Brett seemed unconcerned. Excited even. He'd been working hard these last months. He'd been doing well. They'd all told him so. He'd never done well at anything. And now the big boss wanted to see him.

'Yeah, don't stress about it, fuck,' Fitzy told him. 'Just go tell him, mate, fucken, about all the good shit you've been doing and all that. No one gets the OK to do big, you know, all the decent jobs, without Arnold going yep. I mean, that might be what it's about, man ... that's fucking excellent.'

1

An hour later they were standing in the foyer of Perth's five-star Hyatt Hotel. Plush sofas and bar tables arranged themselves around a stone fountain of elephants, their trunks in a good-luck salute. Smartly attired staff checked in well-dressed professionals. Guests slept in rooms overlooking the Swan River. Manicured gardens and deckchairs surrounded the hotel's sparkling pool.

Fitzy, a short man with a blond ponytail and a surfer's drawl, and Brett, tall and lanky with a drug-user's sunken-eyed sallowness, made their way to the meeting room the big boss had booked for the day.

Arnold dismissed his company — an attractive blonde — as the boys entered the room. He was a big man, dressed in a businessman's suit. Brett took a seat on a long couch, drawing his legs to his chest as he waited for the boss to finish a phone call.

There was a problem, Arnold told him. Brett was a good worker and they wanted him on board. They had a big job coming up. It would be a big earner for everyone. Brett, who'd never had a dime to his name, was looking at big dollars. But the police were sniffing around. Brett was the prime suspect in the disappearance and suspected murder of Sunshine Coast schoolboy Daniel Morcombe. The boy who'd graced television screens, newspapers and milk cartons these past eight years. Heat on Brett meant heat on them. Police scratching about was bad for business for a highly organised criminal gang.

'You're too hot,' Arnold told Brett. 'I'm told that it's deadset that you're the one who's done it.'

Not true, Brett replied. He'd had nothing to do with it.

'I was living in the area in '03 when Daniel Morcombe went missing so I've been interviewed and I was hounded for ages about that and I can guarantee I had nothing to do with Daniel Morcombe's disappearance,' he insisted.

Arnold pushed on. The gang was about trust and loyalty. It's how they'd survived all this time. They all had pasts. They all had a history. Nothing surprised them. Nothing shocked them. They weren't there to judge. They were there to make money, nothing more. He needed Brett to be honest.

'I can sort this for you,' Arnold said. 'You know I can sort things out. I can buy you alibis. I can get rid of stuff, all the kinds of things that can be done, I can do. But I need to know what I need to do, you know what I mean?'

The conversation went back and forth. Brett denied. Arnold pressed. Confess, he said, or they'd drop him. There'd be no big job for Brett. No $100 000 pay day. He'd lose his new mates. His brothers. This new life he'd found. This is what dreams are made of, he'd told them.

Confess, Arnold said. Confess, or walk away.

Brett looked down. His reply was casual. His voice steady. But the words he spoke would change everything.

PART ONE
LITTLE BOY LOST

PART ONE
LITTLE BOY LOST

CHAPTER ONE
DANIEL

TWINS BRADLEY AND DANIEL Morcombe were born on 19 December 1989 at Melbourne's Monash Medical Centre. Both were small enough to fit in the palms of their parents' hands. Bruce and Denise Morcombe would have to wait more than a week to bring their babies home to their two-year-old brother Dean. Weighing just over 1.5 kilograms each, the twins needed careful monitoring in intensive care until doctors were satisfied they were ready to leave.

When Bradley and Daniel were two, Bruce took a redundancy from the Melbourne Metropolitan Board of Works where he'd been employed for 15 years. He used the small payout to buy a Jim's Mowing franchise in Boronia, in Melbourne's eastern suburbs. It was a busy life and the Morcombes worked hard at building their business and raising three young boys.

In 1993, they were offered an opportunity to swap to another franchise territory — on Queensland's Sunshine Coast. Taking up around 60 kilometres of coastline and hinterland, the picturesque Sunshine Coast is 100 kilometres from Brisbane and the third most populous area of Queensland. That number swells in summer months as families descend on beach destinations like Maroochydore and the famed Noosa.

Denise was reluctant to leave Melbourne but it was too good an opportunity to turn down. So the Morcombes moved their young family to Queensland, renting a house in the beachside suburb of Maroochydore for the first few months. The franchise had a small number of mowing clients when Bruce took over, but it was a large district and he got to work building his customer base.

Bruce did well and over the following years broke up his territory to bring in his own franchisees. Denise kept busy booking jobs and running after the three boys. They bought a hobby farm at Palmwoods and made a home there for the family.

Bradley and Daniel developed their own personalities. They were non-identical twins and looked different enough that nobody confused them. Daniel looked more like his mother, inheriting Denise's large, expressive eyes.

Bradley was the more outgoing twin. Daniel was the shy one. More often than not, Bradley would speak for his brother. Daniel was quietly tough. He'd come off his bike, land in a sprawling heap and pick himself up without a word.

He was an animal lover. Bruce and Denise bought ponies for the twins and the boys rode them every second day around the farm. Daniel brought the cats into his room each night and the family's German shepherd, Chief, was his best friend. He'd throw a ball to Chief in the paddocks for hours. They'd sit quietly together, Daniel stroking his fur. Daniel told his mum and dad he wanted to be a vet, and they could see from his quiet, calm manner with the animals he'd make an excellent one.

He was shy around strangers and scared of the dark. Often, at night, he'd come into his parents' room and settle in on the floor.

When the twins were 11 and Dean 13, Keith Paxton, the Morcombes' next-door neighbour, offered them a job. A keen passionfruit farmer, Keith was a commercial grower with vines stretching across his property. He gave the boys work picking ripe fruit off the ground. They would become his best pickers, filling the buckets at the ends of each row with growing speed.

The boys didn't waste the money they earned. They saved and saved, pooling the cash to buy a small motorbike. They'd developed a passion for bikes and would often spend Friday nights at a nearby property owned by a man named Kelvin Kruger, who ran a sandblasting business. Kelvin's property had a natural motocross track in its dips and undulations. On Fridays he had an open-door policy. Workers would drop by and have a beer while bikes skidded around the track.

On 7 December 2003, a Sunday, the Morcombe household was up early. The boys were due at the Paxton farm at 6 a.m. to work on the vines, while Bruce and Denise needed to get ready for the Christmas party they were throwing for their franchisees. They were holding it at Broadwater Picnic Ground in Brisbane's southern suburbs — a large park with play equipment for children and rolling lawn surrounded by trees. It was a busy park, so they planned on leaving home at 8.30 a.m. to make sure they secured a good picnic spot.

The clouds were grey and heavy with water when the Morcombes woke. The phone shrilled through the house just before 6 a.m. Keith Paxton was on the other end. It looked like rain. He told Bruce to send the boys over at 7 a.m. Hopefully the rain would have passed by then. The later start would delay Bruce and Denise, so it was decided the boys would not go with their parents to Brisbane.

The twins were back home just before 10 a.m., hands clutching hard-earned cash. They watched television for a while. Made some food. Wrestled on their parents' bed. It was the beginning of the school holidays and the boys were relaxed and looking forward to weeks on end with nothing to do.

Daniel decided he would go to the Sunshine Plaza — a short bus trip to Maroochydore — to do some Christmas shopping and get a haircut. He asked his twin to go with him, but Bradley wasn't keen to leave the house. He pestered Dean, but he wasn't keen to go either. Dean jumped in the shower and never saw his brother again.

*

At 1 p.m. a little boy in a red Billabong t-shirt and navy blue shorts walked the one kilometre from the driveway of his Palmwoods home to an unofficial bus stop under the Kiel Mountain Road overpass. He followed the concrete path adjacent to the Woombye–Palmwoods Road up to the Nambour Connection Road. There's nothing to mark the bus stop but locals knew the Sunbus stopped at the verge under the overpass, just down from the Christian Outreach Centre.

Daniel arrived in plenty of time. The Sunbus wouldn't come past until 1.35 p.m. His pockets held his wallet with around $100, a phone card with $10 credit and an old-fashioned fob watch he loved to carry around. The watch had been an early birthday present from Bradley. His twin had put money aside to buy it and had had it engraved with the word 'Dan'. Bored, Daniel picked up a stick and used it to draw lines in the dirt. Time passed, 1.35 p.m. came and went. The Sunbus was nowhere to be seen.

After a while, a man came to join him. He was tall and thin and wore his long brown hair in a ponytail. The man lounged against the overpass wall, one leg bent like a stork so his foot rested on the wall. He looked at Daniel. Daniel scratched the ground with his stick.

*

Bus driver Ross Edmonds clocked on at 5.55 a.m. on 7 December 2003 — just before passionfruit grower Keith Paxton, watching the rain clouds gather, picked up his phone to dial the Morcombes.

Ross was nearing the end of his shift when, at 1 p.m., he pulled his Sunbus out of Nambour to head to Maroochydore's Sunshine Plaza. He was driving along the Nambour Connection Road, approaching Woombye's Blackall Street intersection, when he felt the bus give a shudder. The accelerator cable had snapped. He pulled over and grabbed the two-way. They'd need another bus.

The passengers got out and milled around the verge, impatient to get to the shops or catch a movie. It took 25 minutes for a new bus to arrive. It was Sunbus policy to bring a replacement bus to a breakdown, plus a second bus to pick up any waiting passengers.

'You just go direct to Maroochydore,' Jeff Norman, another driver, told Ross. 'We'll do the pick-ups on the other bus.'

They were now 30 minutes behind schedule. Ross boarded the new bus with his impatient passengers, the second bus tailing a couple of minutes behind. Soon, he was driving under the Kiel Mountain Road overpass.

A boy, dressed in a red shirt and dark shorts, stepped forward and waved at him with a stick. A man stood behind him, about three metres back from the road. Ross had to keep going. He pointed behind him, hoping the boy would understand.

'There's another one coming,' he said aloud, knowing his words could not be heard.

Passengers on the bus watched as the boy's shoulders slumped. He kicked at the dirt. Daniel had been waiting a long time and now the bus had left him behind.

Ross picked up the two-way and called the other bus. There was a 'young chap' in a red shirt and a man that needed collecting, he told Jeff. He put the radio down and drove on.

Two minutes later, Jeff Norman slowed his bus as he approached the Kiel Mountain Road overpass. He searched the verge for the passengers. A boy and a man. There was nobody there. He shrugged his shoulders and continued on.

CHAPTER TWO
MISSING

BRUCE AND DENISE ARRIVED home before 4 p.m. to a mostly quiet house. Only Brad was home. He looked up from the computer as they entered.

'Where is everybody?' Bruce asked. Brad told his dad that Dean had gone to a friend's place. Daniel had caught the bus to the Plaza to get a haircut and do some shopping.

They unpacked the car and Bruce settled himself in front of the television. Denise grabbed a clothes basket and made her way out to the clothesline. She stood out in the open with the washing, glancing at the road. Something didn't feel right. Grabbing a load of rubbish, she walked to the end of the driveway. She looked down the street in the direction her son would be walking from the bus stop if he'd caught the early bus home. The road was empty.

Denise went back inside and grabbed the car keys. She told Bruce she was heading to the overpass in case Daniel had caught the earlier bus. She'd save him the walk. The boys were allowed to catch the bus on their own but they had to make sure they made it on to the last bus of the day — the 5 p.m. Buses left every hour from the Plaza and took about 25 minutes to get back to the Woombye–Palmwoods Road. Denise was back within 10 minutes. Daniel had not been on the 4 p.m. bus. He must be catching the 5 p.m., they reasoned.

At 5.30 p.m., Bruce jumped back in the car. He pulled in under the overpass. He sat at the wheel for a few minutes, watching time tick by. There was no sign of Daniel. This time he was worried. Daniel was a reliable kid. It wasn't like him.

Back at the house, he asked Brad about the Sunbus timetable. Was he sure the 5 p.m. bus was the last one? Bruce and Brad got on the computer and looked up an online timetable. It was confusing. They weren't sure.

Denise mentioned she'd seen a broken-down bus when she'd driven to the overpass an hour earlier. She'd taken the long way home and noticed the vehicle abandoned on the side of the road. If they'd lost a bus, maybe the timetable was out. Maybe Daniel had lost his money and hadn't been able to buy a ticket. Maybe he'd run late and hadn't made it on to the 5 p.m. Sunbus. Was he stranded at the Plaza with no way to get home?

They jumped back into the car, Bruce behind the wheel, and drove to the Sunshine Plaza. They pulled in to the bus depot and drove a slow loop. No Daniel. Nobody at all, in fact. It was after 6 p.m. and the centre was deserted. Denise jumped on board another bus and asked the driver about the bus timetable. She came back to Bruce, her face a mask of worry. The 5 p.m. bus had been the last. Where was he?

Now scenarios of snakebites and twisted ankles were going through their minds. Had Daniel taken a short cut and fallen down an embankment? They drove home the same route, looking for any sign of their boy.

'Is Daniel back?' Bruce and Denise asked when they arrived home at 6.30 p.m.

The boys answered no. They hadn't seen him. He hadn't called home either. He knew to call if he was going to be late. He'd done it once before, after missing the 4 p.m. bus.

'Sorry,' he'd told them. 'I'll be another hour.'

Denise picked up the phone and dialled the Sunbus depot. The ring tone shrilled in her ear. She waited impatiently for someone to pick up. Where was he? Where was Daniel?

It rang out. She rang a 13 number, a transport information line. This time someone answered. No, the person said, they'd heard nothing from Sunbus about any problems. They advised Denise to track down a bus and get the driver to contact the depot on their behalf. They got back in the car and headed to the Nambour bus terminus. It was closer than the Plaza. They spotted a bus and Bruce stayed in the car while Denise climbed on board.

The driver shook his head. The depot was closed, he told her. There'd be nobody there to answer his call.

They sat in the car. What should they do next? They decided to drive back to the Plaza. Daylight was waning when they pulled in and they searched through the gloom for any sign of their son. The busy retail hub, by day filled with a cacophony of shoppers, was eerily quiet. They looked at each other. Two people sharing the same concern.

'Let's contact the police at the Police Beat,' Bruce said, referring to the tiny shopfront police station at Sunshine Plaza. They weren't sure what they were going to say. The possibility that Daniel had been taken or lured away hadn't crossed their minds. Daniel was lost. He'd twisted his ankle. Missed the bus. Got sidetracked. They approached the door. It was closed.

They did a quick loop around the centre. Past the cinemas. Was Daniel there, talking to friends? Had he lost track of time? They needed help. They decided to drive to Maroochydore police station.

Bruce and Denise approached the counter together. Were they really reporting their son missing? Sergeant Robbie Munn was behind the counter.

'How can I help you?' he asked.

Bruce told him they were looking for their son. He hadn't come back from a shopping trip. It was unlike him. They were very worried. It had been two hours.

Sergeant Munn started jotting down notes. 'What was your son wearing?' he asked.

They were stumped at the first question. They'd been at the Christmas party when Daniel had dressed for his shopping trip. They didn't know what he'd put on.

Sergeant Munn asked them for a general description. How tall was Daniel? What colour hair? What build was he?

Bruce and Denise gave as much detail as they could. The

questions continued. What was Daniel's state of mind? Was he upset? Suicidal? Did he suffer from depression? Was it unusual for him to turn up late? They were standard questions but completely irrelevant to Daniel. Bruce tried to make the officer see his son through his eyes. Daniel was a quiet, happy, likeable kid. He wasn't selfishly off with friends. His entire reason for leaving home that day had been to buy presents for his family. The Morcombes explained to the sergeant that Daniel had called home in the past after missing the 4 p.m. bus. He hadn't wanted anyone to worry. He'd told them to expect him on the 5 p.m. That was Daniel. He was responsible.

Sergeant Munn took down more notes — a general description and the Morcombes' contact details. He told them he wouldn't log Daniel as a missing person just yet. But he would put out an alert to officers to be on the lookout for a teenage boy. He'd call them around 10 p.m., as his shift was ending, to check in. A patrol car would be sent to their house.

'Look,' he told them. 'I'm sure it's just a misunderstanding. He's running late with his friends, whatever the situation. I'm sure he will turn up.'

*

It was dark when Bruce and Denise arrived back at the house. Daniel was scared of the dark. Denise headed back to the phone and started making calls. Daniel had been to the movies the night before with some friends from school. She called them now. Had they heard from him? One school friend, Scott Balkin, told Denise he hadn't heard from Daniel all day. Nothing had seemed wrong at the cinema. Daniel had been his normal, happy self.

The thought of sitting tight, of waiting for Daniel to come home as the police suggested, seemed ludicrous. Outside it was dark. And Daniel didn't like the dark. Maybe he *was* at a friend's house, they tried to reason. But they didn't believe that. Armed with flashlights, Bruce and Denise went to check the sheds on their hobby farm. They checked the stables, the dam and around the fruit trees. They called his name. Back in the house, they talked some more. Then they searched again.

At 9.45 p.m., 15 minutes before Sergeant Munn was supposed to call, they took the flashlights and headed once again for the car. They'd diverted the home phone to their mobiles in case somebody called, and headed back to the Kiel Mountain Road overpass. Feeling silly, they searched the verge for signs … of what? Discarded clothing? Scuff marks in the dirt? They had no idea what they were doing, but they had to do something. They searched both sides of the road but found nothing.

At 10.10 p.m., the phone rang. It was Sergeant Munn. Had Daniel turned up?

Bruce and Denise were frantic with worry. They told him the places they'd looked, the searches by torchlight.

'I'll get the wheels turning,' he said.

Another call came through just before 11 p.m. This time it was an officer from Palmwoods police station. The conversation was brief. Could Bruce and Denise come in to the station at 8 a.m. to make a report? The promised patrol car never arrived.

*

It was a sleepless night. The worst of their lives. The family sat on the couch in silence.

'I think we should go to bed,' Bruce said at one point.

Fear pressed down on them. Denise wandered about the house. Checked Daniel's room. Looked out the windows at the driveway. Sat on the couch. Looked down the driveway. Checked Daniel's room. Driveway. Daniel's room.

They were up with the sun at 4.30 a.m. Denise jumped in the shower. Bruce jumped in after her. Denise took the car back to the overpass while she waited. No Daniel. An entire night without

Daniel. She drove on to Maroochydore Plaza, not expecting to see him. They were desperate. Was anybody doing anything?

Bruce checked the property again. The sheds. The dam. The fruit trees. The stables. No Daniel. It wasn't far past 5 a.m. when Bruce and Denise met up again. There were still three excruciating hours to wait until the police station opened its doors.

'What the hell are we going to do now?' one of them asked. Maybe he'd been bitten by a snake. Maybe he'd been the victim of a hit-and-run and was lying injured somewhere. Maybe, maybe, maybe.

They walked the length of the driveway together — about 300 metres. When they got to the end they decided they'd walk to the bus stop, checking the sides of the road in case he was lying there. The Woombye–Palmwoods Road had steep embankments and areas of thick scrub. Was Daniel lying in the bushes, unable to yell for help? Their chests tightened by fear, they searched the sides of the road for their son. Nothing. They went home.

Dean had just started a new job and they talked about whether he should go in. In the end, Bruce and Denise decided to drive him the five minutes into Palmwoods for his shift. It was better that he had something to occupy his mind.

*

It was a few minutes before 8 a.m. when Bruce and Denise arrived at the front doors of the Palmwoods police station. It was dark inside and the doors were locked. They sat in the car and waited for someone to arrive.

Sergeant Laurie Davison pulled in spot-on 8 a.m. They cornered him as he walked in the door. To the experienced officer, they looked like nice, normal parents. They spoke to him from under the weight of their worry. He let them inside and asked them to wait in the foyer while he turned on lights and checked overnight reports.

Then he took them to a desk and invited them to sit down.

Sergeant Davison was meticulous and thorough. He took them through the previous day in detail. When did Daniel leave? Why was he going to the Plaza? Where would he normally get his hair cut? The sergeant took notes and then picked up his phone and began making calls. The Morcombes sat patiently as he made call after call, not always knowing who he was speaking with.

Finally, he put down the phone. They needed to go home, he told them, and search through Daniel's clothes. Did he have a red t-shirt? Dark-coloured baggy shorts? Sergeant Davison had called Sunbus. A driver recalled seeing a boy matching Daniel's description standing under the overpass wearing a red shirt and dark shorts.

They were home by 9 a.m. The worry and fear were still there, but for the first time, the Morcombes felt they were being taken seriously. Sergeant Davison had not told them not to worry, that Daniel would be home soon. That it was probably just a 'simple misunderstanding'. It was no longer just Bruce and Denise, searching in the dark with flashlights, looking for scuff marks in the dirt.

CHAPTER THREE
LOOKING FOR DANIEL

IT WAS ABOUT 9A.M. on day two that a missing persons report was filed for 13-year-old Sunshine Coast schoolboy Daniel Morcombe. Two hours later, a Significant Event Message was logged. The Juvenile Aid Bureau was informed and a 'Be on the Lookout For' alert was broadcast to all officers. By 2.20 p.m., Detective Senior Sergeant Paul Schmidt, in charge of the Sunshine Coast Criminal Investigation Branch, was brought in. Police had already been back to the Morcombes' Palmwoods home to pick up a recent photograph of Daniel. Denise had handed it over with shaking hands.

That evening, as radio and television news bulletins broadcast stories of a missing boy, Bruce, Denise, Dean and Bradley drove to the Maroochydore police station so they could be interviewed separately by police. Each sat waiting their turn, looking exhausted and distraught. It was getting dark again and Daniel was gone. It was unbelievable. Inconceivable.

Over the next 72 hours, the search would gain momentum; a snowball rolling down a hill, getting bigger with each turn. Orange-clad State Emergency Services volunteers took time away from work and home and settled in for days of scouring the district for a little lost boy. Police around Australia were notified to be on the lookout for Daniel. Queensland police divers were tasked to check local dams and waterways. Media releases were prepared and sent out to newspapers, radio and television stations.

Forensic crews were sent to the overpass where Daniel had stood, to check for anything of evidentiary value. They found nothing in the way of fingerprints but took plaster casts of footprints left in the dirt. One was confirmed as being a child's Globe shoe. The Morcombes told police Daniel had a pair of

Globe shoes. They still had the shoe box. The Globes themselves were missing from Daniel's room. The box was handed over to police. Broken glass was collected from the ground under the overpass and inquiries revealed a bus had had a window smashed by vandals prior to 7 December. The Sunbus driver had pulled over and cleared the glass away from the frame to stop it falling into the vehicle.

Investigators called the Department of Family Services and checked the Child Protection Register. Had Daniel been abused? Was it his family that had put him in danger? Was he a runaway? The checks showed them what they already suspected: Daniel came from a loving family. His disappearance was very much out of the ordinary.

Forensic crews also scoured the Sunbus vehicles that ran between Palmwoods and the Plaza. Drivers were interviewed. The driver who'd seen a boy in a red t-shirt standing under the overpass had also spotted a 'shadowy' man a few metres behind. He was described as 'scruffy', with messy brown hair. He had facial hair, maybe a goatee. Sunken cheeks. Tanned, weather-beaten appearance.

The Missing Persons Unit was contacted. Task Force Argos — Queensland's world-renowned child sex offender investigation team — was asked to review intelligence on any convicted pedophiles known to frequent the area.

Police officers meticulously door-knocked homes and businesses in the area. Had anyone seen a young boy early Sunday afternoon walking to the bus stop? Or perhaps waiting on the side of the road, under the overpass? Detectives took possession of CCTV footage from the Sunshine Plaza and spent hours scouring the crowds for any sign of Daniel. They checked his bank account for any activity. Nothing. Nil. Zip.

Any computers at the Morcombe home were taken away for examination. If Daniel had been talking to anyone in internet chatrooms, police needed to know about it.

They took camera footage from every service station in a five-mile radius, and from the Nambour railway station. They secured satellite imagery to help with the painstaking ground search. Checked Sunbus ticketing machines and took note of exactly where each bus was at each moment. Spoke to local youth centres about runaways. Called taxi companies to ask about pick-ups and drop-offs in the area.

Daniel's parents looked through his room. It was exactly as he'd left it — tidy, the bed made. A search of his clothes confirmed police suspicions. Daniel had been wearing a red t-shirt — Billabong — and a pair of navy blue shorts. It was the same outfit he'd worn to the movies the night before.

Plain-clothes officers sat on Sunbuses, watching for suspicious characters and identifying any potential witnesses. Soon, calls from the public began to filter through from people who had seen cars parked by the overpass on Sunday afternoon.

Police got hold of a vehicle catalogue. It contained pictures of every single car available in Australia. It would help witnesses identify cars they'd glimpsed parked by the bridge as they drove by on the Nambour Connection Road.

Officers went out to the Sunshine Coast Motor Lodge, not far from the overpass, where drug offenders were known to have been staying. Forensic crews scoured the rooms. There was nothing to connect them to Daniel. They visited 71 pawnshops looking for Daniel's distinctive fob watch or anything else belonging to the teenager.

Nothing. Nothing. Nothing.

CHAPTER FOUR
THE BLUE HERRING

ON TUESDAY MORNING, WHEN Daniel's bed had been empty for two nights, police set up a Major Incident Room. A Major Incident Room is the headquarters of a major investigation. Its walls are lined with photographs, evidentiary material, lists, information on suspects. It's where detectives gather. Where briefings are held.

On Tuesday morning, the more than 50 officers already investigating Daniel's disappearance were joined by four detectives from the Homicide Squad. Police, who two days earlier had described Daniel's disappearance as a 'misunderstanding', were now looking into the possibility he'd been abducted and murdered. Investigators tracked down witnesses and followed up on information filtering through from members of the public.

*

Blake Rogers had been to the beach at Maroochydore on Sunday 7 December and was on his way home for a shower before work when he turned off the Nambour Connection Road. The Morcombes were his neighbours. It was around 1.30 p.m. when he spotted Daniel walking along the Woombye–Palmwoods Road. He told police Daniel was walking along the left-hand side of the road, holding something small in one hand. Something like a phone or a wallet. He'd been wearing a red t-shirt and dark blue or black shorts and a baseball cap.

Blake was home a minute later, washing away the sand and salt in the shower. His shift at the local Red Rooster started at 2 p.m., so he was back in the car 20 minutes later. This time he spotted Daniel standing under the overpass, waiting for the bus. At 1.50 p.m., Blake told police, Daniel had been standing there alone.

*

Craig Beattie's three-month-old daughter, like so many other babies, liked to fall asleep to the hum of a car engine. When she wouldn't settle that Sunday, 7 December, he strapped her in to the capsule and took her for a drive. It was 12.30 p.m. when he left his home at Eudlo, south of Palmwoods on the Sunshine Coast. He'd been on the road for 45 minutes, or maybe an hour, when he found himself on Pine Grove Road — adjacent to the Nambour Connection Road and within shouting distance of the overpass. The boy's red shirt caught his eye.

'He was just walking along, looking up at the trees,' he told police.

*

Peter and Jenny Harth ran the service station on Woombye–Palmwoods Road at Woombye. They knew Daniel — although not by name. He came in to the shop every now and then to buy last-minute items for his parents. Sometimes he'd buy fuel for the motorbike.

On Sunday, 7 December they closed the service station at 1.15 p.m. Soon after, they spotted Daniel walking towards the Nambour Connection Road. He wore a red t-shirt, shoes and socks. Peter remembered something else from that day. After closing up, he drove down Pine Grove Road towards the Woombye turnoff at Blackall Street. He spotted a bus parked on the side of the road. It was drizzling, and people with umbrellas were standing next to the stalled vehicle.

*

Alan Park drove charter buses for a living. On 7 December he was booked to drive a coach from the depot at Tewantin to Dreamworld on the Gold Coast for a private function. He arrived at the depot at 1.45 p.m. and filled out his logbook. Alan marked '2 p.m.' as the time he'd left with the bus and rumbled his way out the gates.

It wasn't long after that that he spotted the boy in the red shirt standing under the bridge. Alan narrowed his eyes. The boy had his back to him as the bus approached the overpass. They'd had trouble with kids throwing rocks at the buses and Alan thought the worst. The boy in the red t-shirt turned around as the coach approached. He looked at the vehicle with indifference and looked away again.

'He's just looking for his bus,' Alan thought, and relaxed.

*

Denise Dance also saw a young boy in a red t-shirt. She drove under the Kiel Mountain Road overpass somewhere between 1.30 p.m. and 1.40 p.m. He was standing close to the gutter. Denise seemed to recall other people standing there too, but couldn't remember anything about them.

*

It was about 2 p.m. when Maureen Martin got into her car to head to the Sunshine Plaza. She took the Nambour Connection Road and was nearing Blackall Street when she spotted a bus pulled over on the side of the road. She continued on, driving under the Kiel Mountain Road overpass. It was here she spotted the boy in the red shirt. He seemed bored, kicking at the dirt.

*

It was about 2 p.m. or just before when Judy Lade left her Palmwoods home to drive her husband to work at a nearby nursery. Her route took her along the Nambour Connection Road and she'd been in the car for only minutes when she drove under the Kiel Mountain Road overpass.

It was the man she'd noticed first. He was tall and skinny and stood right under the bridge, one leg bent up against the wall. There was a boy there too. She saw him as she steered the car around the roundabout.

*

Wendy Burnett had spent the morning at church before treating herself to lunch at a local hotel. But by 1.30 p.m., she was on her way home. She wanted to make it back before her husband left for work. It was around 2 p.m. when she took the Palmwoods exit off the Nambour Connection Road, right near the Kiel Mountain Road overpass. The road was wet and the sky was grey with clouds threatening to dump more of their load.

She noticed people standing near the overpass. They caught her eye because she'd not seen people standing in that spot before, right on the edge of a major road. They were sheltering from the rain, tucked under the bridge.

The man was tall and unkempt. He was gaunt and his hair hung limp on his face.

Not the boy, though. He was wearing something bright and seemed far neater and better dressed than the man. The boy was on the edge of the road, looking down towards the Big Pineapple — a local tourist attraction — while the man stood diagonally behind.

*

Chloe Fooks was in another car that drove past at about the same time. She was sitting in the passenger seat when she noticed the young boy in the red t-shirt and dark shorts. He was standing right by the edge of the road.

They pulled in to the service station nearby and she got out to buy something inside. Many of the times given to police were just estimates. But Chloe's receipt put her at the Forest Glen BP, about four kilometres away, at 2.14 p.m.

*

Jessiah Cocks sat in the passenger seat of his mother's car, nursing his McDonald's. It was a little after 1.35 p.m. when they drove by the overpass, on their way home to nearby Mapleton. He noticed the red t-shirt, standing out against the brown of the clay wall under the overpass. The boy was squatting on his haunches. It was just a glimpse but, like all the others, something made him remember that boy.

He remembered something else, too. On the other side of the overpass was a white 4WD. It was all hard angles. A 1990s model, maybe. He thought it might have had a black snorkel.

*

Then there were the people on the bus. The driver wasn't the only person to see a boy in red trying to wave them down. The passengers who'd waited so long after their first bus broke down saw him as well. Sixteen-year-old Terry Theuerkauf, his sister Fiona and their friends Abby North and Peter Murchie were sitting in the back row. They were on their way to the Plaza to catch a movie.

The boy had a stick in his hand and waved at them as they approached. His shoulders slumped and he kicked at the dirt when the bus didn't stop. It was a long wait for the next bus on a Sunday. They only ran once an hour. There was someone else waiting for the bus too. A man stood a few metres behind the boy in the red top. They all saw him — even though, when it came to describing him to police, they'd seen different things. He was gaunt, with prominent eyebrows. Abby saw a goatee, long hair and a thin face. She saw eyes that were lined and weathered. Two earrings in the one ear. Fiona saw a beanie and sunglasses. A tattoo on his arm and a bag on the ground.

It's called the Rashomon effect. A term often used by psychologists, it's a phenomenon whereby people witnessing the same event recall it quite differently. They aren't lying — they've just been influenced by individual bias, leading questions, time or various other factors.

Fiona would recall something else, too. She felt uneasy about that man. Something about that situation — the boy alone on the side of the road — made her worry for him. After all, when your bus approaches, you usually step forward. But that man didn't move at all.

*

The car was 'squarish', like an old Datsun. Blue in colour. Four doors. She saw it parked on the left-hand side of the Nambour Connection Road, just before the overpass.

Karen Brady also saw people. A young boy was standing in front of the car and a man was behind it. He was tallish, with collar-length hair and wearing jeans and a t-shirt. He was weathered, with tanned skin — like someone who worked out in the sun. She remembered seeing the man staring at the boy. She wasn't sure what time — Karen could only narrow it down as some time between 1 p.m. and 3 p.m.

Keith Lipke saw a blue car, too. But his account was far more strange. It was a little after 1.50 p.m. when Keith spotted it pulled over somewhere between the overpass and the Big Pineapple, further along the Nambour Connection Road. It was a blue four-door sedan. Squarish. About 20 years old with no hub caps. He hadn't seen anybody standing under the overpass but he had seen a man in the driver's seat and possibly a second man seated next to him.

In the back seat, as he drove by, he spotted a tarp. The tarp was moving. He thought perhaps there were kids under the tarp. He told police he spotted a flash of red — but bizarrely thought nothing of it.

Joan Anderson and her husband had eaten lunch later than usual that day. So it was about 1.30 p.m. when they were on their way home via the Nambour Connection Road. They were driving under the Kiel Mountain Road overpass when she spotted the blue car. It was older, with faded blue paint. A boy was standing a couple of metres back from the rear of the car. There was a man beside the rear passenger door. She only got a glimpse, but it appeared as though he was getting out of the car. His hair was unkempt and mousy brown. Her husband noticed he was wearing a checked shirt. She didn't get the registration. But she thought the car had New South Wales plates.

Barry Kelsey had been helping his daughter renovate her Nambour house on 7 December 2003. He was driving under the overpass when he saw a boy standing by the side of the road. The boy looked as though he was waiting for a bus. When Barry pulled level, he noticed a man standing further back. Lean build, dark hair, thin-faced. Wearing a checked flannelette shirt. He'd thought the boy was singing, or talking to himself. But when he saw the man, it occurred to Barry the boy might have been speaking to him. An older-style car was parked on the other side of the overpass. It was a faded dark blue colour.

Gary Mitchell and his wife had spent the weekend with the in-laws at Woombye. But by 2 p.m. Sunday they were headed back home. In 2003 the merge onto the Nambour Connection Road from the Kiel Mountain Road overpass was tricky. There was no bleeder lane. Just a give-way sign. Gary pulled up at the give-way sign and turned to look for traffic.

'I can't see,' he told his wife. A car was parked under the overpass, blocking his view. With the angle of the sun, he could only see it in silhouette. But it was boxy. An older square-shaped sedan. There was a person leaning on the car and another standing up on the footpath. They were in shadow. He got the impression one was a man and the other a child. But he couldn't be sure.

It was some time in the afternoon when Troy Meiers was on his way to a friend's house via the Nambour Connection Road. The blue car with the rough paint job was parked near the overpass. A thin-faced man with a goatee stood at the back, leaning against the tail-light. On the opposite side of the road was a boy in a red t-shirt. A second man stood nearby, his back to the boy. Troy pulled up at his mate's house and banged on the door. There was nobody home. He got back in his car to head home and drove back under the overpass. Fifteen minutes had passed. He noticed the boy in the red shirt again. The man was standing behind him.

There were many inconsistencies in witness accounts. But police felt they could rely on two things: a man had been standing with Daniel as he waited for the bus. And they were looking for a blue car.

*

Bruce and Denise were living a nightmare. They were in an endless state of shock. How could this happen? They waited for answers that didn't come. They jumped at the ring of a phone, at knocks on the door.

Glenis Green was one of the first journalists to staff the *Courier-Mail*'s Sunshine Coast bureau office. She covered an enormous area — all the way up to Bundaberg, if that's where the news of the day took her.

On Tuesday, 9 December 2003, she arrived at work to sift through the events of the night before. A kid had gone missing on his way to the Plaza. Police were looking for anyone who had information that might help track him down. There was a general feeling he'd run off, gone to a mate's place or had a fight with his parents. But the Sunshine Coast had been Glenis's patch for four or five years by then. She'd had missing children come across her desk before. There was something about this one. Something didn't feel right. She picked up the phone and soon had an address for the family.

She would never forget that long driveway. The cottage garden. The beautiful family home. The friendly dogs and the well cared for pony. But most of all, she would never forget the look in Denise's eyes. She was distraught. She looked haunted. *Something has gone horribly, horribly wrong here*, Glenis thought.

Bruce agreed to talk. They would give up their privacy, give up the anonymity of a normal life, to find their son.

'We're just at a dead end,' he said. Daniel, he explained, was a shy kid who knew about 'stranger danger'. He wouldn't have been lured away by a strange man. Talked into a car. 'He was cautious in that regard and this is totally out of character. It's heartbreaking. It's the not knowing that's the dreadful thing.'

Bruce hoped these words would encourage people to come forward with information that could help the police case. But they were just words. They didn't convey that tight feeling in his chest. The fear that gripped them. The blind panic just under the surface. What had happened to their boy?

CHAPTER FIVE
OPERATION VISTA

WITHIN DAYS OF DANIEL'S disappearance, the group of detectives, uniformed officers and support staff working on the case were brought together under the newly named Operation Vista. The unit was responsible for following up an unrelenting flow of leads and tips from the public.

On 8 December— when Daniel had been missing for around 24 hours — police received a report of a boy in a red, long-sleeved t-shirt running through scrub near Peregian Beach on the Sunshine Coast. Pursuing him was a man, or possibly an older boy. The report was given high priority. After all, it might have been Daniel. Detectives met with the witness and took him back to the scene. They walked around, looking for any sign of a struggle. But it soon became clear that the area was a web of walking tracks used by local children to cut through to local bushland. There were many such leads. Countless.

On Wednesday, three days after Daniel disappeared, Sergeant Julie Elliott from the Queensland Police media unit knocked on the door of the Morcombes' Palmwoods home. They needed Daniel's disappearance to stay in the media as long as possible, she explained. The more information coming in from members of the public, the better. Bruce and Denise would need to front a press conference.

They held one that afternoon in a room at Maroochydore police station. Journalists, photographers and cameramen crammed in. Everybody stared at the parents of the little boy who hadn't come home. It was confronting for a couple who'd never had much to do with the media, a couple who were shrouded in shock and living

31

out a nightmare. Denise's parents, Kevin and Monique Beavis, had flown in from Melbourne to lend their support.

The following day the story ran on page 3 of the *Courier-Mail*. Bruce and Denise's emotional public appeal for information came as police confirmed there was a 'real possibility' Daniel had been abducted. Police were 'anxious' to speak with a man seen standing with Daniel at the bus stop, they said.

Calls continued to flood in and the massive team of police assigned to Operation Vista chased lead after lead. One involved a suspicious man seen loitering around the Woombye State School during the last few months of the school year. Parents had spotted the man coming and going in a blue car around the time they came to collect their children. Detectives eventually tracked down a man they believed was the focus of parents' concern. He was a drug addict and would go to the school to collect his own children. He'd also used the school as a pick-up point for drugs, buying or selling them from his blue car. Police found nothing to link him to Daniel's disappearance. The tip was among hundreds that police would have to check and discount.

With no leads on the identity of the scruffy man at the bus stop, detectives began going through a list of names of pedophiles known to frequent the area. There were the two men who had travelled to the Sunshine Coast on 7 December to watch young boys compete at a nipper carnival. They'd planned to use the noisy, public event as an opportunity to groom potential victims. They were there with another man. All three had links to an international pedophile network.

There were registered pedophiles who had attended their regular church service in the area that day. A man with a monstrous background who had just been released from prison for a 'very public' abduction of a child he was caught raping.

And then there was Brett Peter Cowan.

CHAPTER SIX
THE COWANS

MARLENE COWAN MARRIED AN army man. They met in 1959, when Peter was already entrenched in the career he would stick with for life. He loved everything about the army and would discuss it with passion and enthusiasm. They married in Nambour, two years after they met. Peter was stationed at Enoggera, an army barracks in Brisbane's north-west. In 1961, when the Cowans married, the Enoggera barracks already had a history spanning more than 100 years. It began as a collection of four paddocks used for training drills and grew with each world war. In more recent times, the barracks was used as the headquarters for the Australian Defence Force during the 2010–11 floods, when more than 40 people died or disappeared as great walls of water flowed through much of the state.

The Cowans were living in Yandina Creek, a farming area on the Sunshine Coast, when their first son, Robert, was born a year into their marriage. A second son, Michael, was born two years later. Peter's army career meant the family was constantly on the move. By the time their second son was born, the family had been moved to Wagga Wagga in New South Wales.

When Michael was a baby, Peter was posted to New Guinea. He'd remain there for two years, leaving Marlene to care for two small boys. After returning from New Guinea, he packed his bags again and headed to Vietnam. This was around the time Australia suffered some of its biggest casualties of the war, when most troops were in the conflict zone. While their father was away, Marlene took the boys and moved back to Nambour to stay with her parents.

Peter was back within two years and the family packed up to move again. Their third son, Brett, was born in 1969 in Bunbury, Western Australia's third largest city, built around a port 175 kilometres south of Perth. A year later, Peter was posted back to the Enoggera barracks — and their fourth son, Paul, was born. Peter and Marlene bought a house in nearby Stafford Heights when Paul was still a baby. But they wouldn't get to stay there long. In 1974, Peter was told to take his family to Singleton, a town on the banks of the Hunter River a couple of hundred kilometres north-west of Sydney.

Their eldest boy was about 12 when they moved to Singleton. Peter was known as a passionate army man and Marlene threw herself into the local community. The family was well liked. The boys played league for Singleton juniors and the Cowans got to know other parents in the area. It was in Singleton that Brett started school. He hated it. He was an active, restless child. Marlene would later reflect that had Attention Deficit Hyperactivity Disorder been spoken about in the 1970s, he would no doubt have been diagnosed with it.

They moved back to Brisbane in 1976 and Peter and Marlene bought a house in Keperra. The other boys were doing well at school but Brett was behind. He was enrolled in Grade 1 at Mitchelton State School, where teachers had to spend six months catching him up on work.

Peter was a good father. He was strict on the boys when he was home. He wanted them to grow up right.

Brett continued to be difficult. When he was eight or nine, he snuck into the cupboard at their Keperra home and took out a packet of cigarettes. Someone had left them behind in the Cowans' car and they'd been brought in, placed in a plastic bag, stashed in the cupboard and forgotten. Brett knew they were there. He snuck outside and lit one up. His father was away but Marlene caught him at it. He threw the packet out the back door as he came inside. Later, when he checked, he discovered Marlene had put the packet back in the cupboard. Brett had been told not to touch it and he didn't.

It was about that age that Brett started experimenting sexually. It was only touching, he'd explain later. And he was polite about it. He'd usually ask first.

During the school holidays, the boys would go to the army barracks where their dad worked, to swim in the pool. Lots of children did this. Brett was about 10 when he started approaching children at the pool. He'd find boys younger than him — about six to eight years old — and lure them into the change rooms. Others he'd fondle under the water. Sometimes he'd be out riding his bike with other neighbourhood children and he'd coax them into a quiet spot. He'd touch them and ask them if it was OK. It would become a habit, a thrill. And it would continue right through until Brett finished school.

They weren't the only children he targeted. When Brett was around 10, he honed in on a younger female relative. He would abuse the girl for a total of nine years. He would later claim it was only towards the end that he recognised he was doing anything wrong.

He was smoking by the end of primary school. And then he moved on to marijuana. Both those habits, begun as a boy, would continue throughout his life.

In 1978, when three of the Cowan boys were doing well and the fourth was keeping much of his behaviour hidden, Peter was named on the Queen's Birthday Honours list. It was the same list that recognised the Honourable Edward Gough Whitlam, of Parliament House, Canberra, for his 'eminent and meritorious service to politics'. Warrant Officer Class One Peter George Cowan appeared in the *Commonwealth of Australia Gazette* on 6 June, honoured for his 'dedicated service as a company and regimental Sergeant Major'.

Brett dropped out of school in Year 10, saying goodbye to Everton Park's Marcellin College as soon as he was able. He walked out of the classroom and into a panelbeating apprenticeship at a workshop in Eagle Farm. Brett loved cars. He enjoyed tinkering with them. But the apprenticeship didn't last long. The boys at the workshop had an interesting way of initiating young workers. Brett arrived home twice covered in grease. Peter and Marlene were incensed. They drove to Eagle Farm and demanded to speak to the boss. They wanted an explanation. They wanted something done about it. Nothing was — and so Brett left.

It was about that time that Brett started getting in real trouble, and police began calling at the Cowan house. Peter and Marlene were at a loss. They were not used to dealing with police. They went to church. Got involved in community groups. Peter had fought for his country and received one of Australia's highest honours.

When Brett was 18, he was sent to court for break and enter and stealing a car. A few months later he was back on stealing charges. He was fined and put on probation. He was back again a month later, on charges laid early that year: wilful and unlawful destruction of property and stealing.

The list was so long that Marlene would later have trouble remembering all the things her son got in trouble for. They tried their best with their wayward son. If he did something wrong, they'd confront him and Brett would often confess. That was as far as it went, though. He'd keep his mouth shut after that, no matter how much they pressed. He never admitted to the drugs. Marlene could see it in his eyes, when he'd been using. He'd swear he was clean. She went through his room a few times, determined to find the proof. But Brett was careful. He made sure his mother never found anything.

They worried about him. Brett had always been so easily led, easily manipulated. It was a trait he'd take into adulthood — and one that would come in very handy to police.

CHAPTER SEVEN
BLUE JEANS AND DIRTY HANDS

ON 5 DECEMBER 1987, a group of children were dropped off by busy mums at a childcare centre in Stafford, on Brisbane's north side. There were activities inside and a children's playground on their doorstep. It was a Saturday — a day for playing outside, for chasing, hiding and climbing.

The little boy was just seven years old. He had blond hair — almost white blond — and round blue eyes. His mother waved goodbye as he ran off to play with friends.

A young man was there. He'd been there the weekend before, too. The parents didn't know, but 18-year-old Brett Cowan had been ordered to complete maintenance work at the childcare centre — court-ordered community service for the crimes of break and enter and stealing.

He was tall and skinny and wore blue jeans and shoes the same colour. The boys played at his feet as he dug around some pipes in the dirt. He was nice. He gave them jobs to do — especially the little boy with the blond hair. Eventually they got bored — as children do. They ran off to do their own thing. But Brett could be charming when he wanted to be.

'Who wants a golf ball?' he called out. The boys put up their hands.

Brett pointed at the blond boy.

'You have to come into the toilets,' he said to the boy.

When the child told him no, Brett scooped him up. He placed his hand over the boy's mouth and carried him into the toilet block. Brett, his hands filthy from digging in the dirt, undressed the boy and placed him on his lap. The boy noticed the watch on Brett's dirt-streaked wrist. A broken thing, held together with sticky tape.

The little boy was raped in that toilet block, Brett subjecting him to a series of horrific sex acts. He cowered and shook, convinced he would be killed.

'I'm going to tell my mum,' he sobbed to his teenaged attacker.

Brett's hands shot out and grabbed the boy around the throat.

'Do you want me to hurt you?' he asked the child.

It could have gone on. But a childcare worker's voice rang out across the park.

'Are you in there?' she called to the boy.

Brett stood up and walked out, sauntering inside the centre to watch television. The attack was over in minutes. He'd changed a young boy's life forever. And now he stood watching TV as though nothing had happened.

That evening, back at home, the boy went to find his mum.

'I don't want to go to playgroup any more,' he told her.

*

They knocked on the Cowans' door that night. Plain-clothes Constable Mark Hilton left Peter and Marlene's Everton Park home with bags full of evidence — among them, the clothing the young boy had described so accurately.

Brett did not respond like somebody who could be heading to prison for one of society's most detested crimes. He barely reacted. Mark Hilton dealt with child sex offenders every day. Brett surprised him. He was totally relaxed. As though he didn't care at all.

Peter and Marlene were different. They, like Brett's brothers, were good people. They were stunned. Horrified. They were a good family, Mark thought, and Brett was certainly the black sheep.

*

Brett Cowan had never really taken probation seriously. So when a magistrate gave him bail on charges of indecent dealing and sodomy, he didn't take that very seriously either. It wasn't long before he skipped town, fleeing interstate.

Mark Hilton got a call some time after the committal hearing. Brett was gone. He didn't think too much about it. Eighteen-year-old Brett Cowan was one in a long list of pedophiles and child abusers on Mark's radar. Then, a year later, he turned up. Police had come across him in the Sydney beachside suburb of Cronulla. He'd been accused of assaulting someone at a boarding house. Mark packed his bags and flew interstate to bring his wayward offender home.

Visiting police officers picking up prisoners for extradition are traditionally taken out on the town by the locals — and this trip was no exception. Sydney police put on quite the show and it was a tired Mark Hilton who boarded a plane handcuffed to his charge the following morning. Had Brett Cowan been considered violent or prone to bad behaviour, more than one officer would have been sent to collect him. They expected no trouble from the skinny teen.

But staff on board the domestic flight were uneasy. Mark and Brett were bumped up to first class to keep them away from the other passengers. Brett was cuffed to Mark's left wrist when flight attendants led them to empty seats on the plane's left-hand side. He got the window seat, and turned to Mark and grinned. He was the boy next door back then. Butter wouldn't melt in his mouth. Never, in a million years, would you have looked at him and seen a predator.

'I've never been on a plane before,' he said.

*

Brett admitted meeting the boy at the childcare centre but denied any inappropriate dealings. When he faced District Court Judge Brian Boulton, he entered a plea of not guilty. The plea meant the little blond boy had to go to court and give evidence, sitting in the witness box in front of his attacker. It would be something he'd never forget — being asked to look around the court and point to the man who had abused him.

The boy looked up at Brett. Raised his hand to single out the subject of his nightmares. Brett looked back at him and smiled.

The jury returned with a verdict of guilty. But only on the charge of indecent dealing. Inexplicably, they agreed the boy had been abused, but did not feel the charge of sodomy had been proven.

'It's not for me to know what was in the mind of the jury,' Judge Boulton told the court. He went on to say that even though the jury had had some hesitation over the child's story, he had not.

'I should make it clear that I accept the account that was given here by the complainant child,' he said. 'This was a bad instance of indecent dealing.'

Cowan was sentenced to two years' jail. He served about half.

CHAPTER EIGHT
THE BLACK SHEEP

BRETT COWAN HAD SERVED little more than a year in jail when he walked out into the supportive embrace of his family. To Marlene, he was her son and he needed help. They'd organised for him to move in with his grandmother — Marlene's mother — at her home in Maroochydore. The arrangement did not last long. He fell back in with his old crowd, breaking into houses and stealing from people. He moved out with mates as soon as he could.

In 1991, Brett was living in a small block of flats in Nambour. He was always on the lookout for girls. And when two moved in next door — including a young girl who was seven months pregnant — Brett homed in. Eighteen-year-old Tracey Haneveld and her pregnant friend had moved in only days earlier when she opened the door to the tall, good-looking man who said his name was Brett. He was charming. Friendly. He told them he was having a BBQ. That they should come on over.

There were about 15 people in the unit when Tracey introduced herself around. They drank beer and chatted. Someone handed Tracey an acid trip and she took it. She'd never had one before. She put the small square under her tongue and felt it go soggy. After a few hours, they left the unit and made their way to the train line.

They giggled as they pushed through scrub onto the railway tracks. The sugar cane trains chugged their way through Nambour, slow enough for them to jump aboard. When one came rumbling through, Brett and his friends ran alongside until they found a carriage they could climb. They sat on top laughing as the train made its way along the tracks. Brett looked at Tracey and smiled. He liked her. They'd gone about 10 kilometres by the time they

41

jumped off. It would be a long walk back and they started following the train line through the scrub.

Brett walked alongside Tracey and they talked. He was charming and she found him attractive. She liked him. So when he grabbed her and kissed her, she kissed him back.

He came by again the next day. Tracey's heavily pregnant housemate shot her a dark look when she saw their neighbour back on their doorstep. Tracey took off next door again and she and Brett got talking.

'I'm from Brisbane,' he told her. 'I just got out of jail a month ago.'

Brett had a habit of mixing lies with the truth. He told her he'd been in trouble for break and enters. Possession of marijuana. That kind of thing. Tracey nodded and didn't ask any more.

*

Tracey had only ever had one boyfriend before Brett. Her sex life with Brett was normal. He didn't try anything unusual with her. Not then, anyway. It wasn't long before he was talking about moving in together. He knew of a place, he said, in Maroochydore. They could take over the lease with a friend of his named Tim.

So the three of them moved into a house on Bradman Avenue on the Maroochy River. Brett would go out every weekend and buy drugs from a woman who lived near his grandmother. He'd bring home pot and acid. In their spare time, Brett and his mates would break into houses. Tracey knew they were doing it but she didn't say much. They woke her one night. There were three of them, dragging their plunder into the house. They brought in a big money tin and some jewellery. Brett ran his fingers through the jewellery and picked out a charm bracelet. He fastened it onto her wrist. A gift, he said. But the next day he asked for it back.

'You can't have it,' he told her. He was worried she would dob him in. He took the bracelet and walked across the road, tossing it into the river.

Brett's night-time jaunts became more and more frequent. Tracey never had any idea where he was or what he was doing. He'd leave home at 4 p.m., returning in the early hours of the morning. He'd tried pushing her boundaries in the bedroom and she'd brushed him away. Their relationship became less and less intimate.

With Brett away most of the time, Tracey saw more of their housemate Tim and his girlfriend, who stayed over often. She walked into the laundry one day and almost stepped into Brett and Tim's girlfriend. They weren't doing anything at the time. But she knew. Tracey didn't talk to him about it. She rarely confronted him on anything. She just turned on her heel and walked out.

She started spending time with Brett's grandmother. Marlene's mother had taken Brett in at one point and he held genuine affection for her. She did her best by him. And she had welcomed Tracey into their lives with open arms. The older woman became a confidante for Tracey. She often went to her for help.

Sometimes Brett was away for days. He controlled the money and did the shopping. Tracey was lost without him. She'd stay at the house with Tim and his girlfriend, crying, not knowing where he was. Then, one day, they came clean: Brett was with another woman.

'Who?' she demanded. Eventually they told her. The woman lived close by. They gave her the address.

Tracey was there in minutes, banging on the door. A baby was screaming inside. She opened the door and saw a little girl, alone and wailing. A shower was running. Tracey walked through the house and opened the bathroom door. There, standing under a stream of water in another woman's home, was her boyfriend.

'Where is she?' Tracey said.

He just looked at her. She had her answer a minute later. She was slapping Brett's face when the other woman walked in.

*

Tracey was on the phone to her mother, sobbing out her pain, the minute she got home.

'Brett's been cheating on me,' she said, inconsolable. Her mother had her booked on a bus to Dubbo a few hours later. Tracey packed her bag and went to find Brett.

'I'm leaving,' she told him. He tried to convince her to stay, but all the charm in the world wasn't changing Tracey's mind.

She stayed with her mother for three days, talking through her ruined relationship. She called Brett's grandmother, telling her it was over.

But she was back in Maroochydore by the fourth day. Brett's grandmother had offered her a place to stay. Tracey was good for her wayward grandson. She told Tracey she'd like to see them work it out. Christmas was only a few days away and Brett's grandmother convinced them to go along to Peter and Marlene's for lunch.

Tracey had been living with Brett's grandmother, but it was the first time she'd met his mother. He walked her into the kitchen, introducing the two women as Marlene bustled about, preparing lunch. One of his brothers walked in and shot Brett a glare.

'Hello,' said Brett. His brother barged through, shouldering Brett out of the way. Brett was reaching for the ham his mother was slicing when the brother turned on his heel to confront him.

'Get out!' he said, giving him a shove.

Tracey looked on, bewildered. Brett's grandmother took her by the hand and led her away.

'What was that about?' she asked him later.

'You don't need to know,' he replied. 'It's just brother stuff.'

She'd asked his mother too. Marlene hadn't known what to say. She decided complete honesty was not the best approach. She told Tracey Brett's brothers hated him for taking drugs, for breaking into houses. She hadn't lied. Not entirely. But the truth she'd told had been a fraction of the whole.

Brett spent the next few days trying to win Tracey back. He decided being more open with her might work.

'I'm bisexual,' he told her, trying to explain where he went each night. He told her he'd been meeting men for sex in local public toilet blocks. Men would write their phone numbers on cubicle walls and he'd call them and arrange to meet. Strangely, this news did not woo Tracey back to his side. She got on a plane and headed home to family in Perth.

*

Tracey hadn't been in Perth long when she ran into an old school friend, Charmaine. A neighbour was about to leave on an annual driving holiday around Australia and the girls decided to hitch a lift north. They went through Broome and Kununurra, where Tracey called home to tell her mum they were headed to Darwin.

'Brett's been calling,' she said. 'If you don't want to see him, don't go anywhere near the BP Palms Caravan Park.'

But Tracey did want to see Brett. She called him and he arranged to pick the girls up from the bus station.

They arrived at midnight, and Brett collected them in a borrowed car. He was cashed up. On his way to Darwin, he'd swung by his parents' Everton Park home and cleaned them out. He'd stolen their television, their jewellery, his father's alcohol and a valuable coin collection. He also took some of his brothers' tools. Peter and Marlene called the police to report a break-in. It was only later they realised nobody had actually broken in. Brett took Tracey and Charmaine back to the caravan where he'd been staying. Charmaine went to bed while Brett and Tracey sat outside, talking. They talked for an hour, Brett trying his best to charm her back. It was the wail of a baby from inside the caravan that interrupted them. Tracey looked at him, alarmed.

'I'm sorry, Tracey,' he said. 'I haven't told you everything.'

The baby was the same little girl she'd seen when she'd burst in on Brett in another woman's shower. Apparently the little girl, named Crystal, had been left with Brett while her mother travelled with a circus. She'd be back in a few days, he explained.

Their relationship was a roller-coaster ride of Brett's making. Tracey knew how to roll into the bends. She walked away from Brett and picked the baby up off the couch, where he'd left her. She spent the rest of the evening caring for the child of her boyfriend's mistress.

*

They woke in the morning to baby Crystal's cries. Tracey got her up and looked after her while Brett slept in. Then she bailed. She and Charmaine booked into a motel in the city and spent a few days exploring Darwin. But, after three days, they decided to return. The girls moved in to Brett's caravan. Charmaine didn't like him and told Tracey as much. He made her uncomfortable. But Tracey was warming to the idea of taking Brett back. A few weeks later, Charmaine went back home, leaving Brett Cowan and his cramped caravan behind.

*

Tracey settled in to life at the caravan park. She made friends easily. There were people her age there. They'd spend the evenings sharing BBQs and beers. Next door was a woman with two young children. She was friendly. Further along was Liz. She and Tracey became close.

Brett found himself a job. He was pleased to have Tracey back and came home each day happy to see her. But then he started back on the drugs. First it was just dope. Then pills, acid — anything he could get his hands on. He started sneaking out again. Tracey had had enough. She ignored him and spent time with her new caravan park friends.

A group of them were gathered for a BBQ one night when Tracey and a friend decided to drive to a nearby bottle shop to bring back alcohol for everyone. Hands dipped into pockets and Tracey and her friend set off with a pocket full of combined cash. They passed the little boy from next door on their way to the car, his arms loaded with BBQ trays.

'Need any help?' they asked him. He shook his head and continued on.

Brett was quiet when she dropped the keys to their van into his hands. He didn't ask her where she was going or what she was doing. It was unusual behaviour for him.

They were gone for an hour. When she got back to their van, it was locked. Brett was nowhere to be found. She checked in a couple of places, becoming more and more angry with him. He was cheating again, she thought. She went from van to van, banging on doors and yelling his name. She checked the showers. No Brett.

By now it had been two hours and Brett wasn't the only one missing. The little boy with the BBQ trays had disappeared too. People in the park started searching for the little boy. And then Brett turned up. It was just on dusk when they spotted him walking back from the showers, talking to a girl. He was carrying his towel and wore a fresh pair of shorts.

'Where have you been?' Tracey demanded.

'Been trying to pinch some sprinklers,' he told her. He'd been over to a nearby industrial area and got himself covered in mud trying to dig up sprinklers for the lawn he'd planted outside their van. He had a way of convincing her, even when her instinct told her he was lying. Tracey went back to the BBQ and Brett skulked off to the van alone.

She was walking to the shops with Liz when she ran into the woman from next door — the mother of the missing boy. She was frantic. Flashing lights lit up the sky. At the BP service station in the distance was an ambulance and a police car. Her little boy had walked into the service station, the woman explained, naked and covered in dirt and frightened. She was hurrying over to see what had happened.

Tracey and her friend started running with her.

*

Detectives Matt Sodoli and Stan Fensom were cops who did things the old way. Rules were for bending. They acted on the fly and got results. Dealt with the consequences later. Detective Sodoli's reputation followed him everywhere.

'Weren't you the one who once bashed a bloke while you were wearing a Santa suit?' a young police officer once asked him at a party.

He hadn't. But he had burst in on another officer, dressed as a werewolf. The officer had got such a shock she'd jumped clear over the desk. Sodoli didn't believe in the black pants, white shirt and tie uniform so frequently seen on city detectives. He dressed like a bum and ignored the repeated requests from his superiors to sharpen his look. Policing was about getting the job done, Detective Sodoli told them. He couldn't care less how he was dressed.

They were on the road in an unmarked police car when the call came in. It was 23 September 1993, and a little boy, naked, filthy and bleeding, had stumbled into the service station at Palmerston's BP Palms caravan park. He was six years old and so badly injured it was thought he would surely die. The police arrived to find the boy wrapped in a blanket, paramedics just about to bundle him off.

'Go with him,' the detective barked at one of his colleagues. 'Get me something I can use.' He called in uniform officers and told them to surround the park. Nobody was to come in or out. He wanted everyone's name. He wanted everyone spoken to.

Sodoli was waiting at the service station when a call came through from uniform. An officer had knocked on the door of a caravan and the man inside was refusing to come out. The policeman had climbed up the front of the van to yell through an open window — and nearly had his head taken off with a frypan. Sodoli didn't think much of it. There were bound to be all kinds in the park. He told them to keep knocking on doors.

A police officer radioed in from the hospital. The boy had been strangled, doctors had said. That's what had caused the blood blisters all over his face. He had a punctured lung and serious injuries to the lower half of his body. He'd been sexually assaulted and something had cut him up real bad. He'd spoken, though. They didn't know how he was even alive, but that little boy had given them something to work with. It was a man from the park. Tall and slim with mousy brown hair. He lived in a van opposite the toilet block. He kept a bicycle out the front.

Sodoli grabbed Fensom and three or four officers in uniform and marched towards the vans.

*

It was a police officer named Debbie who'd got the boy to talk.

'We've come to help you because you've hurt yourself. Can you tell us what happened to you, honey?' she'd said to this bloodied mess of a boy.

He'd groaned.

'Were you run over by a car?'

'No,' the boy managed.

'What happened to you, sweetie? How did you get all these cuts?'

'When I falled off the back of that car.'

'Which car was that?'

'The one what is burnt.'

'How did you get there, sweetie? Did you walk?'

The boy nodded.

'What happened to your clothes? Did you have any clothes on?'

49

'Yeah,' he said. 'A man took them off.'

'A man took them off? Who is this man?'

The boy didn't answer. His eyes were wide with fear. The police officer tried again.

'Do you know who this man is?'

'Not allowed to tell.'

'Why aren't you allowed to tell? Did he tell you not to tell?'

The little boy nodded.

'But you're allowed to tell the police and I'm the police. So you're allowed to tell me, sweetie. We're going to take care of you now. No one will hurt you.'

The boy nodded.

'Do you know this man?'

The boy nodded again. And told her what she needed to know.

Just before he passed out from the pain, he pointed to his throat. It was sore, he said. It was sore because when he'd cried, the man had put his hands around his throat and choked him until he'd stopped.

*

Things were getting out of control in the park. People were trying to get in; others were trying to get out. A group of about 50 residents had formed a vigilante group, baying for the blood of the monster who could do such a thing to a child. An officer sat on a pine log fence outside the toilet block.

'What are you doing?' Sodoli asked him. It was the officer who'd had to duck a frypan. He pointed at the van. The man inside had dragged his fridge across the door, barricading himself inside. The van was opposite the toilet black. There was a bicycle out the front.

'What does he look like?' Sodoli asked.

The officer shrugged. 'Tall. Brown hair.'

The detective banged on the door.

'What do you fucking want?' a voice from inside said.

'My name's Matt Sodoli,' he said.

'Fuck off.'

'Nobody tells me to fuck off. Open the door,' Sodoli ordered.

'Fuck off.'

The detective turned to the crowd of officers behind him.

'Find me a sledgehammer.'

He had one in his hand a minute later. He had no idea where they'd found it. The first swing shattered the van's flimsy screen. The second smashed in the door. Sodoli kicked the fridge out of the way and dragged the man out by the head. The vigilante crowd was behind him. He shoved the man into a squad car and got them the hell out of there.

*

DNA was a little-known investigative tool in Darwin in 1993. Sodoli had called forensic scientist Joy Kuhl — the same biologist whose evidence had helped put Lindy Chamberlin in jail — for advice.

He was sending some blood samples her way, he said. He didn't know or care about warrants or procedures. They had a van out the front and male residents from the park were being asked to volunteer so they could be ruled out. Anyone who refused would be drawing plenty of attention to themselves.

*

Back at headquarters, Sodoli was the hero. His superiors were slapping him on the back for a job well done. Fensom was in an interview room. Their man was talking and the detective was more than a little furious. Too furious, in fact.

'What's going on?' Sodoli asked him.

Fensom and the man had a history. He told Sodoli the story. Six years earlier, Fensom had arrested the man for attempted murder. The man's partner had left him and fallen pregnant to her new beau. The man sitting in the interview room had cut her phone lines before breaking in and attacking her. The unborn child had been cut from her womb.

'This piece of shit,' Fensom said, pointing. 'That's who he is.'

*

The little boy who wasn't expected to survive did. Shaken residents sat around the park drinking and talking about the animal in their midst. Police continued gathering statements, and Tracey and her friend Liz had their turn. So did Brett.

'I'm going to find this rock spider arsehole,' he'd said as they all sat around.

Tracey thought he was acting strange. Silent. Broody. She told Liz she was having doubts about Brett. After all, he'd been missing when the little boy was attacked. Liz had tried to put her mind at ease.

'Don't be stupid,' she said. 'Brett wouldn't hurt anyone. He loves kids.'

But the strange behaviour continued.

'Let's leave Darwin,' he said to her after a couple of days. 'I'm sick of all the police everywhere. I've got a record. I don't want trouble.'

Tracey stared at him. She asked him if he was hiding anything.

'If you don't come with me,' he exploded, 'I'll go without you.'

*

They were basking in their success when a female officer walked into Detective Sodoli's office with a handful of statements. There was a problem. A discrepancy. A resident of the park — a Brett Peter Cowan — had given a statement saying he'd been in his van when the little boy was assaulted. But his girlfriend and her friend had told police he'd gone missing around the same time. They'd looked for him in the van and he hadn't been home.

'What have we got on him? What does he look like?' Sodoli asked.

'Tall,' the officer said. 'Slim. Mousy brown hair.'

It got worse. Brett lived just a couple of doors from the man they currently had in custody. Opposite the toilet block. A bicycle also sat outside his van. A quick check with interstate authorities revealed he'd been convicted of indecently assaulting a boy about the same age in a toilet block.

'Go pull him in,' Sodoli ordered.

*

They found him at work. He came without fuss. Tracey they found at the park. They pulled up alongside her in a detective's car as she walked to the shops. Sodoli spoke to her through the open window.

'Are you Tracey?' he said. 'Can you come with us?'

Tracey didn't like the police. And anyway, she hadn't done anything wrong. She told them as much.

'There's pot in the van, but that's not mine,' she volunteered.

'Brett needs to see you,' Sodoli told her. 'We've got him at the station.'

He wouldn't look at her when she walked into the room. That's how she knew it was true. She reached over and hit him.

*

Four days had passed between that little boy stumbling his way into the service station and Brett confessing to the attack. They had the boy's underpants, they told him. Whose DNA would they find on those pants? they asked.

Brett folded. But, as always, he did his best to mix truth with lies. The little boy had been looking for his sister, he told them. It had been easy. Brett had swung the boy up onto his shoulders, walked through a gate and out of the park. They'd wandered off into bushland and down a track where a pile of rusting car bodies sat.

'He never struggled,' Brett told detectives Stan Fensom and Scott Pollock during two days of formal interviews. 'Kept on walking down towards the cars. He asked me how much further and I just pointed 'em out and there they were. I went over and sat him on top of the car.'

He'd assaulted the boy, Brett said, before placing him, uninjured, on top of the rusting, jagged car bodies. He'd thrown the boys' underpants into the cars and walked away. The detectives looked at him.

'He — he hadn't had — hadn't had any blood on him?' Fensom asked.

'No. No injuries whatsoever.'

'And what was [the boy] doing at that stage?'

'He was sobbing and crying.'

'Well, what do you think he was sobbing and crying for?'

''Cause he was scared.'

'Did you throw [him] into the — into the wrecks of these cars?'

'No, I didn't throw him in there at all. I placed him, sat him in there. I didn't drop him.'

'Did you throttle him at all?'

'No I didn't.'

'Did you choke him?'

'Not that I can recall, no.'

The detectives didn't bother to say how ridiculous it was to suggest someone could 'forget' trying to strangle a child. They took out some photographs and placed them on the table. It was the little boy, caught in a camera lens, scarred and bloodied. Blood blisters covered his face. They made Brett look.

'Can you tell me what his face looks like?' Fensom asked.

'Bloodied and bruised and scratched,' Brett replied.

'This discoloration and bruising around the eyes and this pinpoint bruising here is a result of asphyxiation, is a result of strangling. Can you tell me anything about that?'

'No, I can't recall doing it at all.'

'Is it possible that you did strangle him?'

'Could be, yeah.'

'Why, why would you ... have strangled him?'

'I don't know. I couldn't recall it happening at all ...'

'OK, is it possible that [the boy] was unconscious when you put him in the — between the vehicles?'

'Could be. He wasn't talking. He was just sobbing and crying.'

'Is it possible that he was barely breathing?'

'Don't know.'

'Is it possible that at this stage, before you put [him] in here, you actually thought he was dead?'

'No, he was still crying and sobbing.'

'Well, is it possible the reason that you put him in here was an attempt to hide his body?'

'No.'

They went over the details again and again, waiting for him to slip.

'What do you think was going through his mind at that time?' Fensom asked.

'I don't know.'

'Do you think he wanted to stay or leave?'

'He probably wanted to leave.'

'How do you know that? Did he try to leave?'

'Nah, not at that stage.'

'Well, what was he doing?'

'He was just sitting there.'

'Why do you think he was just sitting there?'

'He was too scared to move.'

'Would you agree with me he possibly couldn't have moved because, as you said, he was too scared to move? Why do you think he was too scared to move?'

'Cause of what I was doing at the time to him.'

He agreed to take part in a video re-enactment the following morning. Detectives would follow him with a camera as he retraced his steps through the bush.

'As long as there's nobody from the park around,' Brett said. They told him there wouldn't be.

'Anything else?' Fensom asked him.

'There's only one thing I wanna add is, I wish I'd never done it. I wish it never happened.'

'All right.' Fensom was unmoved.

'I'm sorry,' Brett finished.

*

He got as far as the gate the next morning. Surrounded by police, his footsteps captured on film, Cowan stopped at the place where he'd carried the little boy through into the scrub to rape and strangle him.

He told them he couldn't go any further.

*

Tracey was there for Brett's first court appearance. Her mother had flown to Darwin to be by her side. Her mother had walked in first. Tracey sat beside her. She lasted only minutes, bursting out of those courthouse doors to vomit in the gutter.

*

Justice Dean Mildren sentenced Brett on 14 June 1994 on charges of committing an act of gross indecency, grievous harm and deprivation of liberty. The attempted murder charge Sodoli and Fensom had slapped on him was dropped when Brett pleaded guilty to the lesser charges.

'The child was naked, dazed and distressed,' Justice Mildren said. 'He was conveyed to the Royal Darwin Hospital where he was placed in intensive care. It was observed that he had a collapsed and punctured left lung, a deep cut to the back of the head and he had lacerations to the left leg below the knee, a deep cut at the base of his scrotum, a bloodied nose, blackened eyes, scratch marks over his torso.

'He was quiet, withdrawn, tearful, in pain and sedated. His hair, face and body were still relatively dirty with some blood still being present in the nostrils. There were superficial, multiple abrasions present on the legs, arms and the front of the trunk which were generally oblique and in roughly parallel groups. The deeper injuries to the left leg and the perineum were not seen. The injuries of the left scalp was noted to be repaired and surrounded by a blood clot. On local examination of the face, multiple injuries were noted on the front and left side of the face. These took the form of abrasions and bruises, being most prominent around the outer aspect of the left eye.'

The list of the boy's injuries went on. Bruises on his forehead. In his hairline. Abrasions around his mouth and over his lips. Across his cheek. But most tellingly, the boy had haemorrhaging in his left eye.

'[The doctor] says that the overall pattern of injuries indicated widespread repeated applications of both blunt and sharp force.'

The boy had been raped, the judge said. And raped with something. An irregularly shaped object that had left dirt and ash from a recent bushfire in his anal canal.

'The presence of congestion or suffusion of the face with generalised swelling in association with potential haemorrhages in the eyes was highly suggestive of an element of suffocation,' Justice Mildren said.

The boy, now aged seven, was suffering from post-traumatic stress disorder. He would need ongoing help. The judge turned to the subject of Brett.

'The details of his history ... are certainly not flattering,' he said. 'He is a small time drug peddler who uses his peddling to support his own drug addiction and he is a person who lives a parasitic existence, relying on social security and his parents to support himself. He is also a person with the ability to lie. He is apparently noted to be a pathological liar and a person who will steal even from his own parents.' But, Justice Mildren said, Brett had owned up to the attack on the boy. He'd even told police he needed help.

'I have heard evidence from Doctor Walton, a psychiatrist, on the prisoner's behalf, and Doctor Walton's view is that the defendant has a problem in relation to his interest in children but that help is available to him and he considers that he is a suitable candidate for pursuing that help,' the judge said.

Forensic psychiatrist Peter Mals had also spoken to Brett. Dr Mals had raised doubts about Brett's so-called plea for help.

'Mr Mals queries whether the defendant is genuinely remorseful, but so far as that is concerned, I am prepared to give the prisoner the benefit of any doubt that there may be on the issue because of his fairly spontaneous indication to the police that he needs help and the efforts that he has since made to pursue appropriate treatment,' Justice Mildren said. 'Whilst it is difficult to accurately assess his prospects of rehabilitation, I consider them to be at least fair to good as is evidenced by his remorse, his early plea and his own efforts to seek help.'

A difficult assessment or not, Justice Mildren was wrong. Brett Cowan had been abusing children nearly his whole life. And he would go on doing so.

Brett was sentenced to seven years jail with a non-parole period of three and a half years.

CHAPTER NINE
FINDING GOD

MARLENE'S YOUNGER SISTER JENNIFER Philbrook and her husband Keith were pastors at Woombye's Suncoast Christian Church. They taught forgiveness. They taught about helping people who are less fortunate. The Suncoast Christian Church is a large cream building on the corner of Kiel Mountain and Schubert Roads. It casts its shadow over an expansive car park that backs onto an overpass. It's the same overpass where dozens of motorists spotted a small boy in a red t-shirt on the afternoon of 7 December 2003.

Keith and Jenny hadn't ever seen much of their Cowan nephews when the boys were young; the family moved around so much. Sometimes Marlene would send photographs of her children. They would see them at family functions or when Peter and Marlene came to visit. Brett had always been likeable. Charming. He was easy to talk to. But he was also good at big-noting himself. He'd make overly optimistic predictions about his future. He had big plans beyond his capabilities.

When Brett was due for release from prison, it was Keith and Jenny who were asked to take him in. They discussed it at length. Brett was family. It was the right thing to do. But before they made their final decision, they went to see him.

They all met at the jail — Peter and Marlene, Keith and Jenny, Brett and his case workers. Brett had been moved to a Queensland prison, claiming he wanted to undertake a sex offenders' course not available in Darwin. It put him closer to his family, his only support. They sat within the prison's imposing walls as Brett told them what he'd done. He'd sexually assaulted a little boy in Darwin, he confessed. And then he'd left that boy to die. He didn't tell them everything, but what he did say left them stunned. He'd been sexually abusing children since he was a child himself, Brett said. He'd even had a 'relationship' with a younger female relative. But he'd done the sexual offenders course in prison. And he'd found religion. He'd become very interested in Christian teachings.

Keith and Jenny agreed to take Brett in. But in return, he had to abide by some strict rules.

The church pastors lived in a large two-storey house in Bli Bli, near Maroochydore. The property took up roughly an acre. Just off the main house was a besser-block granny flat. It had its own carport, a '70s kitchen with green benches and wood panels, a bathroom and a small laundry. It was here that Brett would live. He was to pay board of $65 a week, and he would attend church and find himself a job. He was to be open with them if there were any problems they wanted to discuss. His behaviour. Alcohol. Things like that.

He agreed. A couple of months after their meeting at the jail, Brett arrived at the Philbrooks' Bli Bli house. He turned up looking clean and fresh. His hair was neat and he was clean-shaven. Sometimes he ate dinner with them and was full of polite conversation. Brett paid his rent in cash and the Philbrooks stashed it away in a drawer. He went with them to church and was enthusiastic about being a Christian. He read the Bible. Learned passages. The church had set up rules for him, too. Keith had been to visit the head pastor, Chas Gullo, and told him about Brett's past. Chas spoke to Brett and immediately laid down the law. He would be constantly monitored. He was not allowed to approach any children. He was certainly not allowed to have anything to do with the church's youth work programs, or Kids Zone, the children's ministry.

It was during the regular church services that Brett met the Davis family. Trevor Davis ran a sandblasting company. His parents, Frank and Hazel, liked Brett. They found him friendly and charming. Brett was a handy sort of person. A jack-of-all-trades and a backyard mechanic. Trevor took Brett on at the sandblasting business. Brett had been using a bicycle and public transport to get around but his parents gave him a ute so he could get to work. His aunt and uncle were pleased to see him making friends at the church and getting into a routine. He seemed to be doing well. And then he wasn't.

The car gave him back his freedom. Brett started going out late at night or during the early hours of the morning. Keith and Jenny noticed men coming to visit the granny flat and suspected they were friends he'd made in prison. And they knew when he left at odd hours; the sensor light in the driveway would come on. The Philbrooks spoke to him about mixing with the right people. Was he making good decisions? Was he getting involved in things he shouldn't be?

'I'm just going fishing,' he told them. They had their doubts.

Then one day Keith noticed the sensor from the sensor light had been redirected. Brett had angled it so it didn't detect his car coming and going down the driveway. They were worried he was misbehaving. His appearance had changed, too. He looked rougher. They worried he was using drugs. They'd never heard from a parole officer. Nobody had come to check whether Brett was staying on the straight and narrow.

*

In 1998, a new family joined the Suncoast Christian Church. A woman named Tracey and her parents started attending services and the Philbrooks decided to invite them around for a BBQ. Brett was home for the BBQ and made a beeline for the young woman standing with her parents. He knew how to work his charm. She'd been told he'd only recently been in prison — for stealing. He seemed to come from a good family, though.

They became friends first. Tracey had a compliant personality. She didn't like to argue or be difficult. She was much more likely to agree, to go along with things, than argue a point. Their friendship continued on for six months before it became something more.

They'd only been dating a short while when he revealed the real reason he'd been in prison. He'd molested a little boy, he told her. It had happened in Darwin. He'd assaulted the boy and then gone to have a shower. Afterwards, filled with concern, he'd gone back and found the child and taken him home. As usual, Brett's attempt at 'honesty' involved more lies than truth. He handed her some court documents to read — paperwork filled with vast areas of blacked-out text. It hardly told her anything. When she was finished, he gathered up the paperwork and burnt it.

'I've reformed,' he told her. 'I've found God.'

Tracey was a good person who believed there was good in everyone. Brett's revelation was shocking but she had been taught to forgive. She was a Christian and so was Brett. Everybody deserved a second chance — and she would give him one.

The Philbrooks were pleased when Brett started dating Tracey. His late-night activities came to a halt and he started looking after his appearance again. He told Tracey he wanted them to wait until they were married to have sex. He knew it was important to her. She was a regular visitor to his granny flat on the Philbrooks' property. She was there one day chatting to him as he took a shower. When he was done, he dried himself off, wrapped the towel around his waist and grabbed her in an embrace. He kissed her and she kissed him back.

Then, suddenly, he spun her around and dragged her shorts down around her ankles. She told him to stop. He didn't. He shoved her against the washing machine and assaulted her. She cried when it was over.

'I'm sorry,' he said. 'I won't do that again.'

His no-sex-before-marriage pledge lasted only days. He wore her down, convincing her by small degrees that it was OK. Tracey was very compliant.

He'd been with the Philbrooks about a year but now that he had a job and a girlfriend, it was time to move on. Tracey helped him secure a lease on a small house in Beerwah on a quiet street of wide green lawns and spacious homes. His was a little cottage on a larger property. At the end of the street was a view of the Sunshine Coast's majestic Glasshouse Mountains. Tracey stayed with her parents while he moved in to the cottage on his own; she promised to join him once they were married.

The wedding plans were underway when the Philbrooks realised Brett's board money was gone. They'd been keeping it in a cupboard drawer in the living area, amassing around $1000. They suspected Brett, of course. Keith and Jenny organised a meeting with Tracey, her parents and Brett. They were all sitting down when the Philbrooks asked Brett if he'd taken the money. Of course he hadn't, Brett told them. Brett knew how to deny, deny, deny.

But Tracey wasn't convinced. She delayed the wedding, giving herself time to think things over. Eventually she decided to go through with it. They met with a pastor at the church for their pre-wedding counselling sessions. They discussed their relationship, their vows to one another. Afterwards, when Brett was out of earshot, the pastor pulled Tracey aside. There'd been a complaint, he told her. A teenage girl from the church had accused Brett of sexual assault. They'd been on the way to a street ministry when he'd pounced.

Tracey listened. She knew Brett was capable of doing some very bad things but she refused to believe what the pastor was telling her. She thanked him for letting her know and went back to her wedding preparations.

*

Melissa Bridges was 15 when it happened. They'd been on the way to help out at a street ministry soup kitchen. Brett had arranged to pick Melissa up from home, as well as another, older, church member.

She'd been a little surprised when he turned up in a van, dressed in overalls and covered in paint. He told her with a grin that he had to drop in at home before picking up the other person. He needed a quick shower and a change of clothes. She could do nothing but go along with it. Melissa waited in the house as he showered. He emerged from the bathroom a short time later, wearing a towel and a healthy dose of aftershave.

He grabbed the frightened girl and pushed her against a computer table, clawing at her clothing and grabbing her breasts. She shoved him off, using her knee to push him backwards before making a dash for the door. It was a lucky escape. Brett was certainly capable of worse.

*

In September 1999, Tracey married the only man she'd ever been with. Brett Cowan was clean-shaven and his hair was short and neat when he met her at the altar.

After the wedding, Tracey moved in to the cottage at Beerwah. When he'd lived alone, Brett had spent a lot of his time watching pornography on his computer. He hadn't tried to hide it from Tracey. She didn't approve and after they moved in together, she told him he'd have to stop.

For a while, life went on. Brett went to work. He tinkered with cars and worked in the yard. He'd shower every night without fail — always wanting to put on a clean set of clothes after dinner. They went to church. They became friends with Trevor Davis and his wife. Trevor spoke about setting Brett up with his own sandblasting business. He wanted to help Brett succeed. Brett's response to the generous offer was lukewarm.

Eventually, Brett fell back into old habits. Strange visitors started coming to the house. Brett was buying drugs and growing marijuana under the house. Tracey did not like this. Sometimes she would be with him when Brett dropped by his drug dealer's house — a woman who lived down the street. Tracey mostly stayed in the car.

Brett started watching porn again. Tracey thought it was disgusting. He showed her the sites he liked to frequent. Images of people having sex with animals or people with no arms or legs having sex.

*

Tracey fell pregnant with their first child in 2002. Brett was excited about becoming a father. She was still pregnant when Brett had an operation for carpal tunnel, a condition where pressure on the nerves in the wrist can cause pain and discomfort. He was off work for some time. While Tracey cooked and cleaned, Brett sat on the couch and drank and smoked marijuana. Her tolerance seemed limitless.

She gave birth to a little boy in July. Brett was a proud dad but not much help. By now, Tracey was seeing the sudden flares of his temper. Someone cutting him off in traffic or someone making a comment he disagreed with could set him off.

He refused to go to church after an argument with a pastor over a sermon. They used to go all the time. Sunday morning and Sunday night services. Tuesday night prayer meetings and Wednesday night home group. Sometimes they'd had home group at their place in Beerwah.

But Brett took exception to a sermon about sin. The pastor told his congregation there was no such thing as an unforgivable sin. All things could be forgiven. All acts. All mistakes. Brett — who needed forgiveness more than anyone — disagreed. That's not what the Bible says, he told the pastor. How could they be preaching things that weren't true?

'They're hypocrites,' he said of the people from the church. 'They're all the same. They're just money-hungry, preaching, brainwashing pricks.'

His relationship with his wife was deteriorating. They were far from intimate. They didn't even really talk any more. She was busy with the baby and he was doing his own thing. They passed each other in the house with barely a glance. He still liked to be home to watch the news each night. Tracey remembered seeing reports of the little boy who'd gone missing in the area. A boy named Daniel Morcombe.

Then, a few days before Christmas, she answered a knock at the door.

PART TWO
PERSONS OF INTEREST

CHAPTER TEN
SUSPECTS

IN 2003, WHEN DANIEL made the walk from his home to the Kiel Mountain Road overpass, there were no cameras to capture his progress. They'd held hope when one was spotted across the road, poised to film activity at a caravan sales yard. But the camera turned out to be a dummy. A deterrent. Police even made inquiries with the military. Was there a satellite recording activity? They checked with commercial satellite operators too. But there was no surveillance captured from above at the exact time they needed.

One week to the day after Daniel disappeared, police set up a mannequin dressed in the same clothing the teenager had worn that day and placed it under the overpass. They pulled over every single car travelling south on the Nambour Connection Road and asked drivers and passengers about their movements the week before. Some had information that could prove useful. Some had already come forward. Some hadn't. In all, 84 people gave eyewitness accounts of seeing Daniel, a person of interest or a vehicle of interest.

A break-in not far from the Morcombes' home was checked out. Images from speed cameras and red-light cameras were downloaded and viewed by investigators.

Detective Sergeant Tracey Barnes from the Sunshine Coast CIB was brought in to be Operation Vista's 'reader', the person responsible for reading over every job log or piece of information coming into the Major Incident Room. A single person could pick up patterns or discrepancies in the enormous volume of information coming in. Individual officers conducting individual inquiries could not.

69

Police began putting together a list of 'persons of interest'. Potential suspects. Some were nominated through Crime Stoppers or by people coming in to their local police station. Others came from a list of local convicted pedophiles Sunshine Coast police had been working on for Operation Butcher.

Operation Butcher was an investigation conducted by the Sunshine Coast District Intelligence Office. It was designed as a means of identifying pedophiles or pedophile networks operating in the area. Anyone with a history of child sex assaults or similar behaviour was added to a database. Information was also gathered on the methods used to target victims. Anyone on the Operation Butcher database was checked out by detectives. Officers from Task Force Argos and State Crime Operations Command were brought in to help local police track each one down and grill them on their whereabouts on the afternoon of 7 December.

*

Detective Senior Constable Dennis Martyn and Constable Kenneth King had been seconded to Operation Vista to help work through the list of pedophiles. Their job was to knock on the door and get an alibi. Martyn was from Task Force Argos. He had years of experience dealing with pedophiles. Some had been bad. Some had been worse than bad. He knew from reading Brett's history that he fell into the latter category.

And if he hadn't known he was knocking on the door of a pedophile's home when he called on Brett, he could have picked it after pulling up out the front. The yard was decorated with colourful little windmills — the type of trinkets a pedophile would use to attract children. Martyn's eyes narrowed. He didn't like it and he hadn't even got out of the car.

The man who answered the door fitted the description given by bus passengers and passers-by. But then, so did countless others. Tracey was home with the baby. She seemed polite and shy. She didn't ask questions or try to intervene and didn't seem like the sort that ever would.

Martyn looked around. Here he had a predator of the worst order with a front garden set up to lure children, and a submissive wife. She was the perfect cover for a man who wanted to slip under the radar. Who would suspect a married man? A family man with a child? And that was another thing. A child was here. A baby. In this house, with this man. Martyn's anger was growing.

Brett was friendly and affable but his eyes slid away. He kept looking at his car as they spoke. King was suspicious as well. Brett seemed too eager to please. After all, they were there to ask if he'd kidnapped and murdered a child. Why was he so relaxed? He seemed like someone who would smile and laugh as he casually tried to talk his way out of trouble.

The officers asked Brett about his movements on the afternoon of 7 December. He told them he'd been to pick up a mulcher so he could get rid of some tree branches. He'd picked it up from his old boss's parents' house in Nambour, taking his and Tracey's white Mitsubishi Pajero up the Nambour Connection Road.

Brett said he'd left about 1.30 p.m. and arrived about half an hour later. He'd grabbed the mulcher, dumped it in the back of the 4WD and driven straight home. He would have been back somewhere between 2.30 p.m. and 2.45 p.m. Brett's voice was casual. But unbelievably, he'd just put himself in a car driving past the exact spot Daniel was last seen — and at the right time. King asked whether he'd noticed a boy in a red shirt standing by the overpass.

He'd noticed nothing, Brett said, except for a broken-down bus on the side of the road. He hadn't thought much about it.

'Bullshit,' Martyn told him. The detective didn't believe a word Brett said.

He let them photograph him. The picture shows a man with short hair who'd recently shaved. He also agreed to them taking a sample of his DNA. It would seem that Brett was being overly cooperative — but in fact, as a convicted sex offender, his DNA had long been on file. It made no difference to Brett if they took it again. They also photographed his various tattoos — a skull on his upper left arm and a skull and scroll on his upper right arm. They noted a large scar on his chest from heart surgery he'd had as a teenager.

Tracey confirmed Brett had been to collect a mulcher from Nambour on the afternoon of the 7th. She'd been to church that morning with the baby, she explained. She would have driven by the Kiel Mountain Road overpass that morning too — although much earlier than the times they were interested in. No, she told them, she hadn't seen anything unusual.

The officers had one more call to make. They dialled Frank Davis's home number. He too agreed Brett had been by two weeks ago. He was there for about five minutes — enough time to load the mulcher into the car. Then they'd waved him off and gone about their day.

They were getting ready to leave when Tracey pulled Martyn aside. She told him she'd washed Brett's clothes that day. He'd arrived home in the afternoon and asked her to wash the clothes he'd been wearing. She had.

King and Martyn looked at each other as they drove away. There was plenty about Brett Cowan they hadn't liked. More than that, they were convinced they'd knocked on the door of Daniel's killer.

*

Two more officers came back two days before Christmas. This time they were there to see Tracey. She invited them in and agreed to answer questions. She told them she had been to church on 7 December. She took the baby but Brett had stayed at home. They'd met through the church but her husband had had a falling out with a pastor and now he refused to attend.

'I went to the morning service from 9.30 a.m. to about 11, 11.30 a.m.,' she said. 'It takes about 25 to 30 minutes on a good run to drive from home to the church, so I would have got home at about midday or a bit later that day.'

She arrived home to find Brett doing chores in the garden. Tracey went inside and made them both some lunch. Brett ate his and told her that he was going to pick something up from the Davises' in Nambour.

Their relationship was strained. They didn't talk much. He drove off in the 4WD and came back as the sun was hitting the cottage's back room. She thought it was about 3 p.m. but couldn't be sure. Perhaps it was 2.45 p.m. Or maybe it was closer to 3.15 p.m. She apologised; she'd had no reason to look at her watch.

They spoke again to Brett. He told them he was sure he'd arrived home at 2.30 p.m. He said the neighbours, John Fragos and his son Eric, had come over to help with the tree branches.

Police went next door. John and Eric told them that yes, they'd been over to help Brett with the gardening. John had no idea what time it had been. Eric seemed to think it was early to mid-afternoon. On the surface, Brett's alibi seemed tight.

'Having regard to the loose times and the inability of those involved to narrow down those times any better, it is not likely that Cowan would have the ability to commit this offence in the time frame outlined, having regard to the fact that he had arranged to do the mulching that afternoon and then did in fact meet those arrangements,' a report compiled by those officers stated.

Detective Senior Constable Dennis Martyn wrote a report too. It went for 10 pages and spelt out in detail why he and Constable King thought Brett was their man. It recommended seizing his car immediately. It recommended seizing his computer immediately. What if Brett had taken photographs of Daniel after kidnapping him and uploaded them to the internet?

Martyn's experience with pedophiles showed they were likely to do just that. He'd been one of the detectives who'd brought a

Brisbane-based pedophile ring to justice. Shannon Lee Voigt, Earl James Henderson and Leigh William Andrews would face court for more than 100 child sex charges. They were given lengthy jail terms for abusing several young boys, forcing them to perform sex acts on the men and each other while being photographed. The images were shared online, eventually coming to the attention of authorities in the US.

To Martyn, Brett was worse than Voigt, Henderson and Andrews. His actions in the past had been far more vicious, more violent. He handed his report into the Major Incident Room, to be passed on to Assistant Commissioner Mike Condon, the officer now leading the investigation. But the report, and the recording they'd made while speaking to Brett, were lost soon after. Martyn would recall Condon did not appear keen to take advice from such junior officers.

*

Some police officers believed Brett's alibi was solid. His movements that day were basically accounted for. When would he have had time to lure a child away from the roadside, murder him and dispose of his body — and then return to do the gardening as though nothing had happened? Besides, the car people had seen at the scene was a boxy blue sedan. Brett drove a white 4WD.

Others could not get past the fact that a convicted pedophile with a history of grabbing and abusing children had admitted to being in the right place at the right time. Whatever the thinking, officers returned on Christmas Eve and asked to conduct a forensic examination of Brett's Mitsubishi Pajero. Brett, of course, agreed, with police noting he was 'extremely cooperative and understanding of [the] investigation'.

They found no visible blood, nothing to show Daniel had been in the car. This was not unusual, the forensic officers told investigators. Someone could sit in a car and leave no trace behind.

An officer used tape lifts in an attempt to capture any DNA. The tape lifts were sent to Queensland Health, where they were set aside and forgotten about. It would be years before someone would remember to test them. They came up clean.

*

There were so many eyewitness accounts of a blue car at the abduction site that investigators set up a 'blue car room'. It was small and plastered with photographs of cars — 37 of them, in fact. They were all blue. Each car had been photographed from the front, back and side. Investigators would bring their witness into the room and ask them to pick out the car they'd seen. The witness was filmed as they walked around the room, looking for the right one. Some were entirely certain the car they were pointing out was the correct one. Others found the room and its kaleidoscope of cars confronting.

Police also looked into the idea that two men had been involved in the abduction. Some witnesses had more than one person with Daniel. Perhaps one of the men had called the other? Police applied to every telecommunications carrier and laboriously checked through the 1600 calls made through 14 different towers around the time Daniel disappeared. It was an incredibly time-consuming task. With the list in hand, police tracked down each and every caller and asked them to explain what they were doing in the area at the time. Their efforts would come to nought. Daniel's killer or killers had not made a call.

As the days wore on, senior police put pressure on investigators to get witnesses to assist with 'comfits'. Without a suspect or a murder scene, it was hoped a sketch of the man spotted waiting at the bus stop would help identify him. Witnesses helped produced several but police were now hesitant to release them to the media. No two were alike. They worried the images might not be accurate enough.

On 14 December — a week after Daniel's disappearance — police returned to the Suncoast Christian Church and videoed all the cars coming and going from the morning service. Nineteen of those cars were boxy blue sedans. The drivers were spoken to and their whereabouts the week before ascertained. Another dead end.

A second doorknock of the area took place a couple of weeks after Daniel's disappearance. Officers completed a questionnaire, jotting down any information from each household. The information was then logged on the Queensland Police database.

Police went to the Big Pineapple, the nearby tourist attraction where some witnesses had reported seeing a blue car or unusual activity. Staff were interviewed and call records checked.

Items were taken from the Morcombe home and sent to a laboratory so Daniel's DNA profile could be obtained and kept on file. They did the same with his fingerprints, managing to obtain a full set that was then stored on the National Automated Fingerprint Identification System.

And all the while, detectives continued to work on their POI list — a lengthy catalogue of child abusers, murderers and sadists.

CHAPTER ELEVEN
DOUGLAS 'RAT' JACKWAY

PSYCHOPATH DOUGLAS BRIAN JACKWAY was walking evil, an incurable sadist without a conscience. His history as a child sex offender and his connections to the Sunshine Coast put him on the list of people who needed to be checked and cleared by Operation Vista detectives. He also drove an older model Holden Commodore — blue in colour.

A month before Daniel Morcombe disappeared, Doug Jackway walked from prison a free man. He'd spent most of his adult life behind bars. He'd had eight years to think about what he'd done to the little boy he found playing with friends. He'd spent those years fighting with prison authorities. Refusing to take part in the sex offenders course — or any rehabilitation at all. Even his family was sorry to see him released.

It was a Sunday in April 1995 when Jackway had come across three little boys playing on a bike track in a country town in Central Queensland. They were school friends — in Grade 5 at the local primary — out riding their bikes on a day when the classroom wasn't calling.

Jackway had been alone in a white car, following them at a snail's pace as they rode towards a nearby bridge. But then the boys changed their minds and steered their bikes the other way. Jackway followed. The path was narrow, a ravine on one side leading down to the water. One of the boys got off his bike to wheel it past the car on the passenger side. He didn't want to fall off the edge. Jackway got out of his car.

'Do you know the way to Gladstone?' he called.

One of the boys turned towards him.

'When you near the intersection, turn left, and just follow the

77

road and you should make it to Gladstone,' the boy, aged nine, said.

Jackway nodded and walked towards them as the boy gave him directions. His friend stood with him. Jackway closed the gap and punched the friend in the head. A grown man with a clenched fist can easily knock a little boy to the ground. The boy stood stunned as his friend went down. Jackway grabbed him by the arm and dragged him towards the car. The boy screamed and Jackway put a rough hand over the child's eyes and mouth. The boy heard the car door open and felt himself being shoved inside. The wheels spun as Jackway took off at speed, holding the terrified child against the car seat with the arm that wasn't steering. He headed towards a nearby park, driving erratically as he neared a wooden bridge.

He was still holding onto the boy when he crashed into the bridge. They weren't far from the other boys, but it was good enough for Jackway. He dragged the child out and pushed him down towards an area of swamp and mangroves.

'Go down here,' he told the boy.

He undressed the child and took off the bike helmet he was still wearing. Jackway looked around. Not far enough, he decided. He dragged the boy further into the mangroves before taking off his own clothing.

It was here that he raped the nine-year-old boy, punching him repeatedly for being frightened in between depraved sexual assaults. Terrified and hurting from a multitude of injuries, the boy thought he would certainly die. Time stood still as the assault went on. It felt like an age. It felt like hours.

In reality, Jackway raped the boy for as long as it took the child's friends to make it back home. They arrived, hysterical, at the boy's father's home, shouting for help. The boy's father called police, and together with an officer, burst his way through the mangroves to catch Jackway, naked, in the act.

Jackway shouted at them for interrupting. And despite the circumstances, denied that he'd done a thing.

*

They came for Douglas Jackway on 10 December 2003 — three days into the investigation into Daniel's disappearance.

They asked him where he was on 7 December. They'd go over the details again and again, tracking Jackway through every moment from when he'd walked out of those prison gates, a box of personal possessions in his hands.

*

Doug Jackway was born in 1976, the third of four siblings, and grew up on the Sunshine Coast. He didn't go to school much, but when he did, he attended Tewantin State School. He sporadically showed up at Noosa High School until they expelled him. He was put on a control order at the age of 15 and was jailed two years later when that failed to curb his behaviour. He was still a teenager when he was accused of the prolonged sexual abuse of a schoolgirl. The girl said he'd used a knife to ensure her submission. But it would be years before she'd find enough courage to take him to court over it.

Jackway was 27 when they released him from Wolston Correctional Centre, a Queensland jail filled with pedophiles, rapists, murderers and high-profile criminals. And despite spending nearly his entire adult life behind bars, he managed to find himself a girlfriend while on the inside. She'd been to the jail to visit her boyfriend but decided Jackway was a better deal. His relationship with Debbie — a single mum from Goodna — had developed through prison visits, telephone calls and letter writing. She'd told him he was welcome to come and stay. And so he did.

He wasn't her only house guest. Aside from Debbie's daughters and their children, a man named Fred was staying at the property too. Jackway ordered him out of the house but was initially content with Fred sleeping in his car, parked down the back of the yard. That was until he found the letters.

79

They were hidden in a bag stashed in the downstairs section of the house and revealed that Fred was the brother of Debbie's former prison boyfriend. They gave Jackway the impression there might be something going on between Fred and Debbie. He was right. Until Jackway arrived, Fred had been her live-in boyfriend.

They had a rowdy argument, broken up by Debbie, who demanded they 'settle down'. A shaky truce was reached.

Jackway made other 'friends', too. A 16-year-old boy named Michael had been hanging around the house. He was the boyfriend of one of Debbie's daughters. Michael was much younger than Jackway, but Jackway didn't mind. They went fishing together, smoked marijuana and drank together. Michael became infatuated with Jackway and soon broke things off with his girlfriend to spend more time with his new, older friend.

Jackway was also spending a lot of time with an old jail mate, Paul Carrington. Paul was a pedophile too. He'd taken a young boy from Bundaberg and driven him to Sydney, sexually assaulting him along on the way. He spent his freedom hanging around Ipswich, offering young men cash in exchange for sexual favours.

Jackway had been out just two weeks when he and Michael headed out in Jackway's Commodore for a day of fishing and drinking. After a while, they left to go driving through Noosa. It was schoolies weekend and a group of girls flagged them down in Hastings Street.

'What do youse want?' Jackway asked them.

'Can you get us alcohol?' one asked.

'Listen,' he told them, 'I'll get youse alcohol. If youse have got the money, I'll buy it.'

Six girls jumped in the back of the Commodore and Jackway did his civic duty for a group of underage school leavers. He dropped them off and parked near a roundabout. A bouncer approached.

'You're not supposed to be drinking here,' he said.

'Yeah, whatever, mate,' Jackway told him, and smashed a beer bottle at the bouncer's feet.

The bouncer grabbed at Jackway, who shoved him off and headed back to his car. He was revving the engine when a police officer approached and pointed at him to stop.

'Turn your car off,' the officer told him.

Jackway gave him the finger and took off — backwards. He was pretty drunk and the car took out a fence in reverse before becoming stuck on a roundabout.

The policeman ran for his car as Jackway revved his engine, driving the car backwards and forwards until he got it off the roundabout. And then it was on. Jackway, with Michael still in the car, put his foot to the floor, the police in pursuit. He hit 170 kilometres an hour in parts until the Commodore hit a set of road spikes laid by police. The tyres of Jackway's Commodore blew out and they soon had him in cuffs.

*

Jackway was not in custody for long. His car would be impounded for longer. He was soon on his way, a date with a magistrate entered into his calendar. He went to collect the Commodore on 5 December, asking his new 'friend' Fred to drive him. His Commodore needed a new set of tyres, so Jackway stole some and stashed them in the boot of Fred's car.

They stopped in at a BP service station where Jackway filled up Fred's car with petrol. He was inside handing over the cash when the service attendant asked him which car he was paying for. Jackway turned around to point. Fred was gone. He wouldn't see Fred — or his stolen wheels — again.

*

A practised thief need not stay empty-handed for long. Stranded at the service station and needing a lift to reclaim his car, Jackway solved his problems by stealing another car. Michael jumped in with him and they drove together to the impound lot at Kunda Park on the Sunshine Coast.

They parked the stolen car nearby and Jackway handed over his hard-earned Centrelink money to get his Commodore back. The stolen car solved another problem. Jackway put it up on bricks while he removed the wheels and replaced the four shredded tyres on his own car. They hadn't been able to take anything out of the car after the police chase ended. It had sat in an impound lot for two and a half weeks, bait and fish rotting inside it. Jackway drove his stinking car home to Goodna to clean it out. Windows down.

On Saturday afternoon, he and Michael were back in the Commodore driving around. They stopped in at Michael's parents' place so he could hassle them for money. They used it to put some fuel in the car and buy a bag of marijuana. They spent the rest of the money on alcohol and headed off to a party at the house of Paul Carrington — Jackway's prison buddy. They drank until they got a call from Debbie. Her daughter needed picking up. She was at another party and falling-down drunk. Debbie's daughter ended up sprawled in the gutter when he tried to get her in the car. Back at Goodna, he left her under the shower in her clothes and went to bed.

He woke at 7.30 the next morning. Debbie was outside, wanting to be let in. She'd been out the night before too and was only just arriving home. A man named Stuart was waiting in a car out the front. Jackway was furious. He yelled at her, and Debbie, who had a broken arm, swung her plaster cast at him. He walked away from her and she followed him through the house, still yelling.

'This is it,' he told her. 'I'm leaving. It's over. It's finished.'

He ran upstairs and grabbed a knife before jumping in his car. He knew where Stuart lived. He arrived to find him on his way out the door, headed to work. Jackway followed him for a while but Stuart wouldn't pull over. He saw him on the phone and figured he was probably calling the police. Jackway gave up and went back to Debbie's house.

It was here that he discovered Stuart hadn't called the police at all. He'd called Debbie. And she was furious. They argued until one of Debbie's ex-boyfriends arrived. Someone had called him for help. He arrived to find Jackway sitting out the front cradling the fishing knife he'd taken with him when he'd tried to chase Stuart down.

'What's the knife for? Can you put the knife away?' the ex-boyfriend asked Jackway.

Jackway eyed him. 'What are you doing here first?'

'Listen, mate, I'm only here to talk to you.'

Jackway stashed the knife and the two men talked.

'Debbie, she's no good for you,' the man said. 'You should just leave. Pack your gear.'

Jackway told him it was none of his business. Eventually the ex-boyfriend left. Jackway stayed. At least for a while. The arguing continued until he could take it no more. In between the arguing, Jackway took a minute out to call his sister. He had to front court on the Sunshine Coast the following morning and wanted to stay at her house for the night, close by. But his sister didn't want him in the house.

'You're going to have to sleep in the car,' she told him.

From here, the remainder of Jackway's day is hazy. He would tell police many versions. In one, he hit the bottle shop and then got in touch with Paul. He needed somewhere to stay. It was over with Debbie. Paul thought about it. Jackway wasn't the best house guest. But eventually he agreed. Jackway packed a bag and headed to his mate's house. He was sitting out the back under the trees when Paul brought him the phone.

'Listen,' Paul said. 'Debbie's on the phone.'

'I don't want to talk to her,' he said. 'You can tell her that, too.'

Debbie gave it 10 minutes and called again. She wanted to work things out. Could he come home? Jackway got in the car once again and drove the 30 minutes back to Goodna. They met in a park and talked for an hour or two. Then they went home. His times were vague. He would claim he went to Michael's parents' house at 5.30 p.m. to collect a mattress. It was also probably the day he dropped in to Super Cheap Auto to steal more items for his car than he could carry.

He never arrived at his sister's house. But when Noosa Magistrates Court opened its doors on Monday morning to a line of drunk drivers, shoplifters and drug-users, Jackway was among them.

*

Jackway gave police from the Sexual Crimes Investigation Unit a statement on 10 December. They hadn't told him much about what they were doing there. They just wanted to know where he'd spent his weekend. Then they methodically checked everything he'd told them.

On 12 December, detectives arrived at Michael's mother's house. She told them she'd seen her son and his friend 'Jacko' on Sunday morning at 10.30 a.m. They'd wanted motor oil for Jackway's car. They were always dropping around asking for money or cigarettes, she said. They had told her Jackway had court the next day, and they would both be driving up the coast that afternoon, staying with Jackway's sister, ready for the morning appearance.

She told the police she didn't see them again until the Monday afternoon, when they'd arrived to collect Michael's mattress. She'd noticed bandaids on Jackway's left knuckles that day. They definitely hadn't been there the day before. He'd also been dressed strangely — he'd worn sandals with long socks, pulled up to cover his calves. Jackway didn't normally dress like that. They'd both looked tired. They'd complained of breaking down on the way back from the coast. No, she told police, she hadn't seen them on Sunday afternoon.

Not long after the police visited, Michael called.

'Have you spoken to the police?' he asked her. Should they ask, he instructed, he and Jackway had been to collect the mattress on Sunday.

'It wasn't Sunday,' she replied.

Police dropped in on Jackway on 10 December, 11 December and 12 December. Then spoke to his friends. Pulled phone records. As they continued to track his movements, Jackway kept busy badgering those who could threaten his alibi. Michael's mother told police Jackway had called her three times demanding she tell them he'd been by to collect the mattress on Sunday. But Jackway's friends confirmed he'd intended to drive to the Sunshine Coast Sunday afternoon but had remained in Brisbane until Monday morning.

In his 12 December version of events, Jackway told police he'd actually been to Super Cheap Auto twice on Sunday. He'd bought spark plugs and a pipe clamp the first time and spray paint for his bonnet scoop on the second trip. He said he'd left Debbie's house at Goodna at 5 a.m. Monday and arrived in Noosa at 7.30 a.m.

Then, later that day, he heard a news report about a missing boy who'd been on his way to the shops when he'd disappeared from a bus stop. He picked up the phone and dialled the police. He told them he knew now why they'd been asking him so many questions. His recollections, he admitted to the officer, may not have been so accurate.

*

By early January, surveillance crews were tailing Jackway. There were many senior police insistent he was their strongest suspect. He had a history of child abduction and rape. He was violent. Unpredictable. A psychopath. He was certainly capable of the crime. They'd lost track of how many times he'd changed his story about his movements on 7 December. Police could place him on the Sunshine Coast the morning after Daniel's disappearance. And he'd gone ballistic when they'd arrived to seize his car — a car that was blue and boxy like the one seen pulled over at the Kiel Mountain Road overpass.

Brett Cowan was a good fit too. But his white 4WD was all wrong and his alibi was tight.

On 9 January, after days of fruitless surveillance came to an end, simultaneous raids were carried out on Debbie's home at Goodna and Paul's Ipswich house. They found nothing linking Jackway to Daniel Morcombe. They came back later with a warrant for the blue Commodore. Jackway was sick of them. They'd been coming at him for weeks. Talking to his friends, asking question after question about where he'd been.

'That's my fucking car,' he shouted at them. 'No cunt touches it!' He ranted and railed and eventually had to be restrained. As the car was loaded onto the back of a tow truck, an officer asked Jackway if he needed a lift somewhere.

'No,' he said. 'I'm not going with no pig in no cop car.'

A forensic search of the car proved fruitless. It had been recently cleaned.

*

Police pulled call charge records from both Debbie's and Paul's houses. A call was made from Debbie's house in Goodna to Paul's at 12.29 p.m. on 7 December. Paul would tell police this was Jackway, asking him for money so he could fill his car with petrol. Jackway needed to drive to the Sunshine Coast for court the next day.

Paul called Jackway back at 1.03 p.m. Debbie answered. She told him Jackway had gone out. At 3.33 p.m., a call was made from Debbie's house to Paul's. Paul told police this was Jackway calling again to say he was on his way to collect the cash. He turned up with Michael a short time later.

This left a three-hour window where Jackway could potentially have been missing from Debbie's home at Goodna. Goodna to Woombye by car takes an hour and a half. A report compiled on Jackway concluded he 'would have had insufficient time to travel to the Sunshine Coast and commit this offence'.

Regardless, some police would remain convinced he was their man.

CHAPTER TWELVE
THE SCRUFFY MAN

IT WAS COMING UP to the first anniversary of Daniel's disappearance when a sketch of a scruffy-looking man appeared on a prime-time television program. It was one of the comfit images put together by witnesses who'd seen a man standing behind a boy in a red t-shirt under the Kiel Mountain Road overpass that day. Police had waited a long time to release the comfits. It was incredibly risky. They were unreliable and often ended up looking nothing like the person they depicted.

In this case, the response was immediate. Among the calls that came in, one named Brett Peter Cowan as bearing a striking resemblance to the police sketch. Brett, the caller said, had offered an 11-year-old boy $5 to suck his penis. He was a welder by trade, drove a white 4WD and had spent time in prison.

*

On 30 November, nine days after the program aired, Detective Sergeant Mick Pownell was involved in serving a search warrant on a house at Moranbah. The occupant, a Brett Peter Cowan, was suspected of having stolen property from his old workplace. They'd also been chasing him over a house fire from 2001 on the same street where he used to live with Tracey. Brett's fingerprints had been found at the scene.

Pownell did a search on Brett's history while he waited to speak to him. It was eyebrow-raising. So too was the fact that he'd once been considered a suspect in the Daniel Morcombe case. The detective had seen something on the Sunshine Coast schoolboy on the television only a few days back. And now the man was standing before him.

Pownell stared at him. Brett Cowan looked exactly like the man in the image he'd seen on television.

*

There were others who would see Brett Cowan's face in the image that was shown again and again in news reports.

'Caller stated that they saw the comfit on Channel 7 and said it looked like Brett Cowan who has previous for sexual assault on children,' a report of one call said in November 2004.

'Caller stated that the comfit re Morcombe looks like Brett Cowan. Caller stated that Cowan was at the Sunshine Coast at the time and has history for raping a 7 yr old boy in Darwin,' another report said. That call came in February 2005; an anonymous tip to CrimeStoppers.

A few months later, police heard from a couple who had been friendly with Brett and Tracey. They'd been watching television one night when a story about Daniel's disappearance came on. As they watched, the police comfit of the man from the bus stop flashed across their screen.

It looked just like Brett, their teenage son said. Later, he confessed to his sister that Brett had touched him inappropriately at a wedding a few years earlier. Then he'd offered the boy money to go further. The boy had refused and run off. The family had contacted police to make a formal complaint but were yet to get any response. Operation Vista detectives got onto it.

In 2007, they heard from a woman who claimed Daniel Morcombe had been kidnapped by a pedophile ring. He was either still alive or had only recently been killed. He'd been brought to Brisbane, the woman said, where he was constantly being drugged and filmed. Brett Cowan was part of that pedophile ring. He was the one who had kidnapped Daniel.

The problem was, the woman gave Brett's name as 'Cohen'. Detectives spent a lot of time tracking down the people in the 'pedophile ring' but couldn't find a Brett Cohen.

Around the same time, a man stole into the foyer of the Ferny Grove police station wanting to give police information on Daniel's disappearance. He was extremely paranoid. He confessed to the officer he'd taken the drug ice that morning. There was a tow truck driver named Brett Cowan — or maybe Brett Cowen — involved in the disappearance of Daniel Morcombe, he said. He was involved in a child porn ring. What's more, the man had seen the sketch of the suspect on TV and it looked just like Brett.

There's no evidence Brett was ever involved in a porn ring. People called up and said all kinds of things. What's interesting is that some of them actually had the right person.

*

In 2008, a 14-year-old girl whose family knew Brett went to her brothers with a secret. Brett had raped her, she told them. The girl's brothers were much more into vigilante justice than reporting the accusation to police.

Brett was working as a tow truck driver at the time. They set a trap, calling his company to request a tow from an address in Clayfield. There were three of them lying in wait when the truck drove up. The driver got out and the boys jumped, bashing him about the head with a wrench. They were mid-assault when the screaming victim convinced them he wasn't the man they were after. Brett had been sent to another job. The brothers had jumped the wrong man.

They would have killed him, they told the driver. They'd meant to kill the man who'd raped their sister. All three were arrested.

*

Tracey Haneveld hadn't seen Brett since he'd gone to prison in Darwin, but she'd seen the news reports of the little boy who'd been taken near Maroochydore. She knew the area well. She even knew the exact spot where Daniel Morcombe had been standing that day. Brett knew it too. They used to stand there on the verge and stick their thumbs out at passing cars, hitchhiking to one place or another.

She spoke to Detective Sergeant Tracey Barnes, who suggested she put her memories of Brett down on paper. So she did, pulling out an old-fashioned typewriter and a stack of purple paper. She typed and typed. Some things about Brett she'd never forget.

I had blocked out a lot of memories of Brett Peter Cowan. He, to me, is not human. I will start from the beginning though so I don't miss anything.

I first met Brett Peter Cowan in Nambour, QLD, Hospital Road if I remember correctly. I had moved there to Nambour from Maroochydore to live with a young pregnant girl that needed a boarder.

The letter went on to describe their roller-coaster relationship. The time she caught him with another woman. The woman's home and the little girl Crystal crying on the floor. The move to Darwin. The talk she had with Brett where he asked her to take him back. Discovering the other woman's child, Crystal, in the van where he was living. The night he raped the little boy.

The day Charmaine and I arrived in Darwin, Brett had the little girl Crystal in his care. I asked where the mother was and Brett said she was in Alice Springs for a while and he had to look after her. This was the same little girl I had seen him with in Maroochydore. The next day after Crystal was gone and I asked Brett and he said the mother had picked her up. I thought OK.

Five years ago, I started having nightmares about Crystal. She is always reaching towards me for help in these dreams. That made me start to wonder what happened to her, so I called [a detective] in Darwin and told him my worries, especially after what Brett had done to [the boy in the caravan park].

[The detective] never called me back. I think he thought I was not all there as he wasn't very interested, then I thought no more of it.

The nightmares stopped until I seen on the TV the disappearance of a boy in Maroochydore a few months ago. The nightmares started. I had a gut feeling that Brett, if he was out of prison, may have something to do with it as Maroochydore are [sic] his old stomping grounds and that is his style.

I could trick him into talking more to me about things as I think I said I still loved him after what he did to [the boy], I was very much in shock, if you understand, so feel free to ask my help on anything.

I know there are a lot of monsters out there like Brett but I think if he was in the area of this boy going missing he was the one who has him or has hurt him.

I better go and post this now. I will call you now too. Good luck with everything.

Tracey Haneveld.

CHAPTER THIRTEEN

THE ALIBI

BRETT AND HIS WIFE were barely on speaking terms when Daniel disappeared in late 2003. But despite the frostiness, Tracey fell pregnant with their second child a few months later.

Brett had made himself even more scarce by then, taking a job in the mines in North Queensland as a fly-in fly-out worker. His old boss, Trevor Davis, had helped him secure the job. But that wasn't the end of Trevor's generosity. The Cowan and Davis families had become friends. They knew Brett was the black sheep of his family, that he had trouble keeping his life together. Trevor and his wife talked about what they could do to help and set their minds on buying another sandblasting business. They would take Brett on as partner and he could run it for them. It cost them a $50 000 deposit — and cost Brett nothing. They were giving him the opportunity to make something of his life. It was an incredibly generous gesture from friends.

In March 2004, Brett came home for his second run of days off since starting in the mines. He wasn't home long. He took off in the middle of the night and didn't come back. The following day he was supposed to pick up a truck for the new sandblasting business. It was to have been the first day of a new life of stability, of job security. Instead, he ran off, leaving the business and leaving Tracey, who was two months pregnant, and their young son.

Two weeks later, Tracey found out he was living with another woman. Later, she'd learn her husband had been cheating on her for some time.

*

Brett met his new woman in a deli in a town called Moranbah, outside of Mackay. Her name was Donna and she served him a hamburger. She thought he was attractive. He was tall with brown hair pulled back into a ponytail and a goatee beard. His left ear had two earrings in the one hole.

Brett ended up back at Donna's that night for drinks. He came back again and again and soon they were a couple — despite the fact he was already married with a second child on the way. He moved in with Donna more permanently after walking out on Tracey. He was good around the yard and set about digging out new garden beds for her. Donna had a tattoo of a wolf and a dreamcatcher on her back; Brett liked it and decided to get one the same. He had the tattoo artist draw it on his arm. Donna paid. He had his tongue pierced, too. Donna noticed he liked to change his appearance a lot. He'd cut his hair off and grow it out again. Sometimes he'd colour it. He'd shave his goatee and grow it back. Once he tried to dye his hair blond. It turned a horrible orange colour.

Their relationship wasn't made to last, though. Trevor Davis and one of his employees travelled to Moranbah one day to write out a quote on a job. Being a small town, they found themselves talking to a friend of Donna's.

'Is it true Brett was in jail for assaulting children?' the friend asked. There had been a rumour doing the rounds.

Trevor nodded. This confirmation of Brett's past soon got back to him and he rang Trevor, furious. He called again and again, shouting abuse and threats. Donna called too, giving the Davises a piece of her mind. But the relationship was soon over. In late 2004, Brett packed his bags and left. He headed for his parents' Everton Park home. No matter what was going on in his life, Brett knew his parents would always come to the rescue.

*

In 2005, detectives pulled out their Brett Cowan file and went back over his alibi. They went to see Tracey to go over times once again. She and Brett were now separated and Tracey certainly didn't feel the need to protect the wayward father of her children.

She told them she couldn't be sure what time he'd arrived home with the mulcher. She'd said somewhere between 2.45 p.m. and 3.15 p.m. at the time, but without having looked at a watch, who knows what time it really was?

'I just estimated the time of day by what I felt the time was,' she told them. 'In reality, this time could be half an hour either side of this. And again, Brett may have been back at home doing stuff in the yard for a time before I realised he was back.'

They went back to Frank Davis, too, the owner of the mulcher. The man whose Nambour home Brett had driven to that day.

Call charge records showed Brett had called the Davis house at 12.50 p.m. to tell them he was on his way. Another call was made from Brett's mobile to his and Tracey's landline at 12.58 p.m. This told police Brett had left home and was surely on his way. He'd arrived about 1.30 p.m. and left soon after, Frank and his wife Hazel confirmed again. Hazel was sure of the time because she'd had errands to run at the Plaza that day and had been in a hurry to leave home.

Eric Fragos, the neighbour who'd wandered over to help with the mulching, could not be sure what time he'd spotted Brett in the garden.

Given that Sunday traffic was not going to cause much of a delay, police estimated the quickest time line as 30 minutes to Nambour, 10 minutes to collect the mulcher and 30 minutes home. That version should have had him arriving home at 2.05 p.m.

If it took 45 minutes each way, and 15 minutes to collect the mulcher, he would have been home at 2.40 p.m.

And if Brett hadn't arrived home until 3 p.m. — as Tracey had estimated — where had he been?

*

On 6 July 2005, Brett Cowan took a seat in an interview room with Detective Sergeant Tracey Barnes and Detective Senior Constable Mark Wright. They asked him again about his trip out to Nambour. How long it had taken, what time he'd arrived home.

Brett sat opposite them at an L-shaped table, his hat discarded in front of him. The two detectives surrounded themselves with paperwork and listed their names, ranks and identification numbers for a rolling camera. They ask him again to 'cast his mind back' to 7 December. What was he doing that day?

'I was home all day, working in the garden in the afternoon … cutting down some trees, tidying up the gardens,' he told them, leaning back in his chair. 'I rang my boss' father up around lunchtime [and] asked him if I could borrow his mulcher.'

He said it would have been 1 p.m. or 1.30 p.m. when he left home. He was at the Davises' for 10 to 15 minutes before he was done loading the mulcher into his car.

'Loaded it in, tied it in, and then left and went straight home,' Brett told them. The drive was half an hour to 45 minutes each way. He stretched out the times enough to explain away any missing minutes. Brett's voice was relaxed. He appeared confident his alibi would hold.

'Did you see a young boy standing under the Kiel Mountain Road overpass?' Barnes asked.

'I didn't see anybody standing there,' he said.

They told him about the phone call he'd made to Frank Davis at 12.50 p.m. Had he left right after making that call?

Brett agreed that he would have.

'So probably more like 1 p.m. that you left home,' Barnes said.

Would he have had a mobile phone in the car with him? Would he have called home from the car after leaving?

'I don't think I called anybody,' Brett said.

They told him they had evidence a call had been made from the mobile to his and Tracey's home number at 12.58 p.m. He agreed that would have been him.

'So that's clarifying, basically, you're on the road at 12.58 p.m.,' Barnes said.

'Yep,' Brett replied.

Barnes told him the 90-minute round trip would have had him home at 2.30 p.m. and driving past the Kiel Mountain Road overpass at 2.05 p.m.

'And you didn't see anything?' she asked.

'Nope. Nobody standing there.'

'You didn't see the broken-down bus?'

'I seen the broken-down bus,' he conceded. There'd been people on it. Maybe a couple inside and a couple more standing around.

Barnes asked Brett whether he'd ever seen any of the comfits released by police showing the man spotted at the overpass. He had.

'Do you think you look anything like those comfits?' she said.

'I thought one of them,' he said, chuckling. 'One of them actually looks more like my brother than it looks like me.'

Wright told Brett he was still concerned about a possible gap in time in his movements that day. Tracey, he said, thought Brett hadn't arrived home until 3 p.m. If he was on the road to the Davises' by 1 p.m., where had the rest of the time gone?

'The only thing I can say ... is that the traffic cameras that are around, like the one in Beerwah and that ... that's it,' Brett had mentioned the cameras before. He'd told them he was on the very road where Daniel had been standing because he believed council-operated traffic cameras had picked up his car driving along the Nambour Connection Road. But police had already tried those cameras. They hadn't been recording.

Wright grilled Brett again. Why hadn't he seen anything at the overpass? Other people had.

'The problem with us is that this is not going anywhere,'

Wright told him. 'We can't write this off and say it's definitely not Brett Cowan, to a point, because until we can get our times right, or something extra that's going to say, well, this is why he was home at 2.30 p.m. ... Anything could happen in half an hour.' They were going in circles. Barnes and Wright decided to wrap things up.

'If you had have abducted Daniel, would you tell me?' Barnes asked him as they were finishing.

Brett paused. 'Probably not,' he said.

*

Brett and Tracey's youngest son was born in December 2004. Brett hadn't been around for much of her pregnancy and he hadn't been there for the birth. She'd well and truly opened her eyes to him now and didn't want him having access to their children. They argued over custody. Brett didn't want the responsibility of having them permanently — or even half the time — but he wanted to be able to visit with them more often.

Tracey complained that her ex-husband was a convicted pedophile and a suspect in the Daniel Morcombe murder. Surely he shouldn't be allowed near any children — even his own. Brett argued that he couldn't possibly have had time to abduct a child while out collecting a mulcher. Any spare time he'd had had been spent at the home of his drug dealer, where he'd stopped to buy some marijuana and share a cup of tea.

This was news to police. He'd never mentioned visiting a drug dealer before. They hauled him back in. Brett and his father fronted the Homicide Squad office at police headquarters on 14 September 2006 for a formal interview with detectives Mark Wright, Howard Hickey and Aaron Walker.

'I'm not gonna give youse names ... I won't dob them in,' Brett said when they brought up the drug dealer.

Mark Wright looked at him.

'I guarantee you, mate … out in front of this door over here [it says] Homicide Squad. It's not drug squad. We couldn't give a flying rat's arse, to be honest. As you'd appreciate, what we're trying to investigate here is something totally different.' Chasing a small-time drug dealer, Wright said, would be a waste of their time. They wanted to ask him about other things, too. But they weren't sure how much Brett's father knew of his past.

'Um, your dad was aware of what was spoken about last time?' Wright asked.

'He's been up front with us,' Peter Cowan said. 'He's kept us informed with everything that's been going on. Shattered us the first time, I might add.'

They got down to business.

'Part of the main thing that we need to discuss with you is … there's a concern there's a period of time that we can't account for,' Wright said. 'And obviously that's important to us because we're dealing with … we're trying to investigate the death of a young boy, or the disappearance of a young boy, and of course with your past and the fact that you were nearby [and] went through the scene at about the time, [it] becomes extremely important to us. What can you tell us now?'

'That I was at my dealer's place,' Brett said.

'We need to know who that person was and where you went,' Wright said.

'Umm, her name is Sandy Drummond,' he told them.

'I know Sandy,' Wright said. 'OK, so what … how long were you … tell us what happened.'

'Oh, well, whenever I went there, I was there for a minimum of half an hour. I didn't believe in going there and getting whatever I wanted and then leaving.'

'Going back to that day specifically,' Wright said, 'can you remember exactly what happened when you got to the Drummonds' place?'

'I parked on the footpath where I normally park. Just went in and sat down. Always talk for a while. Even had a cup of coffee with them.'

'And you specifically remember that?'

'Yep.'

'And how long do you reckon it would have been?'

'Oh, it was … a good half an hour.'

Wright had questioned Brett on his alibi the previous year. They'd gone over and over the times. Brett's movements. Distance and traffic. Phone calls. Every minute they'd tried to allocate, explain. And now here was Brett telling a completely different story, claiming he hadn't been honest the first few times, to protect a low-level drug dealer.

'I just … I just find it hard to … knowing the importance of what we're trying to do, because you know we obviously have bosses that will be interested in what you say and what you've told us in the past … the first thing they're going to turn around and say is, "Well, if it's something as simple as a bag of dope, who gives a flying rat's arse?"' Wright said. 'If you think we don't know about Sandy Drummond, you're kidding yourself.'

'I know she's been raided a few times,' Brett conceded.

'The problem we've got is … here was something that could have been so simply explained away … if that had, had happened back then. It would have been so, so easy to say that's what happened,' Wright said. 'But you've left it till something way down the track and the first thing my boss … is going to say is, "Well, well he just made that up to cover his fucking time" — you know what I mean?'

'As I said, I've had nothing to do with it. Right from the word go. I didn't even see him.' Brett stood firm. The conversation moved on. He told police his ex-wife was using his history as a child sex offender to stop him seeing his own children. He complained she was using past conversations against him.

'Because I've said that, um, I can never say that I'll never reoffend. Because I can't. She's using that against me … ' 'cause

I want more time with my, more access to my kids,' Brett said.

Detective Aaron Walker cut in. 'Well, why does an offender say they can't [not] reoffend again?' he asked.

'Well, you've done it once,' Brett replied. 'What's stopping it from happening again?'

Police spoke to Sandra Drummond the next day. She knew Brett. She'd known him for a while. They asked her about 7 December 2003. Had he been around that day? Sandra had no idea. Not that she remembered, she told them.

*

Geoff Grant's steel fabrication business was doing well in 2006. It had been his father's company and Geoff had only just taken over the reins. His friend Mick, who'd worked for the Grant family for years, had helped Geoff through the transition. It was some time after the new financial year that Geoff spoke to Mick about taking on more staff to help with the workload. They needed more welders, more boilermakers.

'I know someone — he can start right away,' Mick told him. His mate Brett knew how to weld. They decided to get him in for a chat. Brett seemed normal. He was easy going and chatty. He talked about his welding experience and Geoff asked him if he'd do a weld test then and there. Brett agreed. Geoff watched. He clearly knew what he was doing. The job was his, Geoff told his new employee.

Brett was a good worker at first. He turned up on time, put his head down and did his work. Geoff didn't spend that much time on the factory floor but he usually joined the boys for an after-work beer on a Friday. Brett always stood the same way — against a wall with one leg bent and resting on the wall behind him. Like a stork.

He was pretty jovial but would become angry if he disagreed with something. Anyone he didn't like was a 'rock spider'. He said it so many times, Geoff had to ask someone what it meant. It was only much later that Geoff realised the irony of this man calling people he didn't like a word that meant 'pedophile'.

One day Geoff decided it was time to do something about their pigeon problem. There were baby pigeons up in the roof. Geoff wanted them put outside so they didn't mess up the workshop. Brett was only too happy to help. He knocked the nests down in a scattering of twigs and feathers.

'Oh,' Geoff said in surprise. 'Poor birds. That's not nice.'

As he watched on in horror, Brett picked up the birds one by one, twisting their necks so violently their heads tore off. Blood was splattered across the workshop floor. It was gruesome. Geoff had to turn away. He couldn't quite look at Brett the same way after that.

Brett had been with them for around three months when he failed to show for work one day. They tried calling and calling but couldn't get through. One day passed, then two, then a whole week went by and still Brett didn't show.

He had about eight hours' wages owing and Geoff told the payroll girl to hold off sending the money over until they'd heard from him. Eventually, Brett called. He wanted his money. He'd tracked Geoff down at home and the jovial and laid-back Brett who'd shared beers with the boys was gone. This Brett was loud and aggressive.

'If you don't pay me my fucking money, I'll be round there,' he told Geoff. 'I'm going to fucking kill you.'

Geoff was furious. 'Mate,' he said, 'you show up at my place and you'll regret it.' He hung up and dialled the police.

'If you owe him money, you should pay it,' they said.

He told the payroll girl to send the money across. He didn't need the stress.

*

Geoff sat in the office a week later reading through emails. He opened one from an address he didn't recognise. A fake account. Brett Peter Cowan, the email read, is a suspect in the Daniel Morcombe murder. A pedophile with a history in the courts. The email included details of his crimes against children. Geoff stared at it in alarm. He got up and went to find Mick.

'What the hell is up with this guy, Mick?' he said. 'He's being looked at for Daniel Morcombe?'

'Oh, don't worry about that,' Mick said. 'His ex-missus is crazy and just accuses him of all this stuff that didn't happen.'

It wasn't long after that that the front gates of Geoff's business were rammed. It appeared someone with a heavy vehicle or some kind of truck had driven into them during the night. Geoff would later find out Brett had a new job — driving tow trucks.

'Anyone got a beef with you?' police asked.

Just one, Geoff thought.

CHAPTER FOURTEEN

STACEY

THE MISSION AUSTRALIA WAITING room doesn't seem a likely place to meet a man. But that's what happened to Stacey in 2006 as she waited for her appointment with a jobs counsellor. She was sitting in the waiting room, watching the time tick by, when the man next to her said hello. He introduced himself as Brett. He was easygoing and chatty. They talked about inconsequential things. The local leagues club where Stacey spent some of her Friday and Saturday nights. Brett mentioned his father was president of a nearby RSL.

'You should come down one night for a drink,' she said to him

He did. About a week later. She was at a table with a dozen friends, chatting and laughing and sharing a drink. Brett slotted right in. He was wearing a loud shirt and had slicked his hair back with some kind of product. They ribbed him about it in good humour. At the end of the night he drove her home. It was all quite polite.

He started meeting her at the leagues club regularly after that. Stacey's friends would be there too and Brett would talk with them quite happily. He was social and outgoing.

Stacey was nothing like the other women Brett had dated. She was strong and spoke up for what she believed in. She didn't give an inch. She didn't like facial hair so Brett made sure he shaved often. He tidied up his appearance. He told her he used to take drugs. She'd have none of that. She didn't take drugs and didn't like people who did. Any hint of drugs and she was out of there.

They dated for nearly a year. Brett was living with his parents for the majority of that time. Stacey had dinners with them and saw them often when visiting Brett at their home. She enjoyed their company. They were lovely people. She had no idea about his past. No idea he was a convicted pedophile or a suspect in the state's biggest ever missing persons case. He didn't tell her and neither did Peter nor Marlene.

They'd been together for a while when Brett started smoking marijuana again. He started hanging out with an old crowd of friends, including an ex-girlfriend. Stacey didn't like the crowd. They weren't her people. Brett wasn't the person she'd thought he was.

On Australia Day 2007, Brett and Stacey took her 14-year-old son Jacob to a party. It was at the home of one of Stacey's girlfriends. Her son had left with a friend partway through the party. She didn't think much of it until he called her mobile, obviously upset. He wouldn't be coming home, he told her. He was scared.

'Brett tried to punch me,' he said. Brett had grabbed the boy's mobile phone and was trying to look through it. The boy had tried to take it back and Brett had become violent.

'Go home,' she told him. 'It's Brett who won't be coming back.'

Stacey, fierce as a lioness, confronted her boyfriend. He stammered in the face of her rage. Tried to explain. She didn't want to hear it. Not a single word. There could be no reason, no explanation that could justify an attack on her child. She told him it was over. She didn't want to see him again. He wasn't welcome at her place. He wasn't welcome in her life. A few weeks later she walked out her front door to find him mowing her lawn.

'Get lost,' she told him. 'And don't come back.'

Not long after that, she was rifling through her mail when she noticed a letter from Brett. Inside was a ring and the docket to go with it. He'd enclosed a note, telling her to do what she wanted with it.

All right, she thought. She took the ring and the docket back to the store and exchanged it for something else.

He stopped trying after that.

*

In August 2011, Stacey discovered the truth about the man she'd dated for nearly a year. She was furious. Brett was on the news, in the papers, charged with murdering Daniel Morcombe. Later she found out he'd been in prison before for abusing children.

She'd had this man around her children. Stacey would never, ever have knowingly let her kids within a mile of a man like that. Nobody had told her. Nobody had warned her.

CHAPTER FIFTEEN
INCONSOLABLE

DANIEL HAD BEEN MISSING for five months when ABC's *Australian Story* aired a report on his abduction. For Bruce and Denise, it had been an endless nightmare. Every day they'd woken hoping for answers. But despite thousands of enquiries, police still had no idea what had happened to their son. They told the program about the night Daniel hadn't come home. About searching for him in the dark. About asking the police for help.

There'd been a thousand tiny tricks of bad luck. If it hadn't rained, Daniel would have been at the neighbours' on time, picking passionfruit with his brothers. They would have come home and accompanied their parents to the Christmas picnic Bruce and Denise had put on for their staff.

If one of Daniel's brothers had gone with him to the shops. If the bus hadn't broken down. If the replacement bus had stopped instead of driving by. If his killer had driven by earlier or later. If he'd been looking the other way. If Daniel had worn brown instead of red, would he have been noticed by so many? Would he have been noticed by the man who'd steal him away?

Senior Sergeant Julie Elliott from the police media section had taken on the Morcombes' heartbreak. So had Senior Constable Sam Knight, appointed family liaison officer on the first day.

'As Daniel's picture opened up, I just stopped and looked at that and thought, what an angelic face,' Elliott told *Australian Story*. 'What a beautiful smile and beautiful eyes. And we all said to each other, this is not right, there's something different about this one. We all felt that then, the day after. And we were very worried.'

Sam Knight was the go-between for Bruce and Denise and the main detectives working the case. She'd go to morning briefings and pray she'd have something solid, something that would take the pain from Denise's eyes.

'The first time I saw a picture of Daniel was when I walked into the major incident room on that first morning and I mean, he's just beautiful and I looked at him and I thought, this could be my son,' she told the program. She'd gone to the house, a beautiful two-storey cottage surrounded by a country garden, and asked to see Daniel's room. She'd seen how difficult it had been for Denise to open the door.

In the days that followed, she'd come to realise this job, this investigation, caring for this family, would be the most important thing she'd ever do. It was the reason she'd become a police officer. She was the one who'd swabbed them for DNA. DNA samples from the family would be used to help identify human remains. It was one of those moments — like when police divers had come to search their dams — when the Morcombes realised police were preparing to find a body.

'We have built up some sort of picture of what's happened here ... we've got a suspect car, we've got this 20-year-old blue car,' Detective Inspector John Maloney said. 'It is most likely that Daniel was abducted by [a] person or persons in that blue car.'

Police had investigated more than 3500 calls to Crime Stoppers by then. And 300 individual people had been investigated. It was a long list. And the right person's name was on it.

Denise moved through the camera frame slowly, as though she was wounded. Her voice was soft as she thought about her favourite memories of her son. Washing his motorbike. Putting on his motocross clothes. He'd wanted to race and they hadn't got around to taking him down to the local club. They were filled with regret. She spoke about her son in past tense. After so many nights without him, what other reality could there be?

She'd opened letters from psychics. One said he was in a barn close by. Another said he was in a country town. One described how he'd had his head shaven by his kidnappers. He didn't have many days left, it warned. Bruce told her not to look at them but she had to. What if it was true?

'Daniel was good-looking,' Denise told the program. 'And maybe a pedophile has taken advantage of that.' The camera captured her expression as she thought about what she'd just said. She'd stopped talking. Her lips quivered and she bit at the inside of her mouth. But the tears came all the same.

'Every day we part with saying "We will find him",' Elliott said. 'I can't bear to think that we won't.'

Bruce and Denise dedicated their lives to finding their son. They followed rumours and met with people who claimed to have information. It became their obsession.

They asked people to tie a red ribbon to their letterbox. Daniel was on their minds every day and they wanted to ensure others thought of him, too. The more information that came in, the greater the chance police would find that crucial piece of the puzzle. The tiniest detail could be the key to solving the most terrible of crimes.

One day Bruce came across an old door. It had the key still in the lock. It gave him an idea. He took the door down to the overpass and placed it where Daniel had once stood.

'Help find the key to unlock the horror of this crime,' he wrote. The stunt helped keep Daniel's disappearance in the media a while longer.

They sold the investment property they'd worked so hard to buy. The money would go towards finding Daniel. They organised posters and leaflets. Television advertisements. Banners and billboards. It all cost money. They held fundraisers and accepted donations from local businesses and residents. More than 50 printing companies would get together to roll out 1.7 million leaflets about Daniel's disappearance. The first Ride for Daniel was held in 2004, with motorcyclists and bike enthusiasts taking to the road to do their bit for the Morcombes.

In October 2004 the State Government put up a $250 000

reward — the biggest in Queensland's history. The calls came in. Police checked leads. They got nowhere.

People sent cards, letters and emails. They called. Bruce spoke to everybody. Some of the people drove him crazy. They told him horrible or fanciful stories about what had happened to Daniel. He did everything they said, looked into every lead, terrified the one he ignored would be the one that could have taken him to his son.

Daniel and Brad turned 14 on 19 December — just days after Daniel disappeared. It was the first birthday Bradley would celebrate without his twin. The Morcombes were beside themselves. They held a private prayer service. Denise's parents, Kevin and Monique, were still by their side when they gathered around a table of candles and a framed picture of the boys.

Bradley lit three altar candles. One for each brother. As they watched the flames flicker, one went out.

'I know,' Monique said later, 'my Danny is dead.'

*

In 2004, police received an anonymous email from an internet café. The sender claimed to have kidnapped Daniel and was now holding him captive. He was a beautiful toy, a much-loved pet. Police could have him back — if they were willing to pay enough money. The author turned out to be a media and communications student named David Charles Brine. He didn't have Daniel. Disgusted police charged him anyway with making a threat to kill in a document. In January 2005, Brine pleaded guilty to the charge and was sentenced to two years jail, suspended after four months.

It was the same year Bruce and Denise Morcombe began what would become Daniel's legacy. The Daniel Morcombe Foundation became something tangible for them to do. In between chasing pedophiles, well-meaning psychics and time wasters, Bruce and Denise set up a charity they would run in their son's name.

It might help catch his killer. If not, it was an opportunity for them to educate children. Daniel had known about stranger danger and it had not been enough. Children needed to know what to look out for, the signs they could be in danger. Children in schools should be able to see the parents of a boy who'd suffered a terrible fate — and hopefully they'd learn something they'd never forget.

The investigation continued. Senior Sergeant Julie Elliott and Senior Constable Sam Knight formed a tight bond with Bruce and Denise. The women would hold Denise up when she was ready to collapse. They were the closest of friends. But the months and months without answers took their toll on everyone. Elliott and her fiancé split. So too did Knight and her husband. A detective assigned to the case died a short time later of a heart attack.

On the 12-month anniversary of Daniel's disappearance, a crowd gathered at Siena Catholic College to remember the shy little boy whose name was now known for all the wrong reasons. The Morcombes had arranged for 2000 candles to be lit in his honour. Well-wishers wore red ribbons, the colour now associated with Daniel and his disappearance. Afterwards, Bruce and Denise unveiled a large memorial stone they'd had erected under the overpass. It read:

Daniel was last seen waiting for a bus at this spot. He was to travel to the Sunshine Plaza, Maroochydore and purchase Christmas presents. Tragically, he has never been seen again. Red ribbons were openly displayed as a symbol of hope during the search. A red flowering Poinciana tree is planted adjacent to this spot as a growing reminder of this tragedy.

The Morcombe family sincerely thank the many SES volunteers, the Queensland Police Service, Siena College, generous businesses and the large number of individuals for their extraordinary support and sustained effort in our search for answers.

Daniel was a much loved brother of Dean and Bradley (twin) and son of Bruce and Denise.

May peace be with you.

*

Denise was struggling. In 2007, she told *Australian Story* just how bad things had become.

'I started drinking,' she told them. 'Probably after Daniel's memorial I'd go from one drink, [to] two, three, four, five, six. I didn't care how many I had. I just wanted to block out the whole world. Bruce would come home from work and he'd say, "Have you been drinking?" and I would blatantly lie and say, "No, I haven't, I haven't." Probably the worst thing I did to Bruce was the night before Father's Day. I just walked out and said, "I want a divorce." And he was just shell-shocked. He was shattered. He just didn't know that things had got so bad between us. The drinking got worse and worse — probably 18 months.

'One night I said I've had enough of this, so I grabbed a few sleeping pills that I had left and anti-depressant tablets that I had in a jar and I just, I took the lot. Trouble was, I didn't take enough and I woke up again the next morning and it probably wasn't for another week after that Bruce found me drinking again.'

Julie Elliott had spent many nights worrying Denise would take her own life.

'You can't,' she'd tell her. 'Daniel's not found yet.'

Bruce wasn't angry. There was only sadness. Denise knew she was in a bad way and she decided it was time to change that. She got rid of the alcohol, the sleeping tablets, the anti-depressants and let herself feel again.

*

By 2008, more than 18 000 job logs had been filed by police. Thousands and thousands of leads. The State Government reward of $250 000 had got a $750 000 boost, thanks to private donors. A year later, it would expire. There would still be no answers.

INCONSOLABLE

By 2003, more than 18 000 job losses had been tied to police.
thousands and thousands of funds. The Share market, some need
of $250,000 had got a $750,000 boost, three years in salvation, a
year later, it would require. These would

CHAPTER SIXTEEN
RAT IN A CAGE

DOUG JACKWAY WAS NOT good at keeping his freedom. He'd been out only two months — from November 2003 until January 2004 — before he was again arrested and sent back to prison. A girl he'd long ago molested had come forward. She wanted him charged.

Jackway was found guilty of rape after a trial in September 2004. He'd been 14 at the time of the offence. The girl had been nine. A prison psychiatrist would later comment on Jackway's severe personality disorder which brought about impulsiveness and immaturity. Jackway had little ability to problem-solve or make decisions. No respect for social norms. No empathy for his victims. Poor control of his temper. Untrusting.

In 2006, a letter arrived at Wolston Correctional Centre — Jackway's home away from home.

Doug

I can't handle it any more. Daniel Morchams Picture is in the Paper, its on TV. I see him when I sleep, all the time, I going off my head with what we done to him, I have to clear my conscience soon I say ou [sic] so the same, I will go to the Police soon you are in Jail now what dose it matter if you stay there you killed that poor kid. His Parents need to know.

Prison authorities got to the letter before it made its way to Jackway and it was handed over to Operation Vista detectives. The poorly spelt missive had been handwritten in flowing cursive and was unsigned. The list of people who hated Jackway was long but police started with the more obvious candidates. They asked Michael and

Debbie. Both denied writing it and voluntarily provided sets of fingerprints. Police also got a denial from the girl he'd raped. She gave them her fingerprints too. Jackway didn't know either. Only his family called him 'Doug', he said. Everyone else called him Jacko. Detectives were divided into two camps. Some believed Brett was their best suspect. Others believed Jackway was a better fit.

In 2008, senior management of the Queensland Police Service decided to take another look at the man with the blue car. They would conduct a review. Detectives assigned to Operation Golf Avalon would go back over every detail of the Jackway file. Witnesses would be revisited. They also came up with a new plan. They would bug his prison cell.

It was a monumental quest. The chances of successfully planting a listening device in a prison cell were incredibly slim — but they were determined to try. It was not something that happened often. It was probably something that never happened. But in the end it was doomed to fail.

At the same time, Channel Seven's *Sunday Night* program aired an exclusive segment on Jackway — revealing him for the first time as a leading suspect in the Daniel Morcombe case. They didn't call him a suspect, though. Jackway was referred to as a person of 'prime interest'. The episode was timed to run on the very night the $1 million State Government reward expired. More than 300 people phoned police after the program aired.

'He is a truly frightening, evil psychopath,' Channel Seven investigative journalist Ross Coulthart told the *Courier-Mail*.

Assistant Commissioner Mike Condon refused to confirm whether police were actively investigating Jackway. They were, of course. But now it was obvious. It would be obvious to Jackway too. Any chance of gleaning something from an off-guard Jackway chatting within the confines of a prison cell was gone.

*

Detectives Emma Macindoe and Stephen Blanchfield came to see Jackway at the Capricornia Correctional Centre on 27 May 2009. Another attempt to extract something truthful from one of Queensland's worst criminals. Brett, meanwhile, had dropped off the radar.

'Hi, Douglas, how are you?' Macindoe began.

'Yeah, all right.'

'Emma Macindoe and Steve Blanchfield from Homicide. We've got some information and some evidence in relation to Daniel Morcombe. So what we're going to do is give you the information that we have and then invite you to make comment on that. You don't have to answer any questions.'

'Well,' Jackway said. 'You're charging me for it.'

'No,' Macindoe told him. 'We're not charging you. There's just new information that we have and you have the right to know what that information is.'

Before they told him anything, though, Macindoe and Blanchfield asked him to go through his movements again on and around 7 December 2003. He answered their questions, taking them through the fights with his girlfriend, the days of confrontations, ex-boyfriends and knives, stolen cars and stolen car parts and angry security guards. The visit to his sister's house before court. They asked him about the many versions of his alibi. Soon he was losing his patience.

'It's starting to piss me off, I know that,' he told Macindoe. 'I told them last time they seen me, once you get shit, I said come and charge me. Until then, I don't want to know youse. You're wasting my time, you're wasting your own time.'

They gave him a break, Macindoe explaining to him again that when investigators came across new information, it was only right that they let him know.

Two cigarettes and a drink later, the tapes were back rolling. They had taken statements from other inmates, they told Jackway. The accusation was that Jackway and some mates had kidnapped a boy from Noosa. The son of a police officer. They'd put him in the boot of the car with the intention of collecting a handsome ransom. But something had gone wrong. The kid had seen their faces and they'd had to kill him. His body had been dumped in a quarry. This, Macindoe said, was apparently the story Jackway had told to a fellow prisoner.

'I didn't say that. What a liar,' Jackway said.

The prisoner had named some of Jackway's associates and knew about their movements. How would they know that, Macindoe reasoned, unless the conversation had taken place?

'Another inmate,' she continued, 'has said that you stated to him that you'd taken [Daniel] Morcombe and disposed of his body in a mine shaft at Ipswich.'

'Yeah.'

'Have you ever made admissions to anyone in jail?'

'No, I haven't. That's being honest.'

'OK, I'll just go through in chronological order.'

'Yeah.'

'This inmate has approached a prison guard — this is where the information's come from — and stated to the prison guard that "Jackway has just confided in me and told me that he'd killed Daniel Morcombe and disposed of his body in a mine shaft at Ipswich". No?'

'Nah.'

'Another prisoner,' Macindoe read from her list, '"Jackway confided in me of disposing Morcombe at Ipswich".'

'No.'

'Another prisoner has heard two other prisoners ... that Jackway had [boasted] to them that he took Morcombe and that the body had been disposed of at Beaudesert.' She went on. Another prisoner claimed Jackway told him he had kidnapped Daniel in a ransom 'gone wrong'.

'"He stated that he'd killed the kid because he saw their faces",' Macindoe read from her list of allegations. 'There's a young bloke that provided an alibi for him and that bloke has been looked after [by] an older bloke and police will not be able to prove who's responsible. Inmate stated, prior to Jackway's release in 2003, he told him he would abduct a child, rape the child, kill the child and bury the child in an area where the child would not be found.'

Jackway denied it all.

'OK, this one,' she continued, 'prisoner stated that Jackway told him on a number of occasions, there are some things for which he's not been caught for. In a later conversation, Jackway stated to him that he picked a boy up whilst going to his sister's place on the Sunshine Coast. He picked up the boy … [and] attempted to get the boy to perform oral sex on him.'

'I never spoke to nobody,' Jackway said.

Macindoe continued. 'This prisoner says that his girlfriend has knowledge of the Morcombe abduction and has nominated Jackway as one of the persons of interest. Based on information from an inmate … that Morcombe was brought to their house by two male persons, one of them being Jackway,' she said.

'At whose house?'

'Doesn't say.'

'No, I bring him back to no house.' He'd spoken to a couple of people over the years. People liked to ask him if he'd killed the boy. He always told them no, he'd had nothing to do with it. 'I guarantee ya I did not do this to Daniel Morcombe and I hope one day they do find him,' Jackway said. 'You know what I mean? And do find the fucking person who did it. I didn't do it. And there's no way in the world am I doing jail for it. And that's being honest. What do you think? I'm gonna kick back into jail for the next 25 years for something I haven't done?'

They left him to it. Kicking back in jail for something he had done.

CHAPTER SEVENTEEN
LIAR, LIAR

ONLY DAYS AFTER DANIEL Morcombe disappeared from his Sunshine Coast home, police were handed another missing persons case. Elderly pensioner Donald Smith lived in Woodridge, a working-class suburb south of Brisbane, with a long-time crook and drug addict named John Saunders.

Saunders needed money to support his habit. And Mr Smith had money. Police would allege he cooked up a plan to kill his flatmate. He told his girlfriend, a young prostitute, he planned to kidnap and bash Mr Smith or take away his diabetes medication until he agreed to hand over his PIN number.

'Don is dead, he had some sort of fit — I dumped his body in the bush,' he apparently told his girlfriend. Three months later, Saunders took police into bushland on the Sunshine Coast hinterland and showed them where he'd left the body. All that remained were bones. Saunders had stolen $30 000 from his flatmate's account, dumped his body and burnt his car. He'd spent thousands on heroin.

It turned into a complex legal battle. He was initially convicted of murder but changed his plea. A new trial saw him plead guilty to manslaughter. Saunders claimed he'd been high on heroin and speed and hadn't realised Mr Smith's health was in decline. The situation was further complicated because an autopsy had failed to establish a cause of death.

'I don't mind accepting responsibility — Don was my friend,' Saunders told the court. 'I've always had issue with certain things, but at the end of the day a man is dead, and I have to accept responsibility for that.' He was sentenced to 11 and a half years behind bars.

In November 2004, Saunders made contact with police from prison. He had some information for them. He knew who'd killed Daniel Morcombe. He'd been there when Daniel's body was dumped in State forest near Beerburrum, on the Sunshine Coast. In fact, he revealed, he'd even been there when Daniel was kidnapped.

On 15 February 2005, four detectives from Operation Vista arrived at Arthur Gorrie Correctional Centre and left with Saunders sitting in the back of the police car. As they drove him towards the Sunshine Coast, the convicted thief and fraudster told them a story. On 7 December 2003, he and a friend, Dominic, along with another man, had gone for a drive to score some speed. But instead they'd seen Daniel. They'd spotted the little boy in his bright red shirt standing under the overpass and pulled over to speak to him. Saunders told the officers he'd watched on in alarm as his two companions dragged Daniel into the car.

'I don't want to get involved,' he'd told them, and left them to it. He made it back to Brisbane on his own.

Later on, he went around to Dominic's place in Brisbane. There was Daniel. The boy had been abused, he told the officers. People had paid Dominic for a turn. Then, when it was over, Saunders had helped them get rid of the body. Daniel had apparently died after being given heroin. Saunders had got a lift back to Brisbane that day, he told the officers. They asked him for a name. He didn't want to give it at first. And then he did. Police went to that person. Saunders was lying.

'No, OK,' Saunders told the police. 'I stayed in the vehicle.'

This time he told them he'd remained in the car with Daniel, Dominic and the other man. He took the detectives to bushland the day they'd got him out of jail. He had a map he said would lead them to the schoolboy's body. He took them into the State forest at Beerburrum. It was obvious he knew the area well. He knew the rough, winding tracks through the trees. And well he should. It was the same area he'd taken Smith's body.

Queensland Police did not have a trained cadaver dog in 2005. They'd had to fly one up from Victoria. The dog was taken through the forest to see whether it could find any human remains. SES volunteers were brought in to conduct line searches. Nothing was found. Saunders also claimed the clothes Dominic had worn that day had been thrown in Brisbane's Breakfast Creek. Police searched that too. Nothing.

They tried other ways to corroborate Saunders' story. They seized vehicles and forensically examined the carpet and cigarette butts. They examined a mattress. They spoke to friends, relatives, associates. One associate they'd visited had walked away from the door upon seeing detectives and returned a minute later with a photograph.

'This is the person who did it,' she said, and showed them a photograph of Saunders. She'd been at Dominic's house during December and January and heard about what they'd done to the boy, she told them. She'd even seen Daniel's college identification — complete with his picture. Later, she admitted she'd been so affected by drugs she wasn't sure what had happened.

Investigators worked hard to try and stack up any of what Saunders had claimed. They pulled phone records. Tracked alibis. Spoke to dozens of people. Nothing.

In 2009, Saunders' name was again all over the media when a private investigator revealed he was closing in on Daniel's body. And it was Saunders who'd led him there. Private investigator Daniel Legrand told the *Courier-Mail* Saunders had revealed the location of Daniel's remains during a prison chess match. He'd been looking into the case for the past year, he said, and Saunders had been the key.

'I've been told Daniel's remains are actually buried in a five-kilometre radius of his disappearance,' Mr Legrand told the newspaper. 'They are buried in red dirt, possibly close to an old hanger or large shed.'

Legrand said his information had come from another prisoner.

Legrand didn't believe Saunders was responsible for Daniel's murder — but he believed he knew where the schoolboy was.

'They played quite a bit of chess together,' the investigator said. 'That man has provided me with information but is frightened of ever being identified and will not go to the police.'

Bruce and Denise had never heard of Legrand. But they knew all about Saunders. Bruce had even been to one of his court appearances to 'eyeball' the man widely believed to be a person of interest in his son's disappearance.

Assistant Commissioner Condon was not prepared to say much about Legrand's 'developments'. They'd been following Saunders' 'leads' for years — and had wasted much time over it.

'We follow up every piece of information we receive and will continue to do so,' he said. 'And we do not make any statement on persons of interest.'

CHAPTER EIGHTEEN
MORE LIES

SAM SMART USED TWO pages of foolscap paper to tell his lies —
and a third to draw a fake map. He scrawled the words across the
pages, his heavy print an attempt to send police on yet another
fool's errand.

> The 7th December 2003 Daniel Morcome [sic] was abducted
> by me (Sam Smart) and a man who I know. His name is
> Thomas Smart ... It was a simple process take him and leave
> we used a blue Toyota 4 door sedan ...

Sam Smart and his brother first met Thomas in 1987, at a Victorian
caravan park. Sam, at 15, was the eldest of the two boys. Their
mother had kicked them out of the family home and they'd taken
to living in a tent and stealing food to survive. Thomas, a 58-year-
old Aboriginal man with a history of child sex offences, took them
in. Thomas would eventually adopt Sam and Sam changed his last
name to acknowledge his new 'father'. In reality, their relationship
was far from that of father and son. The pair had been involved in
an on-and-off sexual relationship for some years.

On 8 December 2004, Sam made an anonymous phone call to
Crime Stoppers. Thomas Smart, he told them, was the man who
had abducted and murdered Daniel Morcombe. He refused to give
his details but agreed to meet with investigators.

Over the years, Sam would give police long, detailed and
ever-changing descriptions of what happened on 7 December,
claiming he, Thomas and a third man he named 'Mr Stinky' had
been behind the abduction and murder of Daniel. Police spent
some time attempting to prove — or disprove — the claims. They

pulled phone records, tracked movements, checked vehicles and took statements from Sam, Sam's wife, Thomas and many other relatives and associates. Thomas told detectives he believed Sam was trying to seek revenge after Thomas dobbed him in to police for child sex offences.

In June 2005, detectives told Thomas he'd been cleared as a suspect in the Daniel Morcombe case. They thought it was highly likely Sam's claims were a revenge tactic.

But in 2008, Sam, who was now in prison, was at it again. He'd confided in a prison guard, claiming he knew the man who'd killed Daniel Morcombe. Thomas, he said, had told him one day that if he 'kept pissing him off, that [Sam] too would end up in a long line of pine trees in a shallow grave right next to the same little shit who wouldn't shut his mouth'. He claimed Thomas had told him 'it wasn't supposed to happen this way', holding out his hands to mime choking someone. Thomas had told him how he'd offered Daniel a lift to the shops.

'He was just too cute and you know I cannot help myself,' he claimed Thomas said.

Homicide detectives wasted more time interviewing everyone again. They drove Sam from prison so he could point out the place where Daniel was abducted and a supposed shed where he'd been kept tied up.

He directed them to a boat ramp at Pinkenba, on the Brisbane River, where he told them they'd find Daniel's body weighed down with chains and car parts and wrapped in a blanket. In September 2009, police divers were sent in to scour the depths of the Brisbane River where Daniel's body was apparently dumped. They found car batteries on the riverbed. But no body.

In 2012, after wasting countless hours on Sam's claims, police charged him with perjury.

CHAPTER NINETEEN
ROLE-PLAYING

CLARE AND HER FATHER, David, didn't have a lot of money. In 2008, they moved in to a share house together in Durack, a working-class suburb south of Brisbane. It was a two-storey timber house with three bedrooms upstairs and a garage downstairs. The rent was cheap and at first 18-year-old Clare and her dad lived there alone. In April, they found themselves a housemate. His name was Brett. He was 38. Brett's father, Peter, was there the day he moved in, helping his son carry his belongings up the stairs.

Clare was a big girl. And she was young. Brett was happy with both of these things. It took him three months to get her into his bed permanently. She moved into his room. Brett was much more adventurous with Clare. She was young and he could manipulate her into doing what he wanted.

He liked role-playing. He liked being in control, taking the dominant role. Most of his role-playing involved acting out rape and kidnapping fantasies. He'd give her instructions. Tell her exactly what he wanted her to do. He'd tell her to push him away, to cry out. Brett would hold her down. He became more and more forceful. He'd put her hands around her throat and squeeze until she blacked out. He'd grab her and throw her down when she wasn't expecting it. Other times he'd tie her to the bed or to the bars on the windows, using rope to secure her wrists. He was rough with her.

Clare's new man spent a lot of time on the internet. He kept odd hours and often looked tired and drawn. A couple of times she walked in on him looking at pictures of children dressed in adult clothing.

He'd grow a goatee beard for about three weeks and then shave it off. He was in the habit of frequently changing his appearance. He had restless legs. At night he would lie on his back in bed, pedalling as though he were on a bicycle.

They didn't go out a lot. Sometimes a friend of Brett's, a man, would come to the house and they'd disappear together. Clare knew they were having sex. She told Brett it was fine, but secretly she hated it. They went to the friend's house once. Clare was using the computer when she spotted movement at the other end of the house. They were going at it on the bed. And Brett only ever had unprotected sex. He insisted on it. He told her he'd met his friend through the website Gaydar. He was on there all the time. Clare had watched him search for men, typing in the youngest age range he could — 18 to 25.

In late 2008, they went to live with Clare's mother. They were living in a shed. It didn't last long. By early 2009, Brett had found them a caravan at Bribie Island. He loved caravan parks. They were full of families. Children.

They were driving through Brisbane's north one day, Clare in the passenger seat, when Brett turned to her with an idea.

'How 'bout we try a little bit of a, like, role-play tonight?' he said. 'You pretend you're being kidnapped.' He pulled in to a Caltex service station and told her to get out. She was a young runaway, he told her. She was to pretend she didn't know him. She'd taken off and had no idea where to go. Her family didn't know where she was. Brett was a stranger offering her a lift.

'When we get home we are basically going to pretend you're being raped,' he said.

Clare was young. She thought this was what men liked. She went along with it. She stood in front of a coffee shop while he went inside. He came out carrying two hot dogs. Brett was eating one as he approached her.

'Where are you going?' he asked. The role-play had begun.

'Nowhere,' she said shyly. 'I don't have any plans of where I'm going.'

'Well, I'll give you a lift,' he said. 'I'm going up this way.'

She hopped into the 4WD and he handed her one of the hot dogs.

'Here,' Brett said. 'Do you want some food?' He steered the car onto the main road and headed towards the caravan park. They were somewhere near the weigh bridges when he locked the doors.

'You shouldn't trust who you get picked up by, should you?' he asked coldly.

Clare was tense. He was scaring her. Brett was acting stranger than usual. She clutched her seatbelt and looked out the window. White lines and bitumen. They went by in a blur.

He pulled up beside their caravan and walked around to the passenger-side door. She sat in her seat and waited. With one sharp wrench, he yanked open her door and grabbed her by the hair. Clare had long black hair, down to her waist. He grabbed it in handfuls and dragged her out. He shoved her up the stairs as she grabbed at his hands. She stumbled as he pulled her onto the bed, throwing her face down. He ripped her clothes off, tearing the buttons from her shirt.

'Pretend you're being raped,' he said. He was hurting her and she was terrified. No need to pretend anything. She told him to stop.

'No, no, no, just pretend you're being raped,' he told her. He kept her face down as they had sex. In 10 minutes he was done. He lit a cigarette and stretched out calmly beside her. Clare lay beside him and sobbed. Brett was oblivious.

'How was that?' he asked her, smoking his cigarette. 'Was it good for you too?'

'I never want to do that again!' she burst out.

*

In early 2009, Clare discovered she was pregnant. Their son was born in December. It wasn't long before authorities were knocking on the door. Brett had a history, they told her. He shouldn't be around children. Her partner was a convicted pedophile. Clare told them she knew all about it. Brett wouldn't hurt anybody. But the truth was, she'd had no idea. She was a young woman with a baby. She was afraid of being alone.

After they left, Clare asked Brett for an explanation. He was a suspect in the Daniel Morcombe disappearance, he told her. He'd been questioned several times. He told her he'd been working on the road where Daniel disappeared that day. But his alibi was tight. He'd been at his drug dealer's house.

'The police should know I'm not interested in boys that old,' he told her.

She spent a couple of months with his parents after that. Brett stayed away while Peter and Marlene helped care for the baby. After a while, she moved back with Brett. Her father moved in to their place at Bundamba. But after a few weeks, Brett had had enough. He was moving to Western Australia. Starting afresh. His past kept creeping up and causing him trouble. He didn't want Clare to follow him. It was better that he stayed away from their son.

He told Peter and Marlene he was moving to Perth to start again. As always, they were willing to help him get back on his feet. They gave him $5000. Brett packed up his car and drove the width of the country to his new life.

*

He found a caravan park near Perth's airport and hired a van, filling it with a carload of his possessions. He settled in and set about making friends. Brett was good at it. He'd talk to anyone who'd listen. He missed Clare, though. She was the one for him. He called her and told her he was flying her over for a visit. He hadn't been in Perth long but Brett had already run out of money. He paid for her flights with cash borrowed off a mate he'd met in the park.

Clare agreed to make the trip, but had a secret motive for going to see him. She wanted to break it off. Brett was devastated. Furious. He was really angry with her. He'd thought she was the one. The girl he'd dragged from his car by the hair and shoved face down on his bed had been his 'soulmate'.

It was a strange reaction, considering he'd already found himself a new woman. Sharon lived in the park too. She'd found Brett to have an infectious sort of personality. He'd just slotted himself in to her life. He'd told her he had a girlfriend over east but he wasn't sure what was going to happen with the relationship. He'd had to leave Brisbane, he told her, after bashing a 12-year-old boy. She hadn't asked him why he'd beaten a child.

Sharon kept away when Clare came to visit. After she left, Brett locked himself in his van and didn't come out for three days. He told Sharon he'd lost the love of his life.

*

Brett found himself a job as a tree lopper. When he wasn't at work, he sat in his van on his laptop with the blinds drawn. Sharon wanted to know what kept him on his computer for hours each day. What was he doing?

'Playing hunt the cunt,' he told her. She had no idea what he meant.

Sharon thought Brett was incredibly lazy. He wouldn't bother walking to the caravan park's toilet block to relieve himself. He'd just urinate in the kitchen sink.

When Sharon moved out of the park, she left a lot of her furniture and possessions with Brett. He promised to look after them for her. When her ex-husband arrived to collect them some time later, her washing machine was broken and much of the rest was missing. She didn't bother calling the police. What could they do?

CHAPTER TWENTY
WHAT NEXT?

BRUCE AND DENISE MORCOMBE had written many emails to police and other authorities trying to get information on the continuing investigation into their son's disappearance. They thought about Daniel every moment of every day. They worried that others weren't thinking about him at all.

In late June 2009, Bruce and Denise wrote to State Coroner Michael Barnes asking for an inquest into Daniel's disappearance and suspected murder. Coroners have the power to compel witnesses to answer questions in a public forum. The Morcombes thought it was time they had an opportunity to see some of the 'persons of interest' put on the stand.

'We have been told for a number of years that the police report would be presented to the coroner only when all current leads have been extinguished,' Bruce told the *Courier-Mail*. 'But … with new information coming [in] all the time, that may never be the case.'

State Coroner Michael Barnes told the paper: 'Of course I will carefully consider their request.' Two days later, he was interviewed on ABC Radio.

'I'm … aware of the public interest in the matter and as soon as a report is received from the police service, it will be given attention,' Mr Barnes said.

*

The inquest into the disappearance and presumed murder of schoolboy Daniel Morcombe began on 11 October 2010 in Maroochydore, the hub of Queensland's Sunshine Coast where families came to splash in the sea. It was decided that each of the persons of interest would be referred to by number. Clearly not all were responsible for Daniel's disappearance and having their names plastered across newspapers, websites and television stations would be disastrous. Brett was P7. Jackway was P5. Saunders, P1.

Local solicitor Peter Boyce was there to represent the Morcombes, and did so with fiery enthusiasm. He would become a close friend of the family's and would support them for years. Police would change their counsel three times as the inquest went on, starting with a solicitor and ending with a QC.

Counsel assisting the coroner, Peter Johns, started by putting the first 72 hours of the investigation under the spotlight.

'Your Honour,' Johns began, '[on] Sunday the 7th of December in 2003, Daniel James Morcombe, then a 13-year-old from a stable and loving family, set off alone on foot from his house in Palmwoods. His intention was to travel by bus to the Sunshine Plaza shopping centre where he would do some Christmas shopping and have a haircut. Your Honour will hear evidence showing that he did not reach that destination.'

It was the largest criminal investigation in Queensland's history, he said. A report prepared by police giving the coroner an overview of the investigation was more than 10 000 pages long. And that was just an overview. The inquest, Johns continued, would seek to determine whether Daniel was, in fact, dead; how, when and where he had died; and what had caused his death.

Bruce Morcombe was the first witness to give evidence. He took them through the events of that first day. The rain. The work Christmas party. Denise's drive to the overpass to save Daniel a walk home. Then the realisation that something was wrong.

He told the inquest how he and Denise had arrived at the police station at 7.30 p.m. The fear. The frustration as they tried to convince the officer that Daniel was not depressed. Or angry. He hadn't run away. Being told they would not register Daniel as a missing person just yet.

When Detective Senior Sergeant Paul Schmidt — the officer in charge of the investigation in those early days — took the stand, Boyce was ready with some pointed questions. He read from a police report Schmidt had compiled for the coroner.

'Neither officer's actions at the time were assisted by any information that caused reasonable suspicion or immediate concerns for the safety and wellbeing of Daniel Morcombe which may have assisted them in elevating his status to a missing person ...' Boyce read. He read another phrase from the report, 'Did not afford reasonable suspicion.' Police had not turned up to the Morcombes' house that night. They had promised they would.

'Did you make an investigation or any inquiry as to why it was that police didn't bother to attend the Morcombes' residence?' he asked Schmidt.

'No, I didn't.'

'Didn't think that was unusual?'

'That wasn't my charter at the time. My charter was to find Daniel Morcombe.'

The headline in the following day's *Courier-Mail* said: 'Officer did not follow procedure.' Journalist Peter Hall wrote: 'The hunt for Daniel Morcombe could have been launched 13 hours earlier if police had followed missing persons policy to the letter, an inquest has been told.'

The headlines continued throughout the week. On Wednesday, the inquest was told police had sought advice from the FBI in 2005 — and then ignored the advice. Special Agent James Beasley, a crime expert from the Behavioural Analysis Unit at Quantico, was flown to Queensland to review the investigation two years after Daniel's abduction. He found conflicting accounts in the interviews conducted with Saunders and advised detectives on specific areas to focus on when they interviewed him again.

Police at the inquest initially gave evidence Saunders had been spoken to again. But after checking documents on the exhibit list, confirmed he had not. The advice had been ignored.

They had, however, conducted more than 10 000 interviews in the seven years since Daniel disappeared. The investigation had involved more than 100 detectives, and 33 persons of interest had been identified.

The inquest was adjourned after a week. It would resume in March the following year.

*

The Queensland Police Service did not want any of the persons of interest called to the stand when the inquest resumed. They lacked credibility. Some were outright liars who had already wasted considerable police resources. And key POIs had already been grilled before the Crime and Misconduct Commission in secret star chamber hearings. Star chamber hearings were a handy tool when someone showed reluctance to speak to police. The sessions were top-secret and anyone not wanting to answer questions ended up in jail. What was the point in grilling them again?

Peter Johns, counsel assisting the coroner, and Peter Boyce, for the Morcombes, each had half a dozen from the list they wanted cross-examined in a public forum.

The decision came down to the coroner. The police were overruled.

*

They had only a few months to prepare. There would be no room for errors, loose ends or forgotten leads. They had to make sure everything that should have been done, had been done.

In December 2010, a review was ordered into P7 — Brett Peter Cowan. Homicide detectives Grant Linwood and Emma Macindoe were pulled off their normal duties and seconded to Operation Vista. Being pulled from fresher investigations to help a stalled seven-year-long abduction case was never viewed as an easy task, but the pair would leave no stone unturned. They pulled out boxes of documents. Job logs. Interview transcripts and witness statements. Nothing had been done on Brett in years. In fact, in January that year, Detective Senior Sergeant Paul Schmidt had written a report recommending the entire Morcombe investigation be made a cold case.

'I further recommend that this investigation be now forwarded to the Homicide Investigation Group as a cold case investigation at the first available opportunity,' he wrote.

Commissioner Bob Atkinson would not agree.

The file on Brett included a list of reasons why he may or may not be responsible for Daniel's disappearance. The 'pros' column was compelling. He was a convicted pedophile. He'd put himself in the right place at the right time. There were 45 minutes he could not account for. He looked like one of the comfits. He knew the area — his church was metres from the abduction site. And a 4WD similar to his had been spotted on the side of the road.

The 'cons' list was lengthy. Many officers believed Brett just hadn't had enough time. 'The time frames ascertained by investigators of the movements of Daniel Morcombe do not allow for sufficient time for Cowan to commit this offence and get back to his residence,' the report read. His car was white, not blue. There was no evidence Brett had been with anyone else that day and many witnesses had seen more than one person. The clothing he'd worn that day did not match witness descriptions. And, strangely, Brett was not believed responsible because his 'movements that day were as a direct result of home duties he was engaged in'. He couldn't have killed Daniel: he'd been doing the gardening. His movements that day were not suspicious. He'd been cooperative with police and his car had come up clean.

Armed with this information, detectives Linwood and Macindoe decided there was a link they needed to look at. Or maybe it was just a coincidence. When Brett's friend Trevor Davis had bought a sandblasting business, the one he'd planned to hand over to Brett to manage, he'd bought it from a man named Kelvyn Kruger.

It was Kelvyn's property that workers had visited on Friday evenings for a beer while local kids zipped around his homemade dirt bike track. Daniel and his brothers had been there on many occasions. Had Brett been there too? Had he gone to Kelvyn Kruger's for an after-work beer and seen the kids playing on the track?

They spent many hours working on this theory. In the end it came to nothing. There was no evidence Brett and Daniel had crossed paths.

In late January 2011, a few weeks before the inquest was set to resume, the *Courier-Mail* ran an article claiming Assistant Commissioner Mike Condon had pulled up to 40 detectives from their normal roles to review 5000 job logs on the Daniel Morcombe investigation. Some police officers, the paper said, were calling it a face-saving exercise. In late March, POIs like Douglas Jackway and Brett Cowan would be called to give evidence. Condon would not confirm the existence of the task force, but a written statement from the police media section said they were 'committed to utilising all possible strategies and resources to bring the investigation to a successful conclusion'.

The review into Brett's file had been going since December. Linwood and Macindoe had moved on to testing Brett's alibi. Again. They drove from Brett's house to the overpass. It took them 26 minutes in normal traffic conditions. The overpass to the Davises' house where Brett had collected the mulcher was another eight minutes. They knew Brett's history. A few minutes was all he needed to assault and murder a child.

They went to see Brett's ex-wife. Tracey told them she couldn't be sure what time Brett had got home that day. She'd had no reason to look at her watch. She remembered the sun hitting the back room, which it did mid-afternoon. That was all.

They spoke with Frank Davis about the mulcher. The neighbour who'd seen Brett in the garden. Nobody could put an exact time on his arrival back home.

They went back to Sandra Drummond, Brett's drug dealer. He claimed to have spent half an hour drinking tea and buying marijuana at her home. If they could prove she hadn't been home, that she'd been somewhere else, they could prove he was lying.

*

On 14 March 2011, Operation Vista detectives and members of the Covert and Surveillance Unit were called to a meeting by Assistant Commissioner Mike Condon.

They'd come up with a plan. After Brett Cowan's appearance at the inquest, they were putting an officer on the plane back to Perth with him. The covert officer would try his best to befriend him. They all had work to do.

*

They called Douglas Jackway to the stand on 30 March. The inquest had been shifted to Brisbane by then. With POIs coming and going, authorities wanted tighter security in case of any vigilante action. Jackway was aggressive, obnoxious. Reporters stared at this man and pictured him luring a young boy from the side of the road.

The courtroom of lawyers took him through his life, his criminal history and his movements in early December 2003. It was damning. He was a rough-looking man with tattoos. He had a blue car just like the one witnesses had described. Police had him on the Sunshine Coast on the morning of 8 December — the day after Daniel disappeared. His alibi was a mess. He'd changed his story many times. He'd badgered people to cover for him. He'd snatched a boy before. Taken him in broad daylight, in front of his friends. He'd been raping the child when the boy's father arrived. He was a monster.

'I just want to clear my name,' he told the court.

*

Linwood and Macindoe continued their work, even as the inquest went on. Sandra Drummond had a habit of playing the pokies on a Sunday afternoon at the Beerwah RSL. Her daughter worked there. She ran the raffle on Sundays.

Boyce had torn into police at the inquest for never having interviewed Sandra's partner, Kevin Fitzgerald, about whether he remembered Brett stopping by on 7 December. They'd interviewed Sandra. But that had been it.

On 4 April, Linwood and Macindoe did just that. Kevin was sure Brett hadn't been by. Motors fascinated him. Brett claimed he'd taken Kevin out to the car to show him the mulcher. Kevin was sure he would remember that. He'd even have been able to tell them what kind of motor it had.

The detectives were still determined to prove Brett hadn't been by. They checked Sandra's phone and bank records. Investigators who'd been to see the drug dealer in 2006 hadn't done it then. They went to the Beerwah RSL and asked about security footage. But it had been more than seven years. Did they have some kind of loyalty program? Did people swipe in with cards? They did. Linwood and Macindoe were in luck. Gary Gersbach, from Max Gaming, promised to help track down the records. His company had provided the gaming machines and the loyalty card program that went with it. On 5 May, he came back with what they needed. On 7 December 2003, Kevin Fitzgerald and Sandra Drummond had been at the Beerwah RSL playing the pokies. They'd removed their loyalty cards from the machines at 2.20 p.m. and 2.22 p.m., respectively. It was a five- to 10-minute drive from the RSL back home. Given Brett had initially claimed to have been home between 2.30 p.m. and 2.45 p.m., this was significant. A lot of work had gone into proving this small but critical point. Brett was a liar. He'd lied about his movements. He'd changed his story again and again. His latest claim, that he'd spent half an hour with Sandra Drummond, just didn't seem possible.

*

Brett had tried everything he could to escape having to testify. He'd been diagnosed with emphysema, he told investigators. He'd had a lifetime of smoking to poison his lungs. He couldn't possibly fly. It was dangerous. Doctor's orders.

They'd put him on a bus then, they said. They scrambled behind the scenes to make arrangements for an undercover officer to join him on the bus ride home, instead of a plane.

But a bus trip from Perth to Brisbane would be tedious. Brett hadn't exactly come up with a medical certificate proving he couldn't fly. In the end he changed his mind. The plane would be fine.

*

The Brisbane motel had been chosen for its proximity to a busy car park across the road. Late-night diners chasing fast food came and went. Cars parked. Cars left. Nobody would notice the covert surveillance team parked among the hubbub, watching Brett through binoculars. He was a predator. They didn't want him near children. They didn't want him attacking anyone else. As they watched, a man arrived at Brett's door. A late-night caller he'd invited over for a quick visit.

'Good night?' the detective assigned to drive Brett to the inquest asked him the following morning.

'Just a quiet one,' Brett said. 'A bit of TV and early to bed.'

Liar, liar, the officer thought.

*

Twenty-four hours earlier they'd been convinced they knew the answer. Journalists, pens poised, notebooks on laps, had watched Doug Jackway with fascination. This, they thought, is the man who killed Daniel Morcombe. It was in the way he spoke. The way he looked. The blue car he used to drive. He even looked like one of the comfit images. He was rough. Tattooed. His history made him the perfect suspect.

Peter Johns rose to his feet. 'Yes,' he began, 'I call Brett Cowan.'

Courier-Mail reporter Jasmin Lill stared at the man who sauntered into the room. He was tall, with a drug-user's sallow eyes and wiry frame. He wore his brown hair pulled back in a ponytail. Jackway didn't look like the comfit images, she decided. This man did. It was incredible. This man killed Daniel Morcombe.

On the other side of the courtroom, Bruce Morcombe was thinking the exact same thing. It was as though the man in front of him was *trying* to look like the person all those bus passengers and passing motorists had described.

Brett took the stand and gave his name and date of birth. Johns took him through the basic details of his life. Where was he living? Where was he working? What was his relationship like with his parents? What about his children?

Then: 'You have a criminal history?' Johns asked.

'Yes I do.'

'OK. In Queensland and the Northern Territory?'

'Yes.'

'Now, on that criminal history, there's two references to offences that might be termed sex offences?'

'Yes.'

'Is that right? I'm just interested in your description of what those two are.'

Brett gave a brief version of the abuse he'd carried out on the young boy at the childcare centre. Johns asked him to describe the Northern Territory offence.

'Young boy, was my next-door neighbour,' he started. 'He came looking for his sister and I knew his sister was playing on the other side of the caravan park and I took him and — but instead of taking him to his sister, I took him out through the back of the fence and into the bush and molested him on some old car bodies and then went back about my business in the caravan park.'

'Did it involve violence?' Johns asked.

'No, no it didn't.'

Johns moved on. They went over Brett's movements on 7 December 2003. They talked about Sandra Drummond and his apparent visit for marijuana and a cup of tea.

'I always spent time there,' Brett insisted. A cup of tea with his friendly neighbourhood drug dealer. Johns asked Brett whether he understood why that missing time was so important.

'Not really, no. I don't, like, I had nothing to do with Daniel's disappearance at all. Nothing at all. And as I said to the police, and I'm sorry if this sounds bad, but I thought it was funny that they still thought that I still had something to do with Daniel's disappearance over 30 minutes or 35 minutes, whatever it was,' Brett said.

'Why was that funny?' Johns asked.

'Just having, like, to do something in half an hour and get rid of, or, or, you know, anything like that. I don't think that's possible.'

Johns wasn't laughing. He told Brett that if the drug dealer story was excluded, he'd had a 40-minute window to abduct and murder Daniel. Brett was a man with a history of quick, opportunistic offences. Offences where he had quickly committed a crime and continued on with his life as though nothing had happened. When it came to Daniel Morcombe, Brett wouldn't have even had to go out of his way, he'd driven right by the exact spot where the boy had been standing.

'Your Honour, I'm intending now just to ask a couple of

questions in relation to offences that may or may not have been committed by Mr Cowan that he hasn't been convicted for.'

Coroner Michael Barnes explained to Brett that he would be made to answer questions about offences he might have committed — even though he might incriminate himself. But the coroner gave a guarantee those answers would not be used against him.

'Since the Northern Territory offence in 1993, have you committed any sexual offences, even ones you haven't been charged with?' Johns asked.

'No, I have not.'

'What about other offences that don't appear on your criminal history and you've never been charged with? Are there any other offences that you've committed?'

'No, sir.'

'Have you, since 1993, been accused — and by this I mean not only be police but by anyone, accused of any sexual offences which you say you didn't commit?'

'Yes. My wife's auntie accused me of touching their 15-month-old daughter.'

'Right. Any others?'

'Yeah, I was asked in Moranbah about another relation to [a girlfriend's] son, 12-year-old son. I was supposed to have molested him at a party or something.'

'In relation to your earlier years ... had you sexually abused any children prior to that [1987] offence?'

'Before I turned 17? Yes, I had.' Brett admitted to molesting children at the army pool. It started when he was about 10 and went on for six or seven years. It had involved oral sex and younger children, he said.

Johns moved back to December of 2003. He pulled out a list of phone records. They talked about Brett's internet habits. He said he spent most of his time online looking at eBay and pornography. But not child porn, he insisted. Sometimes windows would pop up, but he'd close them right away.

141

'I know about computers being searched, checked, analysed ...'. Brett said.

Johns went through internet dial-up times and durations the night before Daniel disappeared. Someone at the Cowan house had connected to the internet at 8.50 p.m. and continued the session right through until about 4 a.m. Brett conceded that he was the one online until the early hours of the morning.

'Can you tell us whether or not on that late evening, Saturday evening, and through the early hours of Sunday, the 7th of December, 2003, that you were looking at child pornography?' Johns asked.

'I was not.'

'What about some of these pop-ups that showed images of children?'

'Yes.'

Johns was making a point. Brett, whose relationship with his wife was far from intimate, had sat up the night before Daniel disappeared for a seven-hour porn session. They went back over the attacks he had carried out on children in Brisbane and Darwin. They were over in a matter of minutes. Brett was back, carrying on with his day, in a matter of minutes.

'Can you tell His Honour why you find it so funny that the police think you couldn't abduct and sexually assault and potentially murder Daniel Morcombe in a period of half an hour as we discussed this morning, or 40 to 50 minutes, as I will outline later?' Johns said.

'Yeah,' Brett said. 'One, out of my age group. I was interested in six- to eight-year-old boys.'

Bruce Morcombe grimaced. Journalists raised eyebrows. Was he serious?

'Well, sorry, no, we'll come to that, and I'll give you a chance to say that, but I'm worried about the times. This morning you said you found it funny that the police were interested in you because you couldn't possibly do what's alleged within half an hour?'

'Yeah.'

'Well, that's just rubbish, isn't it? You've managed to do it twice, abduct or certainly coerce a boy to somewhere else and rape the boy in a period well within half an hour. That's true, isn't it? You got minutes to spare. So why is it so funny?'

'Where would I have done it? Where would I have taken him?'

'Look,' Johns said, 'I'm asking the questions.' He had another point to make. 'From what's almost certainly a crime that has occurred that's caused the disappearance of Daniel Morcombe, do you know how rare that type of crime is? And to define it, I'm talking about situations where a juvenile boy, a boy under 18 years of age, is snatched or kidnapped from a public area and the perpetrator is never found or isn't found for years — that type of crime. In your lifetime, for instance, apart from Daniel's case, how many times do you think that might've happened in Queensland?'

'I don't know,' Brett said.

'Well, I can tell you, the answer is never. This is the only time. And even if you include girls, who are more likely to be victims of this type of crime, I can tell you, in your lifetime, there's only two cases of girls where they've been snatched from a public area and the perpetrator has never been identified. One of those was in 1972, when, of course, you were only three or four.

'And do you understand that, as of December 2003, that you were one of the very few people in Queensland, if not Australia, who had a proven history of kidnapping and sexually assaulting young boys after taking them from public areas. Do you understand that?'

'Yeah.'

'So if you didn't, in fact, have anything to do with Daniel's disappearance, have you thought about how unlikely a scenario that this actually is, that you, with this extensive history of having kidnapped boys and assaulted them in ways that might lead to their death, happen to be in the very place at the very time that this once-in-a-decade, once-in-20-, 30-year event occurs? Have you thought about how incredibly unlikely that is?'

'No, I have not.' Brett's palms were sweating. Johns was only just warming up.

'You haven't ever cursed at how unlucky you are, that, here you are, someone trying to get yourself back on the straight and narrow, stay away from assaulting children, and you say you don't want to go back to jail, and then this event — this event that's happened only once in your lifetime in Queensland, you, the person with the history who would immediately attract suspicion, happens to be right there, right then. Would you agree that you are incredibly unlucky?'

'Yep.'

'You see, it's not only that. Are you aware that — and I believe it's been put to you — that a man fitting your description, or great semblance to you, was seen by some of the passers-by in the bus that day? As I understand it, you've agreed with police in your interview that you do resemble at least one of the comfit sketches?'

'Yes.'

'I'm suggesting to you that Mr and Mrs Morcombe, who are sitting right there, who have been without their son for seven years, deserve better from you than this ridiculous alibi that you've come up with. See, this is what I say happened during that missing time, that when you were driving along Nambour Connection Road, approaching the Kiel Mountain Road overpass, you saw Daniel.

'Of course you saw him. To have us believe that you didn't see him is like suggesting to us that a snake might slide past an injured mouse and take no notice. Of course you saw him. Of course he attracted your attention. And as such, you parked your vehicle right near the Christian Outreach Centre, which is an area you know so well. That's what happened, isn't it?'

'No.'

'And I say that you approached Daniel and you sat nearby him or stood nearby him and talked to him for quite some time, using your very well-honed skills in convincing children to do things they might not want to do. And that's why people saw a man who looked remarkably similar to you doing just that. And you spoke to Daniel and you had some difficulty convincing him — he was a bit older than your other victims but certainly within the range, I would say.

'And then you had a stroke of luck, you see, because the bus went past him. And he didn't understand why and that's just what you needed to push him over the edge and agree to go with this man who'd been talking to him for about 15 or 20 minutes, who'd been telling him that he would take him to the shops where he wanted to go or drive him back to his house up the road so he didn't have to walk. The missed bus finally convinced him that, all right, this guy sounds OK. You'd had 20 minutes to convince him by then, far longer than you normally need.

'Then you took him to some of the bushland that you know like the back of your hand, from the evidence that you've told us, you assaulted him and in the course of that assault, you either accidentally or intentionally killed him ... I say that you did intentionally kill him because on the previous two occasions you found out that it's very annoying to have the victim survive and come nominate you, and so, this time, you intentionally made sure that that wouldn't happen.

'That's the set of circumstances, more or less, isn't it?'

'No it's not.'

'And if it wasn't intentional, Mr Cowan, today is your opportunity to tell how an accident might have occurred.'

'I had nothing to do with Daniel's disappearance.'

Peter Johns was done.

'No further questions, thank you, Your Honour.'

Bruce Morcombe looked at Brett. This was the man who'd killed his son.

Brett was sweating. His heart raced. But he thought: *They've got nothing.*

Behind the scenes, police were working to change that.

*

Detective Senior Constable Grant Linwood took Brett back to his unmarked police car and drove him to the airport. The detective parked the car and walked his charge all the way to the departure gate.

'Bye, Brett,' he called. And for good measure: 'Don't come back to Queensland.'

PART THREE
THE STUFF DREAMS ARE MADE OF

CHAPTER TWENTY-ONE
MR BIG

THE CANADIAN CITY OF Winnipeg was built where the Red River meets the Assiniboine, near the longitudinal centre of North America. In the late nineteenth century, Winnipeg, like much of Canada, was booming from the completion of the Canadian Pacific Railway. On 17 October 1899, the body of John Gordon was found lying on a Winnipeg street. He'd been murdered. A single wound from a pistol ball had ended his life. Police had a suspect on their radar almost immediately — but Donald Todd would not confess and they needed more evidence.

Two locals were recruited as newly badged detectives. The chief of police gave them the task of pretending to be criminals in order to befriend Todd. William McBean and David Yeddeau drew Todd in with their tales of the criminal underworld. They told him about the gang they belonged to. The violence. The money. The power and the glamour. Todd was enticed. They told him he could join but he'd have to prove himself worthy. They spoke of the enormous fortune he'd make if he was accepted.

Todd, who spent his days drinking and playing cards, was seduced. McBean and Yeddeau told Todd he needed to prove he had the mettle to join a criminal gang. Was there something he'd done, something in his past that would convince them he had what it took?

That's when Todd told them about shooting Gordon. And he didn't just confess to the crime. He wrote it down.

The tactic drew much criticism from the judiciary when Todd was brought before court. The judge used words like 'vile', 'base' and 'contemptible' as he debated whether Todd had effectively been offered money to confess. The *King v Todd* case, which played out well over 100 years ago, is considered the first of the 'Mr Big' stings and the controversy surrounding such policing manoeuvres would follow it for generations.

'Confessions are rejected when obtained by pressure, not because the court presumes the statement is untrue, but because of the principle that the truth of the statement becomes uncertain,' Todd's lawyer observed. 'A bought confession is not free and voluntary. There was everything here to induce Todd to lie.' By confessing, the court was told, Todd stood to make a lot of money.

The judge did not like it. But he eventually ruled that Todd had not been induced to confess to the crime of killing Gordon. He was not even aware he was a suspect. He had only been asked to prove he had the stomach for joining the ranks of a criminal gang. Todd was found guilty of manslaughter and sentenced to two years.

By the 1990s, the Royal Canadian Mounted Police had reworked and modernised Mr Big into an extravagant and often expensive undercover operation.

*

Nelson Hart was a boy in a man's body. Plagued by seizures, the Canadian man had barely learnt to read and lost his driver's licence several times over safety concerns. His mother looked after him until he was in his mid-20s. But after a confrontation between her sometimes-aggressive son and her fed-up boyfriend, Nelson was turfed out to fend for himself.

He didn't do well living on his own and his seizures soon became worse. They became so bad that the government agreed to fund a live-in carer. Jennifer Hicks, a young, brown-haired woman, moved in soon after. Over time, their working relationship progressed to a romantic one and Jennifer lost her job because of it. Without her carer's position, and with Nelson not bringing in an income, the couple lived on government handouts. Soon, Jennifer fell pregnant with twins. Nelson worried how they would care for the children. He worried about money and he worried about his frequent seizures. What if he had one while holding a baby? Was he safe to be around children?

In March 1999, Jennifer gave birth to twin girls they named Karen and Krista. The girls were inseparable. They developed their own little personalities and kept their parents busy. Nelson, meanwhile, was struggling with money. He spent what little he had on gambling. He stayed out late and avoided spending time alone with the girls. Things got so bad that social services threatened to take the children away. They told Jennifer if she wanted to keep the girls, she'd have to leave their father.

On 4 August 2002, while Jennifer showered and got ready for a demolition derby they were attending that day, Nelson took his three-year-old daughters for a drive. It was unusual for the man who'd avoided being alone with them, terrified one of his seizures would cause them harm or frighten them. He strapped them into the car and asked them where they wanted to go. Karen and Krista wanted to go to the park.

Little Harbour is a picnicking area with a boat ramp and a wharf at the end of a gravel road. Swimmers use the wharf area as a diving platform. It's one small corner of Gander Lake, Newfoundland's third largest lake at 56 kilometres in length and several kilometres in width. A swing set had recently been installed — and that's where Nelson took his girls.

In his first version of events, Nelson would tell police one of the girls fell in the lake and, unable to swim, he'd driven home in a panic. Later, he told them he'd taken the girls one by one from the car, shut the door and fallen to the ground with a massive seizure. He told how he woke up to see Krista in the water. In a state of confusion, he got in his car and drove home. By the time he arrived, the confusion was wearing off and he realised in horror that Karen was still at the lake.

Nelson and Jennifer sped back to the picnic area. Krista was in the water, floating away from the shore. Karen was nowhere to be seen. Jennifer didn't know how to swim either, so Nelson took off and called for help from a nearby gas station.

Paramedics got Krista to shore. Incredibly, she was still alive. Barely. She would die in hospital the following day. Karen was found 10 metres from the wharf. She was dead.

Police suspected Nelson immediately. They were suspicious of his changing stories. He insisted he hadn't told them about having a seizure initially because he hadn't wanted to lose his licence. They didn't buy it. But without evidence, they couldn't charge him.

After the death of the twins, Nelson and Jennifer fell on even tougher times. They hadn't even been able to afford a headstone for their daughters' graves. When police quietly moved in to start their sting, the Harts were sleeping on the floor of a tiny flat, barely able to feed themselves.

Then, one day, a French Canadian man named Steph Suave happened upon Nelson and asked for directions. They got talking and Suave — an undercover police officer — pulled out a photograph of a woman he said was his sister.

The woman was young with long, blond hair. She was a drug addict, Suave said. He was desperate to find her. Their mother was terminally ill and wanted to see her daughter before she died. Suave asked Nelson to help him look. There was $50 in it for him if he did. Nelson didn't need to think twice. He barely had a buck to his name. There was another $50 the following day. Nelson had failed to find the missing sister so Suave wanted him to search in another nearby town.

Carefully, inch by inch, Suave wove his web. Soon Nelson was doing all kinds of jobs for him. Suave told Nelson he and some friends ran a transport company. He had Nelson drive a U-Haul for him. A man signed an invoice at the other end.

Nelson and Jennifer found themselves being treated to meals and put up in hotels as Nelson carried out various tasks for Suave. The money was rolling in. Nelson spent $4000 on an elaborate headstone for the girls. It was his first real purchase with the money he was earning.

Some of the jobs Suave was assigning were a little strange and Nelson soon got the impression the organisation wasn't exactly kosher. Before long, he discovered he'd been recruited into an organised crime gang. For months, he carried out tasks for them and was paid handsomely for his efforts. In four months, he made $15 000. Once you're in, they told him, you can't get out. Nelson didn't mind. His new associates had become like brothers to him. They were his closest friends. His confidants.

One day, Suave took Nelson to see the boss. The Mr Big of the crime gang. Nelson was taken into a meeting at a hotel, where the boss told him there was a problem. A rival gang member was going to go to police claiming to have witnessed Nelson pushing his girls into the lake. They were trying to cause trouble, Nelson was told. They needed to know what he'd done. It was a test of trust and loyalty.

He was terrified of the boss. People who crossed him disappeared, he'd been told. Nelson denied it at first.

'I never hurt my daughters,' he insisted.

It was soon made clear that if he didn't come clean, he'd be cast out — or worse. So he confessed.

'This is just about the perfect murder,' the boss said.

'It was pretty well organised,' Nelson replied.

'You must be a thinker, eh?'

'Sometimes it pays to be that way.'

The following day, Nelson went back to the lake with the undercover officers and explained to them how he'd pushed his little girls into the water. He was found guilty of murder and sentenced to life in prison. But he appealed — and the appeal judges had a lot to say about Mr Big confessions.

'The Mr Big technique is a Canadian invention,' their judgement said:

Although a version of the technique appears to have been used more than a century ago, its modern use began in the 1990s and, by 2008, it had been used by police across Canada more than 350 times. The technique, used only in cases involving serious unsolved crimes, has secured confessions and convictions in hundreds of cases. The confessions wrought by the technique are often detailed and confirmed by other evidence.

However, the Mr Big technique comes at a price. Suspects confess to Mr Big during pointed interrogations in the face of powerful inducements and sometimes veiled threats — and this raises the spectre of unreliable confessions. Unreliable confessions provide compelling evidence of guilt and present a clear and straightforward path to conviction. In other contexts, they have been responsible for wrongful convictions — a fact we cannot ignore.

They determined there was a significant risk of false confessions. The subject was put in a position where they'd say anything to hold on to their new life. Perhaps they felt they were in danger unless they confessed?

And so, Nelson's conviction was thrown out. The court ruled that Nelson's recorded confession could not be used in any future trial. The police had nothing. Nelson was a free man.

*

Belinda Romeo was just 24 when she died, struggling against the scarf her killer had pulled tight around her throat. When she was finally still, her short and effervescent life extinguished, her jilted lover unwound the fabric and left her Melbourne apartment with his murder weapon still in hand. Later, he stashed it in an abandoned car and went about his business.

Belinda's mother had contracted rubella while she was

pregnant. Belinda was born with an intellectual disability. But she wasn't one to let that get in the way. She lived a full and independent life.

In 1999, she was seeing a man named Alipapa Tofilau. Alipapa came from a large Samoan family. He worked two jobs and sent money home to his mother. He went to church and played rugby. He was three years older than Belinda. They spent a lot of nights together during their short relationship — but neither of them was serious about it being exclusive.

On the morning of Saturday 19 June, Alipapa got out of bed and drove himself to rugby. He'd stayed at Belinda's flat the night before. And the night before that and the night before that. The post-rugby beers moved from one club to another. Alipapa started calling Belinda, wanting to meet her at a pub in inner-city Melbourne. He'd been calling her constantly. In the past couple of weeks he'd called her 90 times. Belinda had wanted to end things. Alipapa was still hanging on.

Belinda agreed to meet him at the Bridge Club Hotel. She'd spent the afternoon at home with another man but left him in bed to meet Alipapa. At the pub, Belinda got talking to another woman who was also in a sexual relationship with Alipapa. They confronted him together before storming off. Alipapa spent the rest of the night and the following day on a boozy bender with mates.

The following afternoon, full of beer and bourbon, Alipapa rang Belinda from a phone box outside a milk bar. He got inside her flat and walked out minutes later, scarf in hand. Her body would not be found for a week.

Two years later, Alipapa made a new friend. His name was Pat — an undercover police officer — and they soon became firm friends. Pat was a member of an organised crime gang. He lived a fast life of easy cash and glitzy restaurants. They had cops in their pocket. They could find out anything. They could make problems go away. Soon, Pat had Alipapa involved.

The gang had set up a robbery where they gained access to a safe containing a lucrative diamond haul. Alipapa was given a mobile phone and told to stand lookout. He was to call in if he spotted any police activity. In a breath-holding moment for the operatives, a police car did cruise past. Spotting Alipapa loitering, they pulled over to ask him what he was doing.

'I've just finished work,' he told them. 'I'm waiting for a mate to pick me up.' He hadn't missed a beat. The officers nodded and moved on.

The 'crime gang' was impressed. They told him his share of the loot was $10 000. It would be put in a safety deposit box until he'd officially earned his way into the gang.

He'd been working with his new friends for months when police decided to set the ball rolling for their final push. Detectives arrived with a warrant. Alipapa had always refused to give them a sample of his DNA. Now they were taking one, with or without his cooperation. The warrant was designed to let Alipapa know police were still after him. They were putting the pressure on. And considering he'd told his friends in the gang he'd already given investigators a DNA sample, it would put Alipapa under even more strain by having to confess he'd lied.

He called Pat for help. Maybe the DNA sample would match something at the scene?

Pat reminded him about the gang's mandate. Trust. Honesty. Loyalty. They couldn't operate without it. He asked Alipapa whether he'd done it. They couldn't help him, he said, unless they knew the truth.

Alipapa came clean. He'd strangled Belinda in a fit of rage with the scarf she'd been wearing around her neck. Pat took him to see the gang's leader. Their Mr Big. Mr Big needed to know all the details, Alipapa was told, if he was going to fix things with the police. Come clean, Mr Big said, or you can 'get up and walk out now'.

The confession Alipapa gave was detailed and the undercover officers recorded every word. Alipapa was arrested the next day. He denied he'd been at the hotel. When the recording was played, he told the detectives he'd made it up to impress his new friends. The jury didn't buy it. They sent him away for murder.

Alipapa's case would later be one of four taken to the High Court of Australia to determine whether Mr Big confessions were legitimate. The High Court's judgement read:

> All four appellants rely upon the rule of the common law that evidence of a confession … may not be received against an accused person unless it is shown to be voluntary.
>
> A confessional statement will be excluded from evidence as involuntary if it has been obtained from an accused either by fear of prejudice or hope of advantage, exercised or held out by a person in authority'.

The High Court determined that while Mr Big stings have a limited life span, they didn't break the rules. But Alipapa hadn't confessed to a 'person in authority', the court ruled. One judge determined:

> The appellant neither knew nor believed that those to whom he spoke had lawful authority to affect the course of the investigation of or prosecution for the murder of Ms Romeo.
>
> The statements the appellant made to undercover police officers were not made under compulsion. Nothing that was said to or done with the appellant constituted compulsion of a kind that would meet the criteria leading to the conclusion that what was said was not said voluntarily. There was no duress or intimidation.
>
> The police operation was elaborate and took place over an extended period. The appellant thought that he would benefit from saying what he did. More than once the appellant was told how important it was that he be frank about his past and about the circumstances of Ms Romeo's death in particular. He was repeatedly told that if he had a problem the boss

would make it 'go away'. But no coercion was applied to the appellant by those to whom he made his confession. There was no importunity, insistence or pressure of a kind exerted by those to whom the confession was made that would found the conclusion that the appellant had no free choice whether to speak or stay silent.

Observing that the appellant may have felt under pressure requires no different conclusion. What is important is the absence of coercion by those to whom he spoke. That he may have felt under the pressure that he himself generated by his desire to join the gang and thus gain not only the financial benefits said to follow from that membership but also resolution of what otherwise appeared to be his inevitable prosecution for murder is not to the point.

The legal argument had gone on for years. The conclusion was a relief to Belinda's mother.

'Finally,' she told *The Age* newspaper, 'at long last, it's over.' Asked about the Mr Big tactic, she said: 'I think it's wonderful. Without this, we would not be where we are today.'

CHAPTER TWENTY-TWO
THE PERFECT TARGET

IT TAKES A PARTICULAR type of personality to fall for an elaborate operation like Mr Big. The subject has to be vulnerable. They have to be desperate. They are usually aware they are a suspect. Often they've had suspicion hanging over them for a number of years. In one Australian case, police tried Mr Big on a truck driver. It was doomed to fail. The truck driver was busy. He spent most of his time on the road. He wasn't interested in making $50 here and $100 there when long-haul driving was bringing in a much better pay packet.

Queensland Police had tried it on convicted triple murderer Max Sica. On 22 April 2003, Massimo 'Max' Sica made a frantic and tearful call to police from the home of his next-door neighbours. His former girlfriend, Neelma Singh, was dead. He'd found her and her younger brother and sister in the spa of their parents' ensuite. The Singh parents had been away in Fiji.

Police were suspicious. How did he know all three siblings were in the spa? They'd only found Kunal after first removing the bodies of Neelma, her 12-year-old sister, Sidhi, and some bedding that had been stuffed in the still-bubbling tub. Kunal had been placed in the spa first and couldn't be seen at all by someone walking into the room.

In an effort to get Sica's confession, Queensland Police set up a Mr Big operation. Sica, a manipulative and deceitful man who showed all the hallmarks of a psychopath, was onto them almost immediately. The investigative team pulled the plug. They'd find another way.

*

Police had built an intricate psychological profile of Brett Cowan over the years. They had a collection of reports written by forensic psychologists who'd spoken to him during different prison stints.

'Unlike many extra-familial sex offenders, he appears to have been uninterested in any emotional content to his sexual contact with children, preferring fleeting, one-off encounters. This aspect of his offending may, of course, merely have emerged through his desire to avoid detection,' psychologist Dr Steven Smallbone wrote about Brett in 1998.

They also had a pile of Indirect Personality Assessment Questionnaires, filled out by Brett's ex-wife, his ex-girlfriends and his aunt, Jennifer Philbrook.

'The following set of questions was developed to elicit information pertaining to the personality of Brett Cowan,' one read. 'The information obtained will greatly aid in the assessment of his personality. This assessment should provide valuable information to investigators for interviews and other investigative techniques.'

'Internally, he is a little boy looking for attention and acceptance,' Brett's aunt said in hers.

Brett's ex-wife Tracey filled one out after he'd left her for another woman.

Q: Does the subject have any mannerisms or gestures that stand out? (Nervous habits, changes in voice patterns when nervous, upset or angry, etc.)

A: Gets very angry if doesn't get his own way. Constantly lies. Constantly talks to cover up lies and over embellishes. When fear of being caught out, threatens to sue for defamation.

Q: Does the subject have a good vocabulary? Does he/she use it appropriately or to impress?

A: Would try to sell anything to anyone.

Q: Does the subject have any special talents or skills? If yes, what type?

A: Welder, spray painter, sandblaster, picks up trade and skills very easily.

Q: What does the subject do in his/her spare time?

A: Gardening.

Q: What type of reading material does the subject read/view?

A: Pornography.

Q: What type of movies/videos does the subject watch?

A: Action, violence.

Q: Does the subject play any games? (Cards, sports, etc.) If yes, what type?

A: Computer game Sim City.

Q: What does the subject spend his/her money on?

A: Cannabis, car.

Q: Does the subject drive the vehicle as a pastime? If yes, where and how often?

A: When living in Beerwah would always disappear in the car.

Q: What failure has the subject experienced? (Marital, financial, occupational, etc.)

A: Marital (with Tracey Cowan), occupational — is always changing jobs, financial — never good with money.

Q: What is important to the subject?

A: Himself.

Q: Does the subject hold a grudge?

A: Yes. If anybody did anything to/by him wrong, would become very angry but has never committed any violence. Makes threats to sue more than anything.

Q: Is the subject competitive?

A: Yes. Mainly with his mates and what they do, who can drink the most, who can smoke the most, who can tell the dirtiest story.

Q: Is subject's self-image accurate?

A: No. He thinks it is but has high opinion/expectations of himself.

Q: Does the subject display emotion?

A: Yes. Only anger, never showed any emotion with marriage breakdown.

Q: What makes him/her angry, sad, happy?

A: Angry — if he doesn't get his own way, sad — losing his grandmother, nothing else, happy — when he gets his own way.

Q: Does the subject become bored easily/often?

A: Yes. He is like a little child, he can't sit still and needs to be occupied all the time.

Q: Is the subject a risk taker?

A: Yes, mainly his manner of driving, exceeding speed limits.

Q: Does the subject lie frequently?

A: Yes. Will lie about anything to make himself look better.

Q: Knowing what you know about the subject, how would you describe him/her?

A: Manipulative, mean, self-absorbed.

CHAPTER TWENTY-THREE
JOE

FRIDAY, 1 APRIL 2011: Brett Cowan's ticket put him in seat 42D for the long journey to Perth. He sat down, stretched out his legs and tried to shake off the stress of the past 24 hours. He wouldn't forget the way his hands had tried to give him away, that slick layer of sweat making his palms slippery. He looked at the man sitting next to him. He was young and fit. Brett sized him up and thought he looked pretty good.

The man introduced himself as Joe. He was thinking of moving to Perth, he told Brett. Brett nodded. Was this man a journalist? They started talking and Brett changed his mind. Not a journalist. Just a friendly bloke, happy to chat.

Five rows back, another man took his seat. Detective Senior Constable John Carey made sure he had a clear view of Joe. He expected to spend a week or so away from his family, supervising a covert operation. They'd called West Australian Police to let them know they were coming.

The plan was to befriend Brett Cowan. They'd done their research, found out what he liked and didn't like. They'd planned to buy an old car and Joe would ask Brett for help tinkering with the engine. They'd get talking. The car would be rigged with listening devices. They'd capture every word. You never knew what might happen. Maybe Brett would let something slip. That was the plan. The whole plan.

*

On the plane they chatted about Western Australia, about Brett's jobs sandblasting and spray-painting. Brett said he'd flown back to

Brisbane — where he'd grown up — for an access visit with his kids. The lies rolled off his tongue with ease.

'Where are you staying in Perth?' Brett asked his new friend.

'I've booked a motel in the city for a couple of nights.'

'You should look at caravan parks,' Brett said. He told Joe he'd been staying at Crystal Brook Caravan Park, paying $175 a week and around $10 for electricity. If he got stuck, Brett continued, Joe could come crash with him for a couple of days.

Brett was trying it on. Joe was good-looking. It was part of the reason he'd been selected for the job. They talked all the way to Perth. By the time the Qantas jet coasted along the runway, Joe and Brett had exchanged numbers with a plan for Brett to help his new mate find a second-hand car.

*

Joe got off the plane stiff and sore. His legs ached. Later, he'd realise they were sore from trying not to lean away from Brett. He'd smiled and nodded. Laughed and charmed. And the whole while his body, repulsed by this man, was tense as he tried not to flee.

*

He dialled Brett's number at noon the following day. Was he still right to help him look at cars? Brett said he was.

They walked the lot and Brett critiqued the vehicles. On the way home, Joe got his first glimpse at Brett Cowan's over-inflated image of himself. He'd been driving in the area at night, Brett began, when he accidentally clipped a man on a postie bike. He knocked him off the bike and Brett quickly pulled over to see if the man was OK. But the man had said something that Brett hadn't liked. Brett got angry. He went back to his car and found some kind of weapon and chased the man with it. The man made a frantic dash for the bike and tried to ride away. But with Brett in hot pursuit, he dropped the bike and ran off on foot.

'I smashed his bike and set it on fire,' Brett bragged. It was a colourful tale. Maybe it was true, maybe it wasn't. They'd learn quickly that Brett liked to lie.

Joe dropped him off at the park and they agreed to meet again on Monday for another day of car shopping.

*

Brett texted his new friend at 10 a.m. Monday.

'How's things m8? What are you up to today? If you want to go for a tour around let me know I'm free today no work.'

'Hey m8,' Joe replied, 'just at bank sorting cash i'll giv u a call in about an hour. Trip round would b gr8.'

Joe was at the park at 1 p.m. Brett had met him out the front in the past but this time Joe went straight to his van. Brett answered the door sans pants. He was smoking marijuana and asked Joe if he wanted some. Joe resisted the urge to turn and flee. It seemed Brett wanted to be more than just friends.

They bought a 1996 Ford Fairmont for $2650. Brett drove it to the airport so Joe could drop off his hire car. Later, they returned to the caravan park where Brett hooked him up with a new CD player for the Fairmont. He was getting a new and better one, Brett explained.

Joe thanked him. He'd be over on Wednesday with some beers. They'd only been apart an hour or so when Brett called. If Joe wanted to move in to the caravan park, Brett explained, he should bring the application information with him on Wednesday. A couple of hours later, Brett got in touch again. 'Not working tomorrow now either so if you want to do anything let me know cheers.'

'Cheers m8 i got a couple of places to check for work tho. Get bak to u if i get done with that early m8,' Joe replied.

Joe was busy. The Fairmont was with West Australian Police

getting some new equipment installed. Any word uttered in that car would be picked up by state-of-the-art recording equipment. Western Australia had handed over its best technology.

Brett waited all day to hear from Joe and finally sent him a message at 6.52 p.m. 'This is fucked no work again tomorrow will be free all day,' Brett wrote.

Joe waited half an hour before replying. 'Cheers m8 I'm gonna hav a sleep in and we'll catch up b4 lunch. Talk then m8.'

Joe was back at the caravan park at 11 a.m. Wednesday, finding Brett perched on the edge of the bed, pipe in hand, watching the television. A news bulletin was on and Brett paid little attention as the presenter talked about two girls who had died in a boating accident. Then a story about Daniel Morcombe came on. Brett turned around to stare at the TV.

'The largest investigation in Queensland history … twice as large as its nearest rival,' the television intoned.

'Sharron Phillips,' Brett said, wondering whether the young woman with a flat tyre who disappeared from the side of the road in the 1980s would be next on the list for investigation size.

They left the van to tour Perth, Joe stopping in at a bottle shop to buy a carton of Crown Lager as a thank you for the CD player. Joe left Brett at the caravan park just before 3 p.m. He missed a call from Brett soon after. There was a vacancy at the park, Brett said. Joe should apply for the empty van. Brett called him again the following day, a Thursday. He'd lost his job, he told Joe. His boss had gone out of business.

'I need to find work,' Brett said. 'I'm only paid up here for one more week.'

*

They hit a snag on Saturday. Detective Senior Constable John Carey got a call from Brisbane. The *Courier-Mail* had run pages of coverage on Brett and his involvement in the Daniel Morcombe inquest. He wasn't named. The paper could only refer to him as P7. But they'd run an artist's sketch of P7 — and it looked strikingly like Brett.

'P7, who now lives in Western Australia, came to police attention two weeks after Daniel vanished when they generated a list of known child sex offenders who had been in the area,' journalist Kristen Shorten wrote. It was added pressure on Brett and they weren't sure how he'd react. They got their answer an hour later.

'Hi m8 not feeling the best today been a bit sick will have to put off going to freeo [Fremantle] sorry man may be tomorrow if I'm feeling better i'll give you a call.'

'No worries m8,' Joe wrote back, 'hope u feel better in the morning. Let me know if I can grab anything for u.'

*

They tried him again on Sunday.

'Yeah m8,' Brett wrote, 'drop in sorry I missed your call feeling better today cheers.'

Brett had good news. He had a new job already. He'd picked up a spray-painting gig that paid \$28 an hour. The hours were good, too. They had an early knock-off time on Fridays.

'I can lend you some money if you need to get by until payday,' Joe said.

The newspapers were still running stories about P7. That day's *Sunday Times*, a West Australian newspaper, had included an article proclaiming the presence of a predator in their midst.

'Child sex offender lives here,' the headline on page 4 read.

A convicted child-sex offender, who is one of the main persons of interest in the disappearance and probable abduction and murder of a 13-year-old Queensland boy, is living in Western Australia. P7's extensive criminal history includes two convictions for child-sex offences. P7 said he had also been accused of a string of unproven sexual assaults on children, which begun when he was aged 10.

*

Joe and Brett went for a drive to check Brett's post office box. He offered to let Joe use it, seeing as he didn't have a permanent address just yet. It was good news for the undercover team. It gave Joe a reason to keep getting back in contact with him.

Brett got out of the car and went to unlock the post office box, returning with an envelope in his hand. It was paperwork from the West Australian government.

'I'm changing my name,' Brett told him.

'What to?' Joe asked.

'Shaddo N-unya Hunter.'

Shaddo had been the name of Brett's dog. The 'N-unya' was for 'nunya business'. Brett grinned at his ingenuity.

Joe dropped Brett home. They would catch up again soon.

*

Brett called again the next morning. Could Joe pick up some medication for him at a nearby chemist? He could leave the tablets at the caravan park's reception counter.

Sure, Joe told him. The police were now running errands for their number one suspect.

*

The conversations continued. The trips to the post office box continued. Joe gave Brett lifts if he needed to go somewhere. He made calls when Brett couldn't afford to top up the credit on his mobile phone.

Brett was enjoying his new job. But by Tuesday, it was gone.

The boss had apparently lost a contract. It was last on, first to go, he'd told Brett with a sigh. Without work and with a drug habit to support, Brett was struggling.

'Do you need a loan?' Joe asked after Brett told him about losing the job.

Brett did. He asked whether $200 would be OK, warning his friend he might not be able to pay it back for some time. Joe said it was fine. He was going back to Brisbane for a week to spend Easter with his family but would see that Brett got the money before he left.

*

Joe dialled Brett's number on the Friday. It went straight to message bank when he tried it a second time. 'Hey m8 give me a call when you can,' he wrote that night. Nothing. He tried again the following day. No answer. At 4.30 p.m., he went to the caravan park to find him. Brett's car was gone and the van had been cleaned out.

On Sunday he tried calling from a different phone. An unfamiliar number. This time it rang. And rang out. Things weren't looking good.

Then, on Monday, Brett was back in touch. Joe's phone beeped with a text from their AWOL target.

'Hi mate sorry about the fuck around. I have had to move as you know and am still not working. I am staying with family down south. Atm I am not answering my phone sorry but when I have your money in a week or two I will be in touch once again sorry about the fuck around cheers.'

The money was causing problems. It was getting in the way. Brett was avoiding Joe because of it.

'All good, don't worry bout the cash,' Joe wrote back. 'call it a easter present for helpn set me up in Perth. I got some mail coming tho mate so could we catch up and check the po box. Text me back when a good time to call is.'

Joe got his mate on the phone the next day.

'I owe a couple of people money and I don't like owing money,' Brett said of his radio silence. He'd been staying with family on a property, doing farm work in exchange for cash. It was another lie. Brett wasn't with family at all.

*

Michelle Burns met Brett Cowan through an adult dating site. He had a liking for bigger women and role-playing and Michelle ticked both those boxes. They met at his place in October 2010. Brett was living in a caravan park, out past Perth's international airport.

The man who answered the door looked just like the photos from his online profile. Tall, skinny with a gaunt face. He was drinking Scotch and Coke and smoking marijuana. Michelle had been very specific about what she wanted out of the meeting. It was on her profile. She liked to play a submissive role in sex. She liked bondage and spanking. Brett, who once dragged one of his girlfriends from his car by the hair in a sexual role-play enjoyed by one, sat down to talk.

This is unusual, thought Michelle. Normally men she met online were all business.

Brett told her about his interests. He showed her his key collection and told her about his children. He told her he was working as a tree lopper and had moved to Perth from Queensland about six months earlier. He talked and talked. Michelle, quiet and shy, said very little. Eventually, they had sex and she left.

They began meeting fairly regularly. He always wanted to chat before they had sex. One day he confessed he'd done time in prison. He'd assaulted a 12-year-old boy in a fit of rage. He confessed he'd been on speed at the time. But that was a long time ago, he told her. About 18 years earlier.

He disappeared for about three weeks over Christmas. He told her he wouldn't be in touch. Christmas was a hard time, he said. Because of the kids. He told her not to come to the caravan park while he was gone. He said he was having problems with another resident and he didn't want her caught in the middle.

Brett called Michelle after Christmas. He'd moved to a new caravan park, explaining the one he'd been living in had shut down. Over the next few months, he began confiding in her more and more. The real reason he'd been in jail, he revealed, was because he'd been caught molesting young boys.

'I've done all the prison courses and I haven't done anything since,' he lied.

Michelle was too shy to ask him anything else. She searched the internet for information but couldn't find anything. Then one day he mentioned his name had been spelt wrong in media reports at the time. They'd written Cohen instead of Cowan, he laughed.

Michelle went back online and searched for 'Brett Cohen'. The search took her to the 'MAKO/Files' website — an online list of pedophiles collated from news reports. 'It's no secret that sex offenders especially pedophiles are likely to reoffend so public awareness is very important to prevention,' a banner on the site reads. There wasn't a lot of detail. But Brett was listed as having attacked two young boys — one in Brisbane and the other in Darwin.

The revelations continued. Brett told Michelle he was a suspect in a 'big case' in Queensland.

'I had nothing to do with it,' he told her. He was being forced to appear at an inquest but he didn't want to go.

'If you have nothing to hide, you should go,' Michelle said.

Brett begrudgingly agreed. He was trying everything he could to avoid appearing before the Queensland coroner. When he realised he couldn't get out of it, Brett began making arrangements. He asked Michelle to pack away a few things to pass on to his children. He gave her his pet bird to look after. To Michelle, Brett seemed convinced he wasn't coming back.

But he did come back. And Michelle wasn't too happy to see him. She'd been following the inquest on the internet. The reports from journalists showed her the truth of Brett's assaults on those boys. It was a very different story to the one he'd told her. He got back, filled with talk of the new friend he'd met on the plane.

'I can no longer be your friend,' she told him. The things she'd read about him were too much.

'The media made it sound worse than it was,' he told her.

'I'm not coming back to see you,' Michelle said. She stayed away for the next couple of weeks.

Brett had been back a matter of days when Perth's *Sunday Times* newspaper discovered his address and a journalist came calling. He'd ranted about it to Detective Senior Constable Grant Linwood on the phone. Brett had been clearly rattled. He needed to get out of the caravan park. People would find out about his past and he'd be run out of town.

'Child offender tracked,' had been the headline.

A convicted child-sex offender, one of the main persons of interest in the disappearance and suspected murder of 13-year-old Daniel Morcombe, lives in a caravan in Perth's eastern suburbs in an area frequented by children.

But police won't say whether they knew he had been living in Perth or whether they were monitoring him.

Brett asked Michelle whether he could move his belongings to her house. He'd stay until he got his car back on the road. She agreed. Things were desperate. Brett had no job. No car. Nowhere to live. He couldn't afford to pay for credit on his phone. He couldn't afford anything.

*

Munster is a beachside suburb of Perth, south of Fremantle, and home to a wastewater treatment plant and cement works. In 2004, a man named Brett David McDonald lived there in a rented property with his girlfriend and her daughter. McDonald suffered paranoid delusions. In 2004, much of his paranoia was aimed at a man named Steven Peterson — an itinerant worker McDonald's girlfriend had taken in for a while. McDonald was fine with Steven at first. But soon he was convinced that Steven had come into his life to kill him. He believed Steven was part of a bikie gang. McDonald told his girlfriend he wanted Steven out of the house. She obliged.

Some time later, McDonald and his girlfriend were driving in the area when they spotted Steven.

'I could kill him,' McDonald remarked.

'Why?' she said. 'What's he ever done to you?'

'I just don't like the guy.'

It was Steven's sister who reported him missing. It would be four years before they found him, dismembered and hidden in a quarry.

For years the case stagnated. McDonald had been a long-time suspect but investigators lacked the evidence to secure a conviction. They decided to use Mr Big. The covert team was briefed and scenarios prepared. McDonald was deemed a worthy candidate. He had no money and they believed he was the type of person who could be manipulated, who would be open to the opportunities that came with being absorbed into a criminal organisation.

In March 2009, McDonald confessed to undercover police officers.

'I fucking, um, basically fucking, fucking hurt him and hit him and hurt him and then fucking pulled him apart,' he told the covert officer.

'Pulled him apart?'

'Yeah.'

'What do you mean?'

'Fucking, into small pieces.'

'What, you chopped him up?'

'Yeah.'

'That's a smart move.'

The confession led to a conviction and in February 2011, McDonald was sentenced to life in prison.

The win was still fresh in the minds of the West Australian police's covert team when they were brought in to assist Queensland officers with Operation Vista. Joe's work befriending Brett had been first-rate but now the mission was stagnating. Brett had gone AWOL on his new mate. The West Australian covert officers suggested they try Mr Big. After all, it had worked on the Steven Peterson murder.

Victoria Police had used Mr Big more than any other state. They were viewed as the Australian authority on it. Within days, Assistant Commissioner Mike Condon and Chief Superintendent Gayle Hogan met with a Victoria Police psychologist at the team's West Australian safe house.

The psychologist was briefed on Daniel's disappearance. On Brett Cowan and his history. They played her the covert recordings they'd made during his outings with Joe. She found him suitable. Brett was a good candidate for Mr Big. It was time to step things up a notch.

CHAPTER TWENTY-FOUR
FITZY

BRETT WAS STANDING OUTSIDE High Wycombe's post office at 2 p.m. on 4 May 2011 — the time they'd agreed the day before. Joe had been begging to get access to the post office box they were sharing. He was expecting mail, he told Brett. Brett rolled in driving a $500 car — the best he could afford — telling Joe he was looking for farm work anywhere in Western Australia. There was nothing holding him in Perth any more, he said.

Joe had arrived with a friend. Paul 'Fitzy' Fitzsimmons introduced himself to Brett and then left. Fitzy was going in the opposite direction, Joe explained. Could Brett give Joe a lift?

They chatted away as Brett drove Joe to Malaga. Brett still wasn't getting disability benefits for his emphysema. He had no income at all.

'I'll ask my boss if he's got any work available,' Joe said.

Brett was grateful. 'I'll do any sort of work,' he said. 'I've got my own ABN.'

The work would be easy, Joe said. Easy money. Just an hour or two. He'd find out.

'Let me know,' Brett said.

Joe would need to text, though. Brett had no credit on his mobile phone. He could text but he couldn't call. Joe got out in front of the Good Guys store, thanking Brett for the lift. He handed him $50 to cover fuel and waved him off.

A covert surveillance team had been following at a safe distance. They arrived moments later to collect Joe. Brett was desperate. They were in a good position.

*

Brett was in luck. On 5 May, Joe sent him a text message saying his boss had come through. They had two hours' work available the following day. The pay was $150. Joe could pick him up and drive him to the job.

Brett wasn't about to turn down money — easy or otherwise. He agreed. Joe picked Brett up the following day at his local shopping centre and drove them to the airport. There was a man, Joe explained mysteriously, who would get off a flight from Melbourne some time between 2.40 p.m. and 3.55 p.m. All they had to do was make sure he got off the plane. When they spotted him, they had to make a call. That was all. Easy money. Joe gave him a photograph of the man and they split up.

'Text me if you see him,' Joe said.

Brett kept his eyes peeled. Eventually Joe came to tell him they were done. They walked back to the car and Joe got behind the wheel to take Brett home. He handed him $150 and promised to call him if more work came up.

'Any time,' Brett replied, clutching his cash.

*

Joe called again on Monday. Did Brett want some more work? Another job had come up. Brett did. Joe told him to be at the shopping centre again. He'd pick him up at 10.40 a.m. the following day.

They went to Jimmy Dean's diner, a 1950s Hollywood-themed restaurant where you can buy a serve of Memphis fries or American Ribs, and parked out the back. Joe and Brett stayed in the car. They were waiting for a man named Dean, Joe explained. Dean owed money to the boss. When he handed it over, Brett would need to count it. Detective Senior Constable Carey had carefully written the scenario the night before. When Dean arrived, Joe was to tell Brett to stay in the car while he got out to chat. He was to position himself next to the passenger-side door so Brett wouldn't be able to get out and join him. Everything was scripted to avoid unpredictable situations. The words 'trust', 'loyalty' and 'honesty' needed to be worked into the conversation constantly. They needed to brainwash Brett with them. He needed to hear them all the time. He needed to understand what they meant to the group.

Dean arrived and approached Joe standing by the car. The amount was $6000, Joe told him. But there was a problem. Dean, a gambling addict, only had $4000. He pleaded with Joe. He only needed another two weeks to come up with the rest. Joe handed the cash through the window to Brett, who carefully counted it out.

'The boss isn't going to be happy,' Joe told Dean. He let Dean go and got back behind the wheel.

'You think you can trust a guy,' he told Brett. He drove them back to Brett's car and handed him $150.

'How was that?' he asked Brett.

'Good,' Brett replied. 'I don't mind a bit of loan-sharking work.' He told Joe it was probably handy having him there in the car. 'I don't look very nice,' he bragged. Maybe, he told Joe, they should have told this Dean that the loan had gone up by $1000. Failure to pay on time.

'There might be some more work coming up if you're interested,' Joe said.

'I'm very interested,' Brett replied.

*

Joe collected his new offsider from the Midland Freedom Furniture car park at 3.30 p.m. on 16 May. They had another job. Joe drove Brett to the Midland Gate Shopping Centre and found a park outside Coles. They were meeting Fitzy here, he explained.

Fitzy, a short man with a blond ponytail and a surfer's drawl, was driving a black Commodore. He pulled in next to them. Joe introduced them again. They'd met at the post office that time.

Brett would be going with Fitzy to do a job while Joe did a cash pick-up. They were going to Fremantle, Fitzy explained.

Brett switched cars and they headed off. Fitzy was someone new to talk to and Brett committed himself to the task. He told Fitzy he was born in Perth but raised in Brisbane. He'd recently been diagnosed with emphysema. He was trying to get on the disability pension.

'I still have years left in me,' he said. 'I'm happy to do work like this.'

'It's easy work,' Fitzy said. 'Most people give us the money straight up.'

They were off to meet a woman named Cassie. Cassie looked after all their working girls. They'd be picking up their cut of the earnings to hand over to the boss, Fitzy explained.

It was a 45-minute drive from Midland to Fremantle. Brett talked the entire way, a series of mundane and idiotic topics. It was the hormones in chicken giving young girls big breasts, he told Fitzy. Brett knew a woman who only ate organic chicken.

'Flat chested,' he said.

He talked about his kids. He had three. He'd started late — though not for lack of trying. 'Every girlfriend I get, I get them off the pill straightaway,' he said. Brett had wanted a kid ever since he'd been in school. He talked about prostitutes.

'I don't mind paying for it,' he said. He'd pay $30 to $50 for 20 minutes with a girl. 'That's all it takes me,' he said. He preferred Asian girls for their petite build. He liked to 'bang them hard'. 'They don't like it when you really hurt them,' he sighed.

He talked about outlaw motorcycle gangs in Perth. He'd heard they were out of control. They even had access to explosives, he told Fitzy knowingly.

'We stay away from all that,' Fitzy said. 'We run a real business. If you want the attention, become a movie star.'

Finally, they pulled in to the harbour at Fremantle, parking the car outside a restaurant.

'Can you introduce me as "Shaddo"?' Brett asked Fitzy. He explained he'd legally changed his name. 'I'm sick of Brett,' he said.

They found Cassie and she and Fitzy talked business for a while.

'I might get Shaddo to do the money handover in future,' Fitzy told her.

Cassie handed $5000 to the men and they were on their way. They meet Joe at the Burswood Casino, Fitzy handing Brett another $150 for a job well done.

'You'll be needing a collared shirt,' he told Brett, in case they needed to go inside the casino for a job in the future.

'I'll get another pair of shoes, too,' Brett said.

They waved Fitzy off and Brett got back into Joe's car. Joe would be dropping him home. Brett was full of stories of his day.

'Thanks for the work and the introduction to Paul,' he said. 'I'll have to buy you a bottle of Scotch when I get on my feet.'

*

Things were tense behind the scenes. The Queensland team felt they'd received a frosty reception from some of the West Australian officers. There was some tension over which state should be running the operation.

The West Australian police had also declined to undertake the usual task of covert operatives, transcribing each day's recordings. Instead, it was being outsourced to a private company. Having an outsider transcribe — someone unfamiliar with place names and the context of various conversations — was leading to mistakes. There was also the worry that details of a highly secretive undercover operation were being put into the hands of strangers.

Detective Senior Constable John Carey was responsible for writing each day's scenarios but West Australian officers were lending a hand. They seemed keen to phase Joe out. Without him, there'd be no Queensland covert operatives working with Brett.

Maybe none of the Queensland team needed to be there at all.

They came up with a scenario whereby Joe's car — set up with state-of-the-art surveillance equipment — would be set alight. They could tell Brett it had been used in a robbery and now they needed to get rid of it. In the end, the scenario didn't go ahead. But Joe's friendship with Brett would be short-lived.

*

Fitzy collected Brett from the Burswood Casino at 3.30 p.m. on 20 May. They'd be picking up Joe from a nearby bar. He chatted to Brett on the way, telling him about the job, what they were about. He shouldn't discuss his work with anyone, Fitzy warned Brett. It was important they kept a low profile. It was how they did business. They needed to trust the people who worked for them. They needed to trust Brett to do the right thing. Everyone had to be loyal to the business, or it wouldn't work. Trust. Loyalty. Honesty. You look after us and we will look after you.

They arrived at Innaloo and Joe got into the back seat. Fitzy gave them the briefing. They were off to see a prostitute named Brooke. She was doing work on the side. It was against the rules. There was no reason for her to be doing that, he explained. Their girls were well looked after. Brooke had even been given a car by the group.

'We never touch our chicks,' Fitzy told Brett. They were only there to earn them money. It was business.

They were looking for Brooke's car now. They thought she might be in the Sorrento area and they needed to find her to see if she was working. They found the car, a white Nissan Murano, parked near the Sorrento Beach Resort. A moment later, they found Brooke too. She walked up to the Nissan, opened one of the back doors, closed it and walked away again.

'Follow her,' Fitzy told Joe and Brett. 'Find out which room she's in.'

They set off, returning a moment later to tell Fitzy the room number. They held tight, waiting to see whether she had a man with her. Brooke left a short time later, getting into the Nissan and driving to a nearby hotel.

'Follow her,' Fitzy told Brett, giving him orders to observe her, nothing else. He handed Brett $20 to buy a drink while he kept an eye on Brooke.

Brett watched as Brooke scoped the room, moving in on a man. They chatted for a while before the man followed her out. Brett was loving it. He was on a high. He pulled out his phone and dialled Joe to give him the update. Brooke drove her customer back to the resort and pulled in to the car park. Fitzy decided they would wait for the man to leave.

'You should take the car off her,' Brett said excitedly.

When Brooke's customer was done, the three of them went to the room to confront her.

'What are you doing?' Fitzy asked the woman. He told her to hand over the keys to the Nissan and took the cash she had on her — $3650.

'You owe us $20 000,' he told her. 'Pack your things. You're leaving.'

Fitzy sent her off on foot, giving Joe the keys to the Nissan. He and Brett got back into Fitzy's Commodore. That's how the job was done.

Brett, the standover man, was in heaven.

*

Fitzy collected Brett from the local shops on 24 May for the next job. They were off to pick up some crayfish, he explained.

'If there are any jobs that you don't want to do, just tell me,' Fitzy said.

'I am open to anything,' Brett assured him.

Brett chatted away, the usual mix of nonsensical and dirty

topics of conversation. He'd been to the Gold Coast's schoolies event one year, he said. He'd been a 'toolie' — the slang term given to older people who came to hang around with drunken schoolkids celebrating the end of Year 12.

'I hit a bloke for hitting a sheila,' he said. 'If you are going to hit your missus, do it behind closed doors.' Brett thought about what he'd said, then added: 'I don't understand how blokes can hit on their missus.'

He talked about his online dating profiles. He'd check them every now and then but lately the girls all seemed to live too far away. Brett was still seeing Michelle, but was living between her place and a caravan park. He was going to be the park's caretaker, he said.

'Are there good chicks out there or what?' Fitzy asked.

'Most of the chicks who will fuck you are just nymphos and love cock,' Brett told him.

They arrived at the Ocean Reef Boat Harbour in Joondalup, north of the city. Fitzy took Brett to meet Carlos, who opened up a van to show them eskies packed with crayfish. Fitzy made sure Brett could see the cash as it was handed over then asked him to transfer the loot into the boot of their car.

'We're dropping it off to an Asian bloke who owns a restaurant,' Fitzy explained. They got back in the car and hit the road again.

'If we call mums MILF, "mothers I like to fuck",' Brett mused, 'do they call us FILTH, "fathers I like to have ..."? ... Mothers are having C-sections now so they can save their boxes,' he continued. He told Fitzy C-section babies were not as tough as natural-born children.

Fitzy nodded along with endless patience. They were approaching Northbridge — Perth's nightclub precinct — when Fitzy took out his phone and dialled the restaurant owner, Eddie. They organised a meeting point.

'Bring fried rice,' Fitzy told him.

They pulled up in a car park a short time later. The covert officer was of Asian descent and carried two containers of fried rice. 'It's the best!' he proclaimed with an exaggerated Asian accent. The surveillance crew listening in could barely contain themselves. Eddie didn't have an accent at all.

Brett began unpacking the car as Fitzy took the cash from the restaurateur. Later, Fitzy told Brett he was doing well.

'We're a tight group,' he said. 'We don't often let people in.'

Brett was paid the usual $150 for the day's work.

'Call me any time,' Brett said.

'I like your style,' Fitzy replied with a grin.

*

Tuesday, 31 May: They met at the shopping centre again, Fitzy explaining they were doing another cash pick-up. They were going to see Dean, the gambler who'd been short $2000.

'You'll meet my boss,' Fitzy told him. 'I've told him you're doing a good job and that you're not a cockhead.' He told Brett the group had a well-defined hierarchy. If you were good, you could work your way up the ranks.

'Joe rang me last night,' Brett said.

'What did he have to say?' Fitzy asked.

There was a letter waiting for Joe in the post office box. Joe wasn't in Perth at the moment but when he returned, they would meet and Brett would hand his mail over.

They met Dean in a car park. He handed Fitzy a wad of cash and an apology. Fitzy handed the cash to Brett to count. He'd been standing silently by. Brett Cowan, standover man. The money added up. Fitzy and Brett left to meet the boss.

*

Jeff ran the West Australian arm of the crime gang. A higher position in the group earned you both money and respect. It was important, Fitzy explained, that they treated the boss with the respect he had earned. The group had a carefully crafted hierarchy. Everyone was answerable. They were a professional outfit. They trusted one another. Trust. Honesty. Loyalty. They met Jeff in a waterfront café.

'I've heard good things about you,' he told Brett.

'You'll have no hassles from me,' Brett answered. 'As long as you need me.'

Jeff laughed. 'As long as you hang out with Paul, you'll go places,' he said. He reminded Brett he had to want to do the work. They wouldn't make him do anything he didn't want to do.

'There's only one thing,' Brett said. He wouldn't be involved in any violence.

Jeff nodded. They had another job. They needed to pick up some passports. Jeff gave Fitzy the details.

'Take the young fella with you,' he said, nodding towards Brett. The covert team was using carefully crafted language to make sure Brett knew his place. He needed to know he was on the bottom rung. They were making sure that when the time came, he would do as he was told.

*

'He likes you,' Fitzy told Brett as they left the café. 'If he didn't, he wouldn't even give you the time of day.' It was a good life, Fitzy told him. It was a chance to step up in life.

'You hear about things like this,' Brett said, 'but you never expect it to arise in your court.'

'I started where you are,' he told Brett. Now, he worked for Jeff and Brett worked for him. If he worked hard, gained their trust, he would move up the ladder too, Fitzy told Brett.

'Keeping your mouth shut is the biggest thing,' Fitzy said. 'When you're driving, stick to the speed limit.'

He told Brett about their next job. They were going to see

someone from the Department of Immigration. Henry — an immigration official — was waiting for them in Northbridge. They met in an alleyway. Brett stood lookout nearby while Fitzy swapped $5000 for a couple of passports.

With the job done, they headed back to find Jeff.

*

The boss was waiting for them at the Old Swan Brewery. Fitzy handed him the passports and told him the job had gone well. The passports were blank. They'd be used to get a couple of their people out of trouble, Brett was told. They always looked after their own.

'Call me and we'll talk,' Jeff told Fitzy. 'I'll take you out to dinner.'

They left the brewery.

'What did Joey have to say?' Fitzy asked again.

'Not much,' Brett answered. He explained again that Joe had called about a letter that might be waiting at Brett's post office box. Joe thought he might have been done by a speed camera. He'd been going at 50 kilometres an hour through a school zone. Fitzy told Brett he could take the letter off him and pass it on to Joe.

'It's in the car,' Brett said.

'I'll grab the letter and pay it,' Fitzy said. Fitzy taking care of the letter meant Joe needn't have contact with the target. Joe was being written out of the operation.

Brett was dropped back at the shopping centre, where he dug through his car and found Joe's letter. He handed it over. Fitzy gave him $200 for the day's work.

They needed to talk about Brett's appearance, Fitzy told him. They needed him to start wearing better clothes. Wear good clothes, he said, and the coppers won't look twice at you.

Brett was moving up in the world.

CHAPTER TWENTY-FIVE
TRUST, HONESTY, LOYALTY

WEDNESDAY, 1 JUNE 2011: Fitzy collected Brett from the same shopping centre at 11 a.m. They were doing some surveillance work, he explained. There was a bank manager who helped them out getting credit cards. He was handy to have around. But there was a problem. He was using one of their girls. It was against the rules. Their working girls were off limits. They were money earners, nothing more. Fitzy would give Brett a camera. They needed photographs of the two of them together.

They drove to Scarborough and stopped at a café. Fitzy got out the camera and showed Brett how to use it. They found the couple in question and Brett snapped away. Fitzy checked the quality of the images. Not great. He took more until Fitzy was satisfied they had what they needed. He seemed excited.

'I'm a photo freak!' he claimed.

*

'You've taken some good photos,' Fitzy told him. 'The boss will be happy.'

They were on their way to South Perth, where Jeff was waiting for them. Brett chatted away as they drove. He had no respect for armed robbers, he announced. They brought too much attention on themselves. A police officer had been shot in Queensland during an armed robbery. On the Gold Coast. Armed robberies were rife there, he said.

'If you do the crime, you should do the time if you're caught,' Brett said. 'Why fight it? Why make it harder on yourself in court and shit?'

'Have you been in?' Fitzy asked.

'I have done time,' Brett admitted. He'd been in jail for disqualified driving, he told Fitzy. It was his third offence and there'd been marijuana in the car, too.

'Also for a bit of violence up north in the Northern Territory,' he said. He was dealing large quantities of cannabis, he told Fitzy. His supplier had bought himself a new gun and demanded Brett pay all the money he owed. Brett went around to see the man who owed him money. That man had told Brett to 'fuck off' and that he'd never get it.

'He laughed at me — three times,' Brett said. So he went to his car and returned with a baseball bat. He smashed the man across the knee cap.

'Give me the money or I'll hammer ya,' he told the man. He told Fitzy he admired the man. He would have been in pain but he laughed and smiled at him anyway. So Brett busted his other knee.

'I got seven years and did four years,' Brett said.

Fitzy had to play along with Brett's ludicrous story.

'Fuck off,' he said. 'For that?'

Brett told him he'd done the time 'happily'.

'We don't care if ya have done shit — as long as you are honest with us, that's all we can ask,' Fitzy said. Clearly all the talk of trust and honesty was yet to sink in.

Brett told him he was not keen to kneecap anyone else. He'd already been in prison for one act of violence.

It won't be necessary, Fitzy said. 'We look after you,' he said. 'We are not fucking amateurs.'

*

They met Jeff in a car park. Fitzy showed him the photographs.

'Who took these?' he asked.

'Shaddo did.'

Jeff was impressed. There was more work. Jeff needed them

to go to the Canning Vale Markets to pick up $10000 from a fruit seller named Con.

'Con the Fruiterer,' Brett laughed. The covert team had laughed at their joke too.

Con only had $5000 for them. He was having problems with his truck. It needed a new gearbox. There were problems with his neighbour, too. Fitzy told Brett later the real problem was Con's gambling.

'We will work something out,' he told the fruiterer. Jeff would need to be told.

*

They drove to South Perth for some lunch, hanging out on the foreshore to watch the girls go by. Brett, as always, was midway through a marathon of mundane topics. Backpackers. Fish and chips. The price of seafood. Girls with 'small blemishes' on their faces.

'Are you enjoying the work?' Fitzy asked him.

'Jeff asked me the same thing,' Brett said. He was enjoying it very much, he told Fitzy. 'Just don't ring me if you want me to touch someone up. It's the only thing I'd say no to.' Brett took out an old-fashioned cigarette case and showed it to Fitzy. Fitzy took it from Brett's hands and looked it over, opening it up to see inside.

There was a piece of paper taped to the inside. Two names and numbers were written down.

'Is that your missus?' Fitzy asked. One of the names was Emma.

'They are just friends,' Brett told him. The other name, Grant Linwood, was 'Linwood Holdings'. Grant's dad owned a construction company back east, Brett said.

'Don't know it,' Fitzy said, although he knew the names well enough. Lies came easily to Brett.

*

They met Jeff in the car park of the Burswood Casino. He'd had the photographs of the bank manager and the prostitute printed. He handed them to Fitzy with instructions on what to do next.

'Show them to him,' Jeff said, 'and then tell him he owes us $20 000.'

Fitzy and Brett got back in the car to head to the meeting point. Brett asked Fitzy whether the prostitute would be OK. Wouldn't the bank manager think she'd set him up?

'He won't do anything to her,' Fitzy said. That's not how they worked. There'd be trouble from the group if he did. They waited for him outside the Perth Concert Hall. Fitzy showed him the photographs while Brett stood nearby as 'protection'.

'I saw a tear in his eye!' Brett said later. He was loving his role as standover man.

'If he wants to root a girl then he can,' Fitzy said. 'But not the company girls.' They were done for the day. Fitzy took Brett back to his car at the shopping centre.

'You did a good job today,' he said.

'I need to impress you,' Brett said. 'But I need to impress [Jeff] even more.'

Fitzy took out $200 and handed it to Brett. He was doing well, he said again. They were impressed with how he was conducting himself. He was a good bloke. A normal bloke.

'It is good to be called a normal bloke again,' Brett laughed.

*

Monday, 6 June 2011, 10.14 a.m.: 'Mate … got a job on … I know it's a long weekend but if ya free b good mate … let me know mate.'

They met Kristen at the brothel. She handed them their cut — $4000 cash. Brett counted it and agreed it was all there. He was an old hand by now. They met Jeff at Cottesloe Beach to hand over the cash.

'Enjoying yourself?' the boss asked Brett.

'Loving it,' he said. Soon, he told them, he would be able to afford a new car. He had his eye on one for $500.

Stick with us, Fitzy said, and you'll be able to get yourself a real nice car. They looked after their own. The group had even got Fitzy out of trouble when he'd needed it.

'I'm always available,' Brett told them.

*

At 11 p.m. that evening, Fitzy pulled in to Michelle's Bullsbrook driveway. She lived in a small farmhouse with a white picket fence. Brett had told Michelle he was working as a 'pimp driver', picking up girls and clients and driving them around. His temporary arrangement with Michelle had gradually become permanent. He hadn't left. He supposed he was living there now.

They headed off with Fitzy at the wheel. They were doing a burglary, Fitzy explained. If it was OK with Brett, they needed him as a lookout. Brett was fine with that. He had plenty of experience breaking and entering.

'Is Joe back?' Brett asked.

Fitzy said he hadn't heard. It didn't matter, at any rate. Brett worked for Fitzy now. If he worked hard and proved his loyalty, he'd move up the chain. They pulled up outside the Como Hotel to meet another member of the group. Jason was one of their drivers. He'd be helping them with the burglary. Fitzy drove them to the Burswood Casino where Jeff emerged to meet them in the car park.

He gave them the run-down. They had a Customs agent on their books, he said. He'd slipped them the key to one of the warehouses. They had the alarm code, too. It would be active for just one night. Inside, they'd find a haul of cigarettes.

They discussed an escape plan and what Brett should do in case of any police activity.

'You up to it?' Fitzy asked. Brett was. They dropped him off at the lookout position just as a police patrol car drove by. Brett casually sauntered off. Fitzy waited a moment before calling Brett. The coast was clear. A slight diversion from a carefully crafted scenario. Fitzy and Jason went inside while Brett stood watch. Soon, the job was done. They left with the loot. Later, Fitzy drove Brett back home.

Standing outside a warehouse for a few minutes had earned him $150. Brett was doing a really good job, he said. They appreciated that he was always available, that he always answered his phone when they called. He was a good worker.

And if he had trouble topping up his phone credit, Fitzy said, let them know. They'd look after him.

'You're one of us now,' he said.

Brett had never been one of anything. 'Drive easy,' he told his friend. 'Watch out for roos.'

*

Tuesday, 14 June 2011: 'This job's a bit more serious,' Fitzy said when Brett got in the car. They were off to do a pick-up for Jeff. They were collecting guns.

'I don't have a problem with guns,' Brett said.

They drove to a car park where a man slipped into the back seat. He was their gun dealer. They talked briefly before the man slipped out again, leaving behind a green bag containing three pistols.

'I'm more of a revolver man than a semiauto,' Brett said.

They drove again to the Burswood Casino where Jeff was staying and took the guns up to his room.

'Are you all right with moving the weapons?' he asked.

'I have been around bang bangs all my life,' Brett said. His dad was in the army.

*

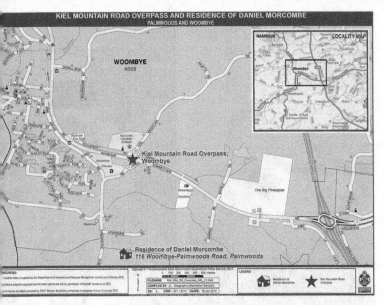

KIEL MOUNTAIN ROAD OVERPASS AND RESIDENCE OF DANIEL MORCOMBE
PALMWOODS AND WOOMBYE

WOOMBYE
4559

Kiel Mountain Road Overpass,
Woombye

Residence of Daniel Morcombe
116 Woombye-Palmwoods Road, Palmwoods

police map of the Morcombe home and the Kiel Mountain Road overpass
ere Daniel was last seen alive.

ove left: Brett Peter Cowan, photographed
police in the weeks following Daniel's
sappearance.

ove right: Brett with his wife and child.

ght: One of the many comfit images
tnesses helped police to create.

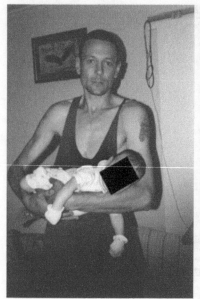
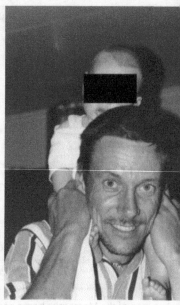

Above: Family photographs of Brett, shown to the court during his trial.

The mulcher in the back of Brett's 4WD.

Detective Senior Constable Grant Linwood leaves the inquest with Brett. Linwood would wave him off at the airport, leaving him to board a plane with the first covert officer to befriend him.
Courtesy Channel Ten

above: A still frame from secretly recorded vision of Brett's conversation with 'Big Boss' Arnold.

right: Brett seems relaxed after his confession to Arnold.

below left: Fitzy (left) with Ian, on the day he was filmed going over what Brett had shown them.

below right: Fitzy (right), Ian (centre) and a Queensland detective stand by the bridge where Brett told them he'd thrown Daniel's clothes into the creek.

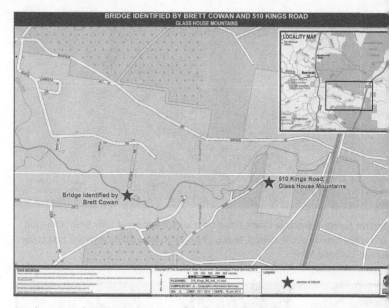

A police map showing the location of the bridge where Brett threw Daniel's clothes in relation to the macadamia farm where he left the teenager's body.

The macadamia farm where Daniel's remains were eventually found.

rs can just be
en on the dirt
ck near the body
water. It's here
at Brett Cowan
ok Daniel's body.

arch teams
ruggled through
ick bushland
the search for
aniel's remains.

lice used
adder to
mb down the
nbankment
here Brett left
aniel's body.

The demountable house where Daniel was murdered

Daniel's Globe shoe, still half buried under dirt and pine needles.

Daniel's Globe shoe, found the macadamia farm during the search for his remains.

Police diver Senior Constable Chae Rowland points to the place where he discovered what remained of Daniel's underpants.

Lawyers Michael Bosscher
and Tim Meehan leave the
committal hearing.
Courtesy Bosscher Lawyers

415 GEORG

Assistant Commissioner Mike Condon speaks to the press after the guilty
verdict, flanked by members of the investigation team.
News Ltd / Newspix

Solicitor Tim Meehan (left) and barrister Angus Edwards (right) and at the trial.
Justice Atkinson said they'd handled themselves with 'courage and perseverance'.
News Ltd / Newspix

Some of those who worked on the investigation receiving an award following
Brett's conviction. Back row L to R: Supt Maurice Carless, D/Sgt Ross Hutton,
D/Sgt Grant Linwood, Commissioner Ian Stewart, D/Sgt John Carey, D/Sen Sgt
Stephen Blanchfield, Insp Arthur van Panhuis. Front row: D/Supt Brian Wilkins,
AC Gayle Hogan, AC Mike Condon, AC Alistair Dawson. Many had received
promotions since Daniel's disappearance.

They met Dougie in the car park of a roadhouse. The outlaw motorcycle gang member drove up on a Harley and greeted Fitzy. Fitzy introduced him to Brett. Brett started talking, telling Dougie the terms of the deal before Fitzy had a chance to open his mouth.

'I prefer the older pistols because they're made of steel,' Brett, the connoisseur, said.

'Keep an eye out for coppers,' Fitzy told him.

'I've been around shooters my whole life,' Brett continued.

They completed the transaction as Brett gave the bikie advice on where to find a cheap prostitute. The place Brett had been visiting was cheap and they gave you a 'blowie' to start, he told Dougie.

Dougie laughed along before driving away with his new guns.

*

'Is it all right that I spoke to him?' Brett asked.

Fitzy said it was fine. Brett was showing he could 'step up'. Working for the group made for a good life, Fitzy said. They were treated well. It was the first time in his life he'd been treated well, he confided to Brett.

'It makes you want to be more loyal . . . put more effort in,' Brett said. He was getting the message.

'These blokes are like my brothers,' Fitzy said.

'Is Joe back yet?' Brett asked again.

'There is some shit happening that you don't need to worry about — we are just looking after him.'

He dropped Brett home, handing him $200 for his efforts.

CHAPTER TWENTY-SIX
EXIT JOE

BRETT WAS WEARING HIS best outfit when Fitzy met him at the car park on 16 June. He'd even showered for the occasion.

'Jeff is taking us to a good restaurant for lunch,' Fitzy had explained on the phone.

'McDonald's?' Brett had asked with a laugh. He'd been on a shopping spree the day before. He'd sold his old Ford for $700 and treated himself to a pair of Kmart shoes for $50.

'Jeff must be happy if he's taking us out for lunch,' Fitzy observed. They met Eddie in Chinatown, collecting $10 000 from the restaurateur.

'Shaddo boxer!' he exclaimed on seeing Brett. He punched the air for good measure.

They met Jeff at Coco's in South Perth. Fine dining with waterfront views. Crisp tablecloths set with wine glasses.

'This is the first restaurant I've been to since getting to Perth,' Brett said. They moved outside to a table with a view of the city.

Only one beer, Jeff told them. He needed them to work that afternoon.

'There is a lot more work coming up,' he said. They ordered lunch and sat back to enjoy the view.

'We're going to help Joe out,' Jeff said to Fitzy. 'He's a trusted and loyal worker.'

Joe had been written out of the covert operation. From now on, only West Australian operatives would have contact with Brett. They would tell Brett that Joe had got himself into trouble. He needed to go overseas, change his name.

It was an important lesson for Brett, though. They were

showing him how they looked after their own. Joe was loyal. They trusted him. They were sending him to London with $10 000 while they took care of whatever problem he'd run into. They were showing him there was nothing they couldn't fix. They could even make someone disappear. They could give him a new identity. A new life.

But they were also making sure Brett no longer had any contact with Joe, who'd befriended him so effectively. Jeff told Brett and Fitzy to delete Joe's number from their phones. He gave them both new sim cards for their phones, complete with $30 credit. Brett was told not to try to call Joe.

'If any mail comes for Joe, give it straight to Paul,' Jeff instructed. 'I'll call Joe soon and he'll come down and have a beer.'

The food arrived and Brett tucked in. He looked out over the water at the city skyline. At the spread in front of him. It was fine dining, better than he'd had in a long time.

'Why can't all the days be like this?' he said.

Jeff talked about work they had coming up. He was happy with how Brett had been performing and hoped he'd stick with it. He hadn't heard one bad word about him. They'd been working on something big and Jeff's boss, the big boss, was happy with their progress.

Joe arrived once they'd finished eating. He hadn't been invited to sit down with them for a meal. He ordered a beer and greeted the boys.

'We're going to sort that thing out,' Jeff reassured him. 'We'll look after ya.'

'I appreciate what you've done for me,' he said.

They handed him $10 000, making sure Brett caught sight of the cash. Jeff instructed Fitzy to take Brett and drop Joe at the airport.

But first, Brett was handed a wad of cash and told to pay the bill. They'd spent up, wanting to show Brett the lifestyle he was coming into. Fine restaurants. Nice cars. They wanted him to see the receipt, to see how much they spent on a casual lunch. He was impressed. Just shy of $300.

'It's not the sort of restaurant I would take a girl to unless I really wanted something from her,' Brett, the romantic, said when they were on their way to the airport. They talked about Joe's impending trip to London.

'R and R — rest and rooting,' he joked with Brett.

'How good is it how Jeff looks after us?' Fitzy said. The boss knew a lot of people.

'You do the right thing by the group,' Joe added, 'and you'll be looked after.'

They waved him off outside Qantas and headed back to Brett's car.

'Don't forget to text me when you've set up your new sim card,' Fitzy said, handing him $100.

That night, as he wrote his final report, Queensland's covert operative Joe Emery signed off with a short comment. He wanted to report West Australian police for bullying.

CHAPTER TWENTY-SEVEN
THE BROTHERHOOD

FITZY AND BRETT MET at the Bunnings car park in Joondalup at 3.40 p.m. on 21 June. Fitzy had reminded Brett to bring his old sim card. The boss wanted it, he'd explained. Brett handed it over and it went in the centre console of Fitzy's car. Brett told his mate he'd been staying up until the early hours of the morning trawling for women on a dating site. He'd got a hit — a 36-year-old woman who didn't mind having her husband hang around and watch.

'The body is tidy but the face has a few cracks in it,' Brett commented. He talked about his sex life with Michelle. It wasn't an exclusive relationship, he said.

'I'm a try-sexual,' Brett laughed. 'I am willing to try anything … within reason.'

They drove to Kings Park where Jeff was waiting for them. He handed over $30000 and told them to take it to the Perth District Court. There might be a country trip coming up, he told them. Not a problem, Brett said.

*

The group's influence was everywhere. They could do anything.

'Jeff has his finger in every pie,' Fitzy told him. The boss had court officials in his pocket. Corrupt police who'd do whatever he asked. They could find out anything about anyone.

'There's nothing Jeff can't fix,' Fitzy said.

They were at the District Court, the same building where Brett had gone to change his name. Even his mother called him Shaddo now, he said. He called her once a week. He never spoke to his brothers, though. They didn't get along.

'My younger brother could easily put a bullet in my head,' Brett said.

Fitzy handed the keys to Brett and told him to park the car while he took care of business. He'd arranged to meet the court official in the coffee shop. He sauntered away, $30000 in hand.

He met Brett back at the car. A woman walked by and Brett whistled.

'She needs more meat on her,' he said. He liked his women big.

Their next job was a cash pick-up at the brothel. It was easy work and Brett was enjoying the power it brought. He and Fitzy were a team. At the end of the day, Fitzy drove Brett back to his car. Brett spent the drive suggesting Fitzy join him in a threesome with a woman he'd met online. He told Fitzy she wasn't too pretty.

'You don't look at their face when you are doing them doggy,' he reassured his mate.

Fitzy told Brett he was probably going away for the weekend.

*

Tuesday, 28 June 2011: Fitzy and Jeff had discussed the possibility of Brett doing an away trip. Sometimes they had business to take care of in regional areas — or even interstate. Brett, of course, said he was up for anything.

They were going to Albany, a coastal centre five hours south of Perth. Albany is the oldest settled town in Western Australia, predating Perth and Fremantle. Stunning coastlines and historic buildings made it a popular tourist hub. In June 2011, the people of Albany unknowingly hosted Brett Cowan and an undercover police officer who called himself Paul 'Fitzy' Fitzsimmons for a night. The drive was long and filled with Brett's chatter.

'I have worked out I am a bit of a brainy cunt,' he told Fitzy at one point. 'I have a wealth of knowledge.' He talked about his mum and his dad. Brett often talked about his dad. His father had started off as an army 'grunt' and worked his way up, he explained proudly. He was the president of his local RSL and still heard from people he'd recruited. He'd known two of the soldiers killed in Afghanistan.

Brett moved on to the Catholic Church. There were priests, he lamented, who abused children in the church. And those children weren't even paid any compensation. The irony. He told Fitzy churches weren't short of money. People handed their money over to churches all the time.

'It's a business just like our business,' Fitzy said. 'Our bosses do not care what you have done before, as long as you are making money for them and are honest to them.' It was an oft-repeated message. They reminded Brett of it every single day, drumming it into his head.

'It helps if you got a little bit of form to do this,' Brett agreed. He told Fitzy he loved the work, the brotherhood. 'I always wanted to do something like this,' he said. 'You need to pinch yourself … am I dreaming?'

He talked about a scrap-metal yard he'd had dealings with in Queensland. He'd spoken about it before and Fitzy was always keen to hear more. Brett had described a 'mechanical arm' that collected old cars and moved them into a shredding machine. His job as a tow truck driver had taken him there often. It would be a good place to dispose of a body, he'd told Fitzy several times. Nobody would check the boot of the car, and blood would simply mix in with oil and other fluids. The high-powered shredding machine would cut through anything. There'd be nothing left.

Is that what he'd done with Daniel? The undercover team thought it was a possibility and were happy to keep him talking on the subject.

'I am surprised that people … they probably have tried to get rid of a body,' he said.

'You could do a trial run with a sheep or something,' Fitzy suggested.

'It's also a good way to get rid of a shooter,' Brett said. 'Getting it shredded instead of throwing it into the water.'

'You're an ideas man,' Fitzy told him.

'I'm a problem-solver,' Brett replied.

They drove on, the open road ahead of them. Crosses dotted the side of the road, some with flowers placed beside them by grieving friends and family. They were the places where people had died, where tired drivers had left the bitumen, ploughing into trees or wildlife or a passing road train. Brett had been to such crash sites while working as a tow truck driver. Sometimes bodies had still been inside the cars. He bragged of stealing things from the dead. Once, a driver had had a key ring with a $5000 casino chip hanging from it. Brett's light fingers had slipped it into his pocket.

Brett was never short on words and every one of them was being captured by recording devices set up in the car. Behind them, a covert surveillance team followed, listening to everything he said. Brett had belonged to a church back east, he told Fitzy. The church was on a bad intersection so the congregation liked to pray for those driving through. When crashes stopped occurring at the intersection, other bad things started to happen instead. People started going missing.

Fitzy was listening. 'Were they dead?' he asked.

'I am not saying dead,' Brett replied. 'But they disappeared from a main road.'

Brett's phone rang before they could go on. It was Michelle.

'Are you religious?' Fitzy asked him after a while.

'I'm a firm believer in the spirit world,' he said. He told Fitzy he'd almost become a Krishna. He loved the food they served at their temple.

*

They arrived in Albany, pulling in to the Albany Holiday Park where Fitzy booked them into separate cabins.

'We'll work tonight,' Fitzy said, handing Brett $50 to spend on dinner. He told Brett he needed to see a few people. He'd be in touch soon. The covert team met for a briefing. A reconnaissance of the area was done while Brett entertained himself with his $50.

'Mate … relax goin 2 b at least 1 hour,' Fitzy texted him.

'All good m8,' was the reply.

Brett was waiting out the front of the park for Fitzy at 9.30 p.m. They were off to see a woman named Ali. She worked for their bank manager in Perth. Ali met them in the McDonald's car park with a small stack of credit cards. Fitzy showed the cards to his offsider. Brett was impressed. They had more work to do that night. The next job was the real reason they'd come to Albany, Fitzy said.

The Albany wharf was in darkness when they pulled up. The port manager, a man named Simon, seemed nervous.

'There are coppers everywhere,' he told them. He didn't think it was a good idea to use their phones.

Fitzy told Brett there were two metal canisters in the boot of their car. He needed to get them out and put them in Simon's car. Fitzy took a stack of cash out of his pocket — $8000 — and handed it to the port manager.

'It's a relief to have those canisters out of the car,' he said once they'd left.

*

They hit the road back to Perth at 10 a.m., Brett settling in for five hours of mindless talk as rain battered the car.

'They want to change the name of fairy penguins,' Brett said, so 'the gays' weren't offended. He talked about not having seen his children for two years. His parents saw them, though, and had them every second weekend. His youngest didn't even remember him. He talked about liking larger women.

'If I want something on the bony side, that's what [the brothel] is for!' he laughed.

They drove past the Midland railway yard and Brett pointed it out to Fitzy.

'There is where my daddy started,' he said. He talked and talked. Fitzy, with endless patience, thanked him for the company, telling him it was nice to have someone along for the trip to Albany.

After hours on the road, Fitzy pulled in at Brett's girlfriend's house. He handed him $400 for a job well done. They talked about an interstate trip. Brett was more than happy to help out.

'I am up for it all,' he said.

*

Wednesday, 6 July 2011, 10.26 a.m.: 'Mate…pik u up 1130 at Bunnings …'

Brett slid into the passenger seat of Fitzy's car, talking a mile a minute. His new dog wouldn't stop barking. He was trying to track down an anti-bark collar. One of those ones that delivered an electric shock. He could probably put it on a woman too, he joked. Brett had been spitting in the kelpie's mouth, convinced it would help the dog recognise him as its owner.

Fitzy's phone rang and rang. They had two jobs on that day.

'We have been busy,' he said.

'That's good for us all,' Brett replied.

Fitzy took them to a café in Claremont where they were joined by Cassie, the group's brothel madam. They ordered coffee, a proper business meeting, and Fitzy gave Brett the money to take to the counter.

'We might be going away next week,' Fitzy told Cassie. He and Brett could be off on an interstate mission.

Western Australia was in the midst of a mining boom and the money was flowing through to everyone. Business was good for Cassie. When their coffees were drained, Cassie handed Fitzy $7000 cash and waved them goodbye. Just another cash pick-up. A chat with mates in a nice café. This was the life. Brett was getting used to seeing large amounts of cash waved around. He was still struggling though. He'd applied for a credit card and been declined.

'You have to wait three months before you can apply again,' he complained to Fitzy.

'In a few months' time you won't need to care about money,' Fitzy told him. He was right.

*

The next stop was the Perth Concert Hall. They were there to see the bank manager who they'd caught with one of their prostitutes. It was time for him to pay up. He handed Fitzy the $20000 he owed. Brett thought the whole situation was hilarious.

The boys were now carrying $27000. It was time to drop the loot off to Jeff. Fitzy arranged to meet him in a café and stuffed the notes into a Commonwealth Bank bag. He handed the bag to Brett to carry inside.

'This is the most money I've ever had in my hands,' Brett said.

Jeff was waiting for them, ready to discuss the interstate trip. They'd be going to Melbourne if Brett was up to it.

'He is more than ready,' Fitzy said.

Brett was excited. 'I've never been to Victoria before,' Brett told Jeff.

'It's a bit of a step up,' Jeff said. He took some time to explain to Brett how he should behave on the trip. He wasn't to tell anyone about where he was going or what he was doing. He shouldn't be talking about the group at all, he reminded him. They needed to trust each other. It was how they operated.

'I understand what you're saying,' Brett assured him. 'You won't have any problems with me.'

There was a lot of work coming up, Fitzy told Brett. Jeff had a boss to answer to as well — a man named Arnold — and everyone wanted things to run smoothly. All Jeff expected, and all Jeff's boss expected, was trust, honesty and loyalty.

'You need to be honest with Jeff and Arnold,' Fitzy said. 'They don't give a fuck about what you've done in the past.'

*

Sunday, 10 July 2011: Fitzy dropped off Brett to meet Jason, the group's driver, in Northbridge late at night. It was a last-minute call-up for Brett. The person supposed to be working that night had let them down.

'I'll never let you down,' Brett told Fitzy when he'd asked if he could step in.

Jason set Brett up as lookout across from a restaurant. He was to wait for an Asian man to come out. He had to warn Jason if the man was leaving. Jason took off to steal the man's car — a sports model Mercedes worth $100 000.

'I used to [steal] cars over east but nothing like this,' Brett said when he saw the car.

The covert team had hired the Mercedes earlier that day. They'd been stoked to get behind the wheel. The Asian man, of course, did not exist.

*

Tuesday, 12 July 2011: Brett arrived at Perth's domestic terminal with his mate Fitzy by his side, happy to be travelling to Melbourne for the first time. Michelle thought he was off to Brisbane to see his kids. She hadn't doubted his story. Brett's ticket said 'Shaddo Hunter'. It didn't feel awkward any more. His new name had 'gelled'. He talked about his dad as they waited for their flight. Peter Cowan was writing his memoirs, Brett said.

'He's only spoken about his experiences for the last nine years,' he told Fitzy. He talked about going to dawn services with his father, about wanting to see Canberra's war memorial because his dad had told him it was worthwhile. Brett was proud of his dad. So were his brothers. One day they'd get miniatures of Peter's medals.

'He's kicking back now,' Brett said of his father. Peter was enjoying retirement, spending his days fishing and crabbing. Brett was happy with what he'd achieved in his own life, he said. He'd done so many different jobs, learnt so many different skills. He was a 'jack-of-all-trades'. He liked working with wood, with steel.

'Or you can just do what we do,' Fitzy said.

'Yeah,' Brett said with a laugh. 'Kick back, drink coffee and eat at fancy restaurants.'

Jeff came to meet them as they waited to board. He had a bag with $40000 inside to give to Fitzy. He'd be joining them in Melbourne, he explained, but would be catching a different flight. He'd see them later, he said with a wave.

'I wonder if there are any slutties on the plane we can join the mile [high] club with?' Brett said.

*

A man named Ronnie met them at the other end. He was the group's Melbourne operative, equal in rank to Fitzy. Ronnie drove them to Melbourne's famous Lygon Street restaurant strip. They'd all be staying in different hotels. Better for business, they explained to Brett. It's all about keeping a low profile. Fitzy pointed out a kebab shop and a bottle shop next to Brett's hotel.

'What more do you want in life?' Fitzy asked him.

'A slut on the bed,' Brett laughed.

They checked him in to his hotel and left him to it, promising to meet him for dinner in an hour or so.

*

'There are no digital channels on my TV,' Brett complained when they arrived to collect him. The rain fell steadily as they drove up and down Lygon Street, looking for a park. They found an Italian restaurant with a free table and ordered a round of beers and some oysters Kilpatrick.

'Don't hold back on the food,' Fitzy told Brett.

Brett was having trouble understanding the menu. The only time he went to nice restaurants like the one they were in, he said, was when his parents took him.

Ronnie, the Melbourne lieutenant, told Brett he was impressed he'd been sent on an interstate trip. He must have earned a lot of trust to be catapulted up the ladder so quickly.

'I need to thank Joe for it all,' Brett said. 'I'll have to buy him a beer when I next see him — in 18 months' time.'

'Yeah,' said Fitzy. 'But you've also made your own luck.'

CHAPTER TWENTY-EIGHT
ARNOLD

COVERT OPERATIVES FROM THREE states met on the morning of 14 July as Brett Cowan ate breakfast alone at a Lygon Street hotel. It was an important day. Three West Australian operatives and five from Victoria would play their roles to convince Brett he was meeting the organisation's national head. The 'big boss'. The Mr Big.

The Victorians led the country on Mr Big operations. They'd been consulting with Queensland and West Australian operatives from the beginning.

Fitzy and Ronnie met Brett outside the kebab shop across the road from his hotel. They'd told him to keep his head down the night before but Brett had managed to scope the street for girls. He'd found five standing outside his hotel and wolf-whistled at them. One of them had told him he was rude.

'That's not rude. You wanna see rude? Come up to my room,' he'd said.

There'd been no takers, he lamented. His parents had called that morning. They'd phoned from the airport, about to board a flight to Malaysia.

'I'm the black sheep of the family,' he explained to Ronnie. He'd asked Peter and Marlene to bring him back a lighter and a key ring, even though he rarely, if ever, saw them. He collected such things.

They got to work. Ronnie was a man down and there was a lot happening that day. The Melbourne crew was tight, he explained to Brett. Their work was based on trust. They would have to trust Brett to do the right thing by them.

They pulled to a stop outside a well-known Melbourne brothel where one of the group's girls was waiting outside. The covert operative playing the role of a sex worker was stunning. She'd got out of a surveillance car moments before Fitzy and the crew pulled up, walking down the footpath as though she'd strolled from the brothel. She wore the tiniest skirt and leaned in the window of the car to talk to Ronnie.

'I'm a bit short,' she said, handing over $10000.

Ronnie wasn't happy with her excuses. He told her they wanted the rest of the cash the following day. They stopped around the corner to count it out. Ronnie made a call, advising his boss they were 'two short'.

They stopped at a second brothel soon after. Another prostitute with another wad of cash. They drove to the Footscray Markets, meeting a fruit seller named Kostya. He handed them his protection money in a box of fruit. They counted it in a nearby street — $20000.

They met Ronnie's boss at a café near the Melbourne Cricket Ground. He handed them a black case containing $40000 and instructions to take the lot to a gaming manager at Crown Casino named Robbo. Robbo was their man on the inside who'd help them clean the money. He was a handy contact. It was more money than Brett had ever seen. The $27 000 he'd carried not all that long ago seemed like small change now.

'We should put it on black,' he joked.

Ronnie told them Robbo had been wanting to join the group for some time.

'He's not in that position yet,' he said vaguely. 'Some people are cut out for it and some are not.' He turned to Brett. 'What we're doing is just the tip of the iceberg,' he said. 'You could be running your own blokes over here some day.'

'Cool,' Brett said.

Robbo met them out the front, telling them he'd be about 20 minutes. He returned with a casino cheque for $72000. Arnold — the big boss — was named as the recipient. They left Crown to head to the Hilton. Arnold was waiting for them.

'I'm getting a sore neck,' Brett said as they walked away, 'from looking at all the good-looking girls.' Brett liked Melbourne a lot.

*

Fitzy and Ronnie, the two lieutenants, walked with Brett into the Hilton's lounge bar. It was the first time Brett had ever walked through a revolving door. They ordered a round of beers. Brett refused. He was on his best behaviour. They sat at a table. Ronnie and Fitzy looked around the room, spotting Arnold and his bodyguard sitting across the hotel lounge. They were talking to a detective, his Victoria Police lanyard hanging from his neck. Another one on the books willing to dig out information for a price.

The bodyguard was huge and dressed for the part. He wore expensive chains and rings on his fingers. Straight out of *The Sopranos*. He crossed the room to Brett's table, shaking hands with the men as they sipped at their beers. Victor, Ronnie and Fitzy explained, was Arnold's Russian bodyguard.

'I know a Russian over east,' Brett announced.

He was particularly impressed with Russian mail-order brides, too, he told Victor. They were trained in various sexual acts before bedding their husbands. It was part of their culture, he advised knowledgeably. Victor nodded along and returned to his table.

'I'm still spinning out that Arnold is here,' Ronnie said.

'I haven't glanced or looked up there,' Brett replied.

A minute later, Victor was back. He took out a piece of paper and slid it across the table to Brett.

'Write down your name and date of birth,' he instructed.

Brett took a pen and wrote 'Shaddo N-unyah Hunter', his birthdate and his mobile number.

Victor looked at it. 'Write your other name,' he said.

He wrote 'Brett Peter Cowan'. 'I changed my name recently,' he explained.

'We need to be very careful,' Victor said and returned to Arnold's table.

Ronnie told Brett they were always cautious about who they accepted. Brett's name would be given to the detective seated at Arnold's table. The detective would be running a background check. Brett's days of being a knee-capping drug dealer would soon be over. Soon, his new friends would find out exactly who he was.

'Are there toilets around here?' Brett asked. 'I really need a piss.'

*

Victor returned to their table one more time. Arnold wanted to meet Brett. Brett followed the Russian across the room where the big boss gave him a hearty handshake.

'I've heard good things about you,' Arnold told him. 'It's only early days yet. I'm good to my people but I expect them to be good to me in return.'

Brett was chuffed. It was an opportunity to tell Arnold how much he'd been enjoying the work. He'd developed quite a passion for photography, ever since he and Fitzy had done the surveillance job on the bank manager and the prostitute. He told Arnold how he planned to buy his own camera equipment when he'd earned a bit more money.

Brett was filled with pride when he returned to the table where Fitzy and Ronnie were drinking their beers. He told them Arnold had heard about his 'good work', that they'd spoken about his photography.

'My pictures speak mountains,' he declared.

'The bosses don't give a fuck what we've done or where we are from,' Fitzy said. He'd started where Brett was, Fitzy said. He remembered when $100 was a lot of money. Now it was a meal at a restaurant.

'You wouldn't be in Melbourne if I didn't think you were right for the job,' Fitzy told him.

'Thank you,' Brett said. 'I love hearing my name in praise.'

They talked about the job all the way back to Brett's hotel. Ronnie was more than happy with Brett's work. It was great working with someone with a bit of maturity, he told Brett. He was the sort of worker they'd be happy to have in Melbourne.

They were part of a brotherhood, Fitzy added. They had people who could do anything, find out anything, make trouble go away. There was nothing they wouldn't do for one of their own. The detective Gary who'd been with Arnold — he was part of it.

'There's nothing that can't be sorted out,' Ronnie said. Fitzy agreed.

'I remember sitting where you are,' Ronnie continued to Brett, 'thinking they wouldn't let me into the group because of the shit I've done.'

They stopped at a red light. The steps of Melbourne's Parliament House rose beside them.

'Arnold will probably be in there tonight,' Fitzy laughed.

Ronnie agreed. 'He knows everyone.'

'I'm on the bottom rung,' Brett said, 'and I've met the top rung.'

They pulled up outside his hotel where Fitzy handed Brett $50 for dinner.

He shook his head. There was still $100 in his wallet. They gave him the box of fruit from the markets that had earlier hidden thousands of dollars. He took it with a grin and waved them off from the footpath of Lygon Street. Life was good. Brett had landed on his feet.

*

Brett took himself out for pizza that night. He'd ordered it takeaway, walking back along Lygon Street with the box in his hands.

'That smells nice,' a girl commented as he walked by.

Brett wasn't one to waste an opportunity. He invited the girl and her friend back to his room. They giggled and walked away.

'Something smells fishy — your box,' he called after her.

He recounted the story as Ronnie drove him and Fitzy to their next job the following morning. The patience of the covert operatives was endless. They had a job to do. A very important job. They laughed along at Brett Cowan's wit.

*

They arrived at the Royal Hotel for a prearranged meeting with a man named Tom. Ronnie's boss — the head of the Victorian syndicate — was there waiting for them. This was the reason they'd come all this way: they were smuggling blood diamonds back to Perth.

Tom came in and greeted the team. He was carrying the diamonds in a bag. They were worth somewhere between $900000 and $1 million, he told them. They'd already been sold. The men discussed the profit the deal would bring to the group — upwards of half a million dollars.

They'd needed Brett to come to Melbourne because smuggling the diamonds back to Perth was a 'two-man job', Fitzy explained. They needed two for safety. He asked Brett whether he was happy doing the work.

'More than happy,' Brett said.

*

Fitzy stood outside Melbourne Airport's Qantas terminal while Brett smoked a cigarette. It had been a 'cruisy' trip for Brett, he explained. He was new this time, so they hadn't been able to take him along on all the jobs. But Brett was thinking about that piece of paper, and the name he'd written on it. The name he'd tried to put behind him.

'I hope they have enough ink in their printer when they print out my record,' he said. He laughed at his joke.

'You don't need to worry about it,' Fitzy said. 'They just need to make sure.'

'I'm not,' he replied. 'It's two and a half pages.'

'Don't worry about it.'

'No I'm not. I'm not worried about it. There's been nothing in 20 years.'

Nobody cared what he'd done, Fitzy said. And if there was a problem, they certainly had the people to sort it out. Arnold knew people, he reminded Brett.

Brett took his seat on the Qantas flight back to Perth next to a 14-year-old girl and her mother. He spotted a USB port alongside the TV.

'Should have brought porn,' he said to Fitzy. He settled for comedy sitcoms instead, watching them between chatting mindlessly with Fitzy as the plane took them home.

Jason the driver was there to collect them at the other end. Fitzy flashed him a look at the diamonds, making sure Brett got a look as well. They dropped him home. Brett had earned $500 for the trip away. He'd met the boss, he'd seen the inside of the Hilton and had walked through a revolving door for the first time. It had been a good trip.

*

Thursday, 21 July 2011, 10.58 a.m.: 'Hey mate … u good 2 work 2day … let me know …'

They met at the usual shopping centre car park, Brett filled with stories about what he'd done with his $500. He'd spent $110 on a bottle of Scotch with an alcohol content of 60 per cent — the highest he'd been able to find. He'd taken a mate out to dinner and bought them two buckets of mussels.

'I need to get in the habit of saving,' Brett said.

It was an average working day for an above-average organised crime outfit. They met Cassie, their brothel madam, at a café on the South Perth foreshore where she handed them $9000 in takings. After that, they headed off to meet Jeff to hand the cash over. Brett was excited to see the West Australian boss. He told Jeff he wanted to buy a camera so he could do more surveillance jobs. Jeff thought this was a good idea. They talked about tracking down some brochures so they could look at buying both a still camera and a video camera.

But first, he said, there was a big job in the works. They might need Brett's help on it, if he was keen. They were busy. Lots of work meant lots of money to be made. Brett was more than keen. Jeff walked them back to their car and handed Fitzy $3000. They were off to see Craig, the Perth police officer on their books. The $3000 was for him.

The bundle held $3050. Fitzy handed it to Brett to count. The covert team had slipped the extra note in to see if Brett would say anything.

He counted it out. 'It's all there,' he said.

Fitzy took the cash and counted it again. There was an extra $50, he said.

'I thought there was one too many notes but I wasn't sure,' Brett said.

Fitzy handed the $50 back to Jeff. They gave Brett the talk again. Trust, honesty, loyalty. It's what they were all about. They helped out their own. They fixed problems. Brett was a slow learner.

*

He hadn't meant to get the money wrong, he told Fitzy on their way to meet Craig. He'd known they weren't under, at least.

'Don't worry about the money,' Fitzy told him.

Brett coming along to meet their crooked cop meant they trusted him. They wouldn't let just anyone deal with Craig. Brett was 'coming into the brotherhood', Fitzy said.

'I like to aim big,' Brett bragged. 'I'll get Jeff calling me sir one day.'

'I don't know about that,' Fitzy said.

'That will probably never happen,' Brett agreed. He was keen to buy a new car once he'd made more money though. Brett was thinking a panel van. He'd put a sling in the back for the girls, he told Fitzy. A dungeon on wheels.

'Shaddo's sex caravan,' he laughed.

They pulled in to meet Craig. The men shook hands and Fitzy gave him the cash.

*

Brett was becoming more and more enamoured with his new life. He had money. He had friends. And he had the prospect of even more money as time went on.

'I have found my calling,' he told Fitzy. 'I have found the job that I have been waiting for, for all these years. I always wondered how the other side lived and now I can find out for myself.'

They arrived back at Brett's car and Fitzy handed him $200 for the day's work. He told Brett they couldn't be happier with him, with the way he conducted himself.

It was the way he was brought up, Brett explained. His dad had always taught him 'little boys should be seen and not heard'. It was a respect thing.

*

Friday, 22 July 2011, 4.41 p.m.: 'Mate ... u good 2 work 2night?'

'I had fun last night,' Brett announced when he slid into Fitzy's car. He'd been in contact with a couple through an adult dating website and met them at a hotel. The girl had been skinny — not his usual taste — but he'd had a wild threesome. The girl had given him $50 afterwards and he'd spent the night at the casino on the blackjack table. Brett chatted as Fitzy drove them to the job.

Fitzy called the contact on the way. A man named Barry. Fitzy used the word 'mess' as he spoke and Brett announced in delight that he knew where they were going. They were heading to the army barracks. Fitzy agreed they were. They met Barry, an SAS soldier, in a car park.

'I couldn't get them all,' Barry said, and showed them eight pistols.

'Are you cool with that?' Fitzy asked Brett as they drove away with a carload of 'stolen' guns.

'Fucking oath,' Brett said.

'Don't tell ya dad,' Fitzy laughed.

'I stole a box of hand grenades when I was a kid,' Brett said. Maybe he had. Probably he hadn't.

They met Dougie, the bikie, at another car park. Brett was happy to have someone else to brag to about the previous evening's threesome. Fitzy handed over the guns and they went on their way. He dropped Brett back at his car, handing him $200.

'I like gun jobs,' Brett said. 'It's something about steel.'

*

Tuesday, 26 July 2011, 2.10 p.m.: 'Mate ... meet me at casino bout 3 p.m., got wk 4 u if u want it ...'

Jeff was waiting for them at a café inside the casino. They ordered coffees and sat down to discuss business like regular businessmen. Jeff needed Brett to conduct surveillance for them. It was the very thing he'd been asking for. His dream job. Jeff handed Brett a hand-drawn map of an airfield. It was about 50 minutes' drive from Perth, Jeff explained.

Arnold was concerned about security. He wanted to know how many planes landed, how many took off. Who came and went. Brett was to start the job that day, taking a photograph with his mobile phone to show he was in position. He should return the next day and the day after, always going at different times.

'There's a big job coming in,' he told Brett. 'I'm hearing good things about you but you need to be looked at first.' There was potential for Brett to get a cut of the big job — likely more money than he'd earned before.

*

Fitzy and Brett left Jeff behind, Fitzy handing his offsider $100 for fuel to get out to the airfield. He made sure Brett was happy to do the job. Brett was. He'd been dreaming about the money he would soon make, all going well.

'I have been dreaming about a new car. Literally, I have been dreaming about it,' he said.

'There are a couple of steps to do yet,' Fitzy said. 'We got to get the OK from Arnold.'

Brett knew they'd soon be discovering the truth of his past. The lies that he'd told.

'It was 20 years in the past ...' he said.

'If anything pops up, you just tell them the truth,' Fitzy said. 'It's not hard.'

*

Brett called from the airfield. It was 5 p.m. and he was in place. He'd decided to tell anyone who asked that he was a plane watcher. He'd used the excuse on an elderly man who was there watching the aircraft take off and land. The man had been excited to find another plane enthusiast. He'd invited Brett over to a row of sheds to talk to his fellow club members about planes, should he wish.

'I saw a kit plane land,' Brett told Fitzy. The elderly man had told Brett there was no security during the day and a single guard at night.

Fitzy praised him for his good work.

*

Wednesday, 27 July 2011: Brett was becoming an accidental plane enthusiast. He'd spent the afternoon spying on the airfield while talking to another enthusiast. He'd told the man he was staying in the area and was thinking of bringing his kids down to see the planes. He'd asked about joy flights and spoken to a man who'd spent 28 years building his own plane.

There was a 'club day' the following Sunday, he was told. Bring the kids down then.

*

Thursday, 28 July 2011: 'The old bloke from the first day pulled up,' Brett told Fitzy after spending two hours at the airfield. It had been a windy day. There'd been little activity on the runway but Brett and the old bloke had spent the time discussing different kinds of planes.

Brett had told the man he was interested in taking his kids on a joy flight.

*

Friday, 29 July 2011, 11.34 a.m.: 'Mate ... meet ya at casino carpark at 1230 ... bring the map bro ...'

'This will be a big job for Arnold,' Fitzy told him when they met in the car park. They'd do a small run first. If that went well, they'd be doing the big run. Brett's surveillance would be invaluable to their plans.

Brett had been researching cameras, he told Fitzy. He'd been searching the internet and looking at brochures. He pulled one out and handed it to his mate. He'd circled several options — one was $1499 and the other $1799. He'd also like a pocket camera, he told Fitzy. For the more covert jobs. Fitzy took the brochure, promising to take a look at it. He took out $500 — Brett's pay for the three days he'd put in at the airfield. Brett's enthusiasm was boundless.

'I wake up in the morning wondering if Paul will call today,' he told Fitzy. '[I think] c'mon Paul, ring me!'

Their group was a brotherhood, Fitzy explained. Brett was a brother. He shook his hand to seal the sentiment.

'It is the first time I feel part of a family in a job,' Brett said.

CHAPTER TWENTY-NINE
BIG JOBS, ECSTASY AND JETSKIS

TUESDAY, 2 AUGUST 2011: Brett opened the passenger-side door of Fitzy's car and jumped in, chatting away as they drove to meet Jeff. He'd decided he wanted his new car to be a 4WD. Something he could take fishing. A LandCruiser in black, or maybe dark blue. They looked schmick, he said.

They met the boss at a café in the city, discussing business over a brew. The big job was coming up, Jeff said. It was worth 'over a mill'. Those who worked on the job would get a cut of 10 per cent.

Simon, their port manager who'd taken the canisters from them some time back, would be driving a 'sample' from Albany to Perth for them. Jeff gave Fitzy $5000 and told him to take it to Armadale and hand it to Simon as payment.

They hit the road. Fitzy needed to make sure Brett understood the payday that was coming. Ten per cent of $1 million, he said. That was $100 000 for anyone working that job.

'Not a bad payday,' he told Brett.

'That's a third of this property I've been looking at,' Brett said.

'Once Arnold gives you the OK, it will all be cool,' Fitzy said. 'When ya in the brotherhood,' he continued, 'it's not just all about work. We party on as well.'

Fitzy was thinking of going on a surfing trip to Indonesia when their payday came round, he told Brett. Travel hadn't been much of an option for Brett. Until now.

'I'd love to go away,' he said, 'but that would have to be something someone fixed.' The possibilities were opening up in front of him. It was a life he never thought he'd have. Money, mates, holidays. A brotherhood. A family. His own brothers hated him.

His new ones had only praise for him. He'd dreamed of going to Africa or South America. He'd never believed he'd actually get there — not with his two and a half pages of criminal record.

'I am 100 per cent there for you, Paul,' he told Fitzy. He chatted away about what he'd do when he had money. He'd buy land for Michelle. He'd send her mother on a cruise. He'd get his pilot's licence. Imagine how useful he'd be to the group if he could fly a light plane, landing on small airstrips around the country.

'I'm always checking my phone to see if you've called,' he told Fitzy.

*

They met Simon in the car park of a hotel in Armadale. They were there to collect the 'sample' — 5000 ecstasy tablets in a metal canister. Brett took the canister from Simon's car and placed it in their own while Fitzy handed over the cash. The drugs were worth between $50000 and $70000, Fitzy explained. They had a plane that would bring their big shipment in. The one that was worth more than a million dollars.

Brett was hooked on the idea of becoming a pilot. He told Fitzy it should cost about $10000 to get his licence. He could fly to Alice Springs. To Uluru. Maybe he'd fly a helicopter, too.

'If you can pat your head and rub your stomach, you can fly a helicopter,' he said knowingly. He'd be safe from the cops, too. Cops can't pull you over in the air.

*

They returned to the café where Jeff was waiting. Jeff thanked Brett for his work and turned to more important matters. They were looking at booking the penthouse, he told Fitzy. It was time to let their hair down. The parties were for group members only. And Brett was close to being one of them. So close.

Fitzy drove Brett back to his car with the canister of 5000 ecstasy tablets rolling around in the boot.

'I'd cop it on the chin,' Brett said, 'if police stopped us now.' He'd put his hand up immediately. Tell the cops the drugs were his. It wouldn't worry him. He knew Jeff would be able to sort it out. The bosses could fix anything.

'It means a lot to me that you'd do that,' Fitzy said. 'We do not hang people out to dry.'

'I'd do a little bit of time for you,' Brett told his mate. 'I'd go to the police, "Solicitor, please — fuck off".'

Fitzy grinned. Brett was hooked.

*

Thursday, 4 August 2011, 4.36 p.m.: 'Mate ... meet u at the normal meetn place in bout 45 ...'

Fitzy turned on the recording device and went through the usuals.

'OK,' he said. 'Five, four, three, two, one. I'm a sworn member of the West Australian Police, currently conducting duties at the undercover police unit. My covert operative number is 452 and I'll be using the assumed name of Paul. I'm currently working on Operation Vista in relation to the Daniel Morcombe homicide. Today's date is Thursday the 4th of August, 2011. That's Thursday, the 4th of August, 2011.' He was in the car, waiting for Brett. A moment later, the door opened. Brett was all smiles and freshly shaven.

'G'day, brother, how you going?' Fitzy said.

'Not bad, yourself?' Brett replied.

'Hey, fucken hell! Hello, you look like a different bloke, mate! What's going on?'

Michelle hadn't liked his new, clean look. 'Where's my dirty old man?' she'd complained.

Brett got in the car and Fitzy handed him a carton of cigarettes.

His favourite brand. The boys had done a job, he explained. Fitzy had picked up some of the loot for him. Jeff had said it was OK to give some to Brett. Fitzy steered the car onto the road and they headed off. They were meeting Craig again.

'That's Rottnest out there, mate,' Fitzy told Brett as they cruised by sand and surf. The surf was small, and stand-up paddle boarders were making the most of the clean conditions.

'They're scared of getting wet,' Brett said. 'I don't see how you could have fun standing there, cause it'd ... surely you'd be pulling the muscles in your back the wrong way doing that.'

They spotted Craig's unmarked vehicle in the Cottesloe Beach car park. Fitzy pulled up alongside to find Craig sitting in the back seat.

'Hey, mate, how are ya?' Fitzy greeted the cop. 'You remember Shaddo, yeah?'

Craig nodded. 'Yes, yes. Mate,' he said, 'I've gotta give this stuff to Jeff. It's all ... she's got a fair bit of history.' He handed Fitzy a package of documents. Dirt for the boss on a female target. And another thing, Craig said, the silver Hyundai being used by the gang had to go. Police had their eye on it.

'It's fairly hot,' he warned. 'There'll be some sort of shit maybe even happening tomorrow. Just don't let it be where it is tomorrow.' The conversation seemed to be wrapping up. And then: 'Ah, and the one other thing which is ... might ahh, raise your hackles, there's a ... subpoena from Queensland for Brett ... do you know about that?'

It was a surprise for Brett, as they'd known it would be.

'For coroner's court,' Craig continued.

'That's been and gone,' Brett said.

'No, it's ... this is fresh.'

'Fresh, is it?'

'Yeah.'

'Oh, I didn't know about that.'

'But that's something we can fix as well,' Craig said.

Fitzy didn't say a lot. They would have to let Jeff know, he said. Craig was relaxed, confident it could be sorted out.

Could it be fixed up? This thing, this enormity that had been hanging over Brett's head for so long, reduced to some casual remarks. No hassle. No hassle. Gotta make sure everyone's looked after. How would Fitzy react to the truth of Brett's background? What would Jeff say? He hadn't been honest with them. They waved Craig off and got back in the car.

'What's that about, mate?' Fitzy asked.

'I was living in the area that that Daniel Morcombe went missing from,' Brett told him. 'And that's how I fucking met Joe — on the plane back from being subpoenaed over there for coroner's court in Queensland. And, um, I know I had nothing to do with it, I'm, my alibi is 100 per cent, you know?'

Fitzy nodded.

There was more. Brett had convictions for two sex offences. He'd molested young boys. But it had been 20 years and he hadn't touched a kid since.

'There's nothing we can't get fixed,' Fitzy said. 'But the thing what they want, I know the bosses make sure ... nothing can come back on us, cause, you know we work as a good group, man. There's shit that's been fixed. There's nothing they can't fix. So don't stress about shit, man, it's just ... you gotta be honest, man, you gotta be 100 per cent honest to us, you know. You can't fucking lie to us.'

Their subpoena probably wouldn't work anyway, Brett mused. He wasn't Brett Cowan any more. He'd changed his name to Shaddo Hunter. Their paperwork would be wrong. Fitzy didn't know about that. But he was keen to push the honesty line one more time.

'Oh, man, as I said, I don't give a fuck what you've done or fucking anything, man. As long as you do the right thing by us and you're honest to us all the time, man,' he said. 'And I, I've fucking talked you up. You're not even rude, mate, you don't even swear, dude, you know? We're in this as a business, mate. I mean, we're mates, you know?'

Brett agreed. They were mates. He'd never felt so much a part of something as he did with Fitzy and the guys.

'If I'd known that there was going to be another subpoena, I would've said something to you or Jeff,' he said.

'Don't fucking stress, dude,' Fitzy told him. He took out his phone and dialled Jeff's number. They'd see him in an hour. In the meantime, they had business to attend to. A cash pick-up at the brothel. Easy work.

'Don't even fucking think about it, dude, I can see you thinking,' Fitzy said as he steered the car through Perth traffic.

'I am thinking about it,' Brett said, 'but I'm not letting it get to me. It'd be the only thing that stuffs me up with youse. This'd be the only thing that stops me from coming in, coming in with youse would be that.' He'd done the sex offenders program in prison. They'd told him not to hide it from people. He'd hidden the fact that he was bisexual for a while. But then he'd 'come out of the closet'. He wasn't gay though, he told Fitzy.

'I don't care if you are gay,' Fitzy said.

'That's why I offended against kids,' Brett said. He hadn't had the 'guts' to go and see a man.

They would fix everything, Fitzy assured him. They were a team. A brotherhood. They'd do anything for each other.

'This is the first family I've ever had, mate,' Fitzy told him. 'That's why it fucking means so much to me. Because they've always fucking looked after me … that's why I do everything they want me to do and they, they fucking call me in the middle of the night, if I gotta do it, I do it, you know. They're my family, mate, you know what I'm saying?'

Brett knew. He felt exactly the same way. He'd never belonged anywhere before. But he belonged with them. He felt it.

*

'Hello, boys,' Jeff greeted them. They were later than planned. Traffic had been a nightmare. The West Australian boss took a better look at Brett and grinned.

'Look at you all trimmed up!' he exclaimed. 'You look about five years younger mate.'

'He looks like a different dude, eh?' Fitzy agreed. They chatted away, Fitzy giving his boss the run-down on Craig's warnings about the 'hot' car they needed to get rid of.

Then: 'The only other thing is, umm, what Craig said — I've told Shaddo not to fucking worry, but —'

Brett cut him off. 'Brett's come up with a flag in Queensland,' Brett said, talking about himself in the third person. 'A subpoena for coroner's court. It's about the Daniel Morcombe disappearance,' he continued. 'The boy that disappeared, you know? I was living in the area where Daniel Morcombe disappeared. So, I'm one of their suspects. I was told that it was all sorted and dealt with back then, so that's why I haven't mentioned anything about it to you.'

Fitzy told Jeff that Craig would come by to talk to him about it over the weekend. The police officer had been confident he'd be able to sort it out, Fitzy said.

'Well,' Jeff said, 'I appreciate you being honest with us. As I've always said from the start, Shaddo ... the best way to work is honesty, OK? I'm not about judging people. We've all got a task to do. Don't feel like you can't tell us these things because at the end of the day, [there's] probably nothing I haven't heard before or whatever. You know what I mean? Don't stress about that. I'll speak to Craig and find out exactly what it's about and what's going on, all right?'

They talked for a bit longer. Brett explained again that he'd thought it was all over. That's why he hadn't said anything. Jeff seemed to accept the explanation.

'Are you happy to keep working?' he asked Brett.

'Yes, mate.'

'All right, and if a spot comes up on a big job, are you happy to …?'

'Yep.'

'All right. Let me speak to Craig and find out the guts of it all. Let me get the, the whole story from him … and then I'll talk to you later. But don't stress, OK?'

'Yep.'

'At the end of the day you've been honest with me and I appreciate that.'

Trust. Honesty. Loyalty. They wove those words into the conversation 100 times a day. They'd seeped into Brett's brain. It was all about trust. It was all about loyalty. You just have to be honest with us. Be honest with us and we'll be loyal to you. We can sort this. We can make it go away. By the time their carefully constructed subpoena scenario played out, Brett was already brainwashed.

*

On 5 August 2011, Brett Cowan dropped in to a car dealership and took a Toyota FJ Cruiser for a test drive. It handled a little differently to the $200 Hyundai he currently drove. The Toyota was worth around $50 000. He told the dealer he was waiting on an inheritance. There was a Monaro he wanted to look at, too. Soon he'd be able to walk into a showroom, point at a car and hand over the cash.

He told Fitzy about his day when he called him that afternoon. He hadn't heard from his mate that day and was happy to hear Fitzy was with Jason, their driver, and another car enthusiast. Jason got on the phone and said g'day too. Then Fitzy was back. Brett asked if he could work the following day, a Saturday. He was available the whole weekend in fact.

'Everything cool?' Fitzy asked him.

'Everything is cool,' Brett replied.

*

Monday, 8 August 2011: Brett had seen Craig on the television news over the weekend. He'd thought it was hilarious. It was a news item about a murder and there he was! The very same cop they had on their books. He and Fitzy were driving to a cash pick-up, Brett chatting away as Fitzy drove.

'I was thinking about what happened the other day,' Brett began. He'd decided he could walk away from his life, if need be. Cut ties with his family. Cut ties with his children. Disappear and start again with a new identity. Brett Cowan would be dead. If that's what it took to stay with the group, then that's what he'd do.

'I am loving this,' he said. 'I am happy. I haven't been happy like this before. It's not just the money, it's what I am getting from yas — the mateship.' He interrupted this sentimental line of thought to wolf-whistle at a girl in the car beside them.

'I was a bit pissed off,' Fitzy told him. Brett should have been honest about his past. It didn't look good for Brett to have lied. 'We don't want shit like that popping up,' he said.

'I'm not proud of my past,' Brett said. He'd made a decision in jail to never offend again. 'I do not want to be behind bars for the rest of my life,' he said.

'We all have a past,' Fitzy told him.

'It's hard to tell someone you have molested children,' Brett said. 'You know it all now.' Then he figured that perhaps his past could be a selling point to the group. 'With those sorts of convictions under my belt,' he said, 'you know I am well and good to do virtually anything.'

*

They met Cassie for the cash pick-up at Fremantle's famed Little Creatures Brewery. The madam gave Brett an affectionate hug when she saw him. They sat down to lunch and chatted away like old friends, Brett telling Cassie about the car he'd taken for a test drive. He was thinking about buying a boat, too. He bragged about his French polishing skills, explained to her how to do it. He talked about his approaching birthday. He'd be turning 42 in just a few weeks. Fitzy paid for the meal and he and Brett headed back to the car.

'She's a nice chick but if she wants her sewing machine French polished, I won't go out of my way to do it,' Brett said.

Fitzy steered him back to the topic of work. There was another country job coming up. Jeff needed them to go to Kalgoorlie, a mining town out east.

'Only if you want to come,' Fitzy said.

Brett was keen.

'Don't worry about that shit the other day,' Fitzy told him.

They pulled in at a Toyota dealership on the way home so Brett could take another look at the FJ Cruiser. A salesman approached and handed them a brochure. There was a Great Wall dealership next door and they wandered over to peruse the cars there. The talk on the way home was of cars and boats and a new place to live. Brett talked about renting a unit, away from his old friends and life, after the big job was done.

His new life would be all about the brotherhood, his brothers in the group, Fitzy told him.

The only other business where you rely on your 'brothers', Brett said, was in the army. His dad had had to rely on his brothers in Vietnam.

'This is the stuff only dreams are made of,' Brett said.

*

They spotted a jetski store on their way home. Toys for the boys. This was Brett's life now. They chatted to the sales staff about makes and models, Brett commenting how 'cheap' they were. Brett, who drove a $200 car. When they were done window-shopping, Fitzy dropped Brett back at his car and handed him $100. He'd pick Brett up at 9 a.m., Fitzy said. They were going to Kalgoorlie.

Brett told him he was sorry. He'd lied about his past and he was sorry for it. There was nothing else he hadn't come clean about though.

'Nothing I know of,' he joked.

*

Fitzy collected Brett from Michelle's house just after 10 a.m. on 9 August. It was an overnight trip. Another cash pick-up. It would be hours of Brett's mindless chatter. Brett talking about Brett. Sex. Murder. His father. His brothers who hated him. His many trades, his many skills. Complaints about his ex-wife, his ex-girlfriends. Hours of Fitzy's immeasurable patience.

Brett got onto the topic of James Bulger. The little boy was just two when he became one of the world's most famous murder victims. In 1993, James was led away from an English shopping centre by two 10-year-olds who tortured and murdered him. Brett believed one of the killers was now living in Perth under a new identity.

'The Australian community,' Brett said, 'needs to know who he is.' He moved from one topic to the next. His parents didn't call him as much as they used to. His latest cover story for his job — driving a limousine. He'd spoken a lot in the past of his habit of collecting various items. Key rings. Hats. He'd once had over 2000 hats.

'I collect watches,' he said to Fitzy. 'I've got four fob watches over east.'

Fitzy's ears pricked up. Daniel Morcombe had been carrying a fob watch when he disappeared. It was an unusual item to have.

'What's that?' Fitzy asked.

'A fob watch is, you know, your old pocket watch,' Brett explained. Brett's were a couple of hundred years old but you could buy them brand new, he said. His mother had his stashed away somewhere.

'They're fucking wicked, those things,' Fitzy said. 'You see all fucking scientists and shit have them in their pockets.'

It was an hour before Fitzy's phone rang. It was Jeff. There'd been a change of plans. Arnold was in town. He'd be needing them to turn around. The big boss wanted to see Brett.

*

It might be about Brett getting a spot on the big job coming up, Fitzy mused.

'Is that all what Craig brought up the other day?' Brett asked. The inquest. The subpoena. The missing boy, murdered all those years ago.

'Yeah, I mean, [if] it's about that, man, just tell him the fucking truth, hey? That's all you can do. Could be about that, could be just about how to fucking make it all go away or whatever. Just gotta be honest with the dude, mate ... You know what Arnold's like, he's fucking awesome.' Fitzy looked at the open road ahead of him. The miles he'd travelled. The miles in front of him.

'Fuck, I wish they'd rung me about two hours ago,' he said. 'Fucking typical.'

CHAPTER THIRTY
THE TRAP

COVERT OPERATIVE NUMBER 483, Arnold, was in position in the Swan River Room of the hotel. Next door, in another room booked out by the investigative team, was a handful of detectives, monitoring every word on a screen. They had eyes and ears on Arnold and Brett. This was it. Months of carefully constructed scenarios. Of tension and arguments. State versus state for control of one of the biggest investigations in the country's history. Months of careful manipulation. They'd taken a man on the edge — jobless, homeless, without a penny to his name, without enough cash to buy credit for his mobile phone — and shown him another life. They'd shown him stacks of cash. Power. Cars and women. He could be anything he wanted to be. Brett the standover man. Brett the covert surveillance operative. Brett the photographer.

They'd given him dreams. Brett the pilot. Brett the homeowner. The landowner. The man who took his 4WD on fishing trips. Who towed his boat on interstate trips with mates. Who took his jetski out for a spin. Brett, the man who walked into a car dealership and paid $50 000 cash for a brand new car. They'd shown him a brotherhood. A new family where he was respected instead of detested. Where his mates stood by him with steadfast loyalty. Trust, honesty, loyalty. They trusted him and he trusted them.

Detective Superintendent Brian Wilkins, the head of Queensland's Homicide Squad, fixed his gaze on the television screen. So too did Detective Senior Constable Grant Linwood. They held a collective breath as Brett walked into the room. It was down to this. The last roll of the dice.

*

Brett folded himself onto the couch while Arnold gave him the score. Brett was a liability, Arnold said. He was a suspect in the Daniel Morcombe disappearance. He was their number one suspect. It was too much heat for the group. He was putting them in danger. Brett would have to front the inquest again. He might even find himself arrested, facing a charge of murder.

But there was a solution. They could buy him an alibi. They could buy police. Brett had seen that with his own eyes. They could make it go away. He was a good worker. They'd invested time and trust in him. They had the big job coming up.

They needed him to tell them what he'd done. They couldn't help him unless they knew everything. Every detail. Every risk. Every mess that needed cleaning up. If he didn't — they'd have to let him go. The mates, the money, the car, the jetski, the boat — it would all be gone. They'd cut him loose. He'd never hear from any of them again. He'd be back living in a caravan park, struggling to pay the bills. He'd have nobody. He'd be nothing.

'I'll be straight with you,' Arnold said, 'I'm here on other business but I got some information through early this morning which has kind of made me postpone that stuff.'

'OK,' Brett said.

'Is there something you need to tell me, or …?'

'Umm …'

'Bearing in mind that this whole … what we do is based on respect and honesty, right? I'll let you know that I don't care what you've done. I've got no qualms at all, you know? I've had a lot of real bad cunts on my books. What they do, what they get up to, doesn't faze me at all. All I'm looking for is loyalty, respect and honesty.'

'Yep, I understand that,' Brett told him.

'So, go on.'

Brett rattled off his criminal history. The fraud charges when he was young. Stealing. And the two child sex offences. He'd spent time in jail for those.

'There was other offences that I haven't been caught for ... which is something I haven't told other people,' Brett said.

'If you don't want to tell other people, that's fine,' Arnold said. 'It's just between you and I. As I said, I pay good money to a lot of people and I take a lot of risk in doing that [and] from the information I've got, I'm told you've done, you've done the Daniel Morcombe murder.'

'Yep,' Brett said.

'I'm told it's dead set that you're the one who's done it.'

'Yep.'

'And like I said, it doesn't bother me at all, but what concerns me is that I need to, I can sort this for you.'

'Yep.'

'I can sort things out. I can find alibis. All the kind of things that need to be done, I can do.'

'Yep.'

'So if you say to me, look, I had nothing to do with it, that's not what I've been told. And that brings me in a real dilemma, in a crossroads, because I want to move forward with what we're doing.'

'Yep.'

'So look,' Arnold said, 'what happened and how can I sort it out?'

Brett was cornered. 'I don't know,' he said.

'Like I said, right? Honesty, trust, respect, right?' Arnold said.

'Yep.'

'You know where you're going. You know what your options are here, right? And you know the information I've got and I said I've paid good people good money ...'

'Yep.'

'... to keep us clean and if I've gotta postpone what we're gonna do for a few months to sort this out ...'

'Yep.'

'... I'm happy to do that for your sake.'

'Yep.'

'Right. Because I'm told that you're pretty loyal.'

'Yep.'

'You built up a good relationship with some of the boys and they speak very highly of you.'

'Yep, I appreciate that.'

'So what do I need to fix?'

'Yeah ... OK,' Brett said. 'No, yeah, I did it.'

*

A couple of metres away, in the next room, the gathering of detectives stared at the screen in astonishment. Jaws dropped. It was an all-encompassing astonishment. They couldn't shout, so they stuck to whispers of jubilation. Phone calls were made.

'Fuck!' they said, wide-eyed in shock.

And then came the chaos. They'd hoped for it, but not really expected it. Nothing was ready.

*

Arnold didn't miss a beat. There was still work to be done.

'All right, OK, so you did it,' he said, matter-of-factly. 'But what I'm saying is, you know, I need to kind of know, I need to step you right back to the whole thing ... so if there's anything like, I don't know, if they've got any DNA or that kind of shit?'

'There's no DNA,' Brett said.

'You know,' Arnold said, 'obviously they haven't found the fucking body.'

'They took my car, they searched my car, did all forensics in my car, they got nothing out of my car.'

'Well, look, just lead me through the whole fucking thing, how it happened, from whoa to go. Then I'll think about things that we need to sort and fix.'

It was the secret he thought he'd take to his grave. Now he needed to find the right words. He'd always told versions of the truth when cornered, admitting only to the barest of details. With the boy at the childcare centre, he'd always denied putting his hands around the child's throat. In Darwin he'd always denied causing the horrific injuries that covered his victim's body. Would he do that now?

'Umm,' he said. 'I don't know how it … I seen him standing there. I did a loop around and came back. I was going up to my boss's father's place to pick up a wood mulcher. [I] picked it up and on the way home there was a broken-down bus and then I seen Daniel.'

He'd parked at the church, Brett told Arnold. The same church where he'd spent many hours listening to sermons. The church where his wife had been with their baby that morning.

'I walked down and sat there and then … I didn't talk to him at all when I got there, maybe just lookin' as though I was waiting for the bus. Umm, the bus drove past and that's when I said I'm going down to the shopping centre, do you want a lift? And he's gone "yep".'

'So he missed the bus or something, did he?' Arnold asked.

'No, the bus drove past.'

'OK, so you asked him if he wanted a lift and he said yeah.'

'Yep, he's jumped in … instead of taking him to the shopping centre, I took him to a secluded spot that I knew of.'

'Where was that?'

'It's at Beerwah.'

Arnold made him spell it out. It was right by where he used to live, Brett explained.

'OK, so you know the area,' Arnold said. 'You've taken him to Beerwah … how far away is that from where you picked him up?'

'Oh, half an hour,' Brett said.

'Did you talk to him along the way?'

'Yeah, just chatted.'

'No, no problems?'

'No.'

'All right. Well, like I said, I'm not judging you at all. So bear that in mind, all right? Just tell me what I need to fix. You've taken him to Beerwah?'

'Um, yeah, [we] went to an abandoned house thing that I knew where …'

'Do you know exactly where that was?'

'Yeah. End of Roys Road.'

'We're gonna need to get that sorted.'

'There's nothing there,' Brett said. He'd gone back a week later to look for Daniel's body. There'd been nothing left.

'What happened in the house?' Arnold said.

Brett paused.

'Like I said, I'm not judging you, all right?'

'I never got to molest him or anything like that. He panicked and I panicked and grabbed him around the throat and before I knew it he was dead,' Brett said.

Daniel was dead, it seemed, before anyone had known he was missing. Long before Bruce and Denise began their frantic search. Before the police were alerted. Before the Sunshine Plaza shut its doors. Daniel was dead.

'All right, and how long did it take to strangle him out, do you know?' Arnold continued.

'Lost track of time … it didn't seem, it didn't seem long.'

'All right. So you grabbed him around the throat. Were you still sitting in the car?'

'No, no … we were out of the car.'

'You've taken him to the house?'

'Yeah.'

'Whereabouts in the house?'

'There's not furniture or nothing. It's just in the first room.'

'Did he fucking spit any blood, anything in that room?'

'Not that I know of, no.'

'What about his clothing? Did he have his clothing still on?'

'Yes, he had his clothing on then.'

'All right, so you've choked him out.'

'Yeah.'

'He's, he's, he's died.'

'Yep.'

'In that room.'

'Yep.'

'What have you done then with him?'

He'd taken Daniel outside, Brett said, and put him in the back of his car, arranging his little lifeless body around the mulcher he'd collected earlier. He'd driven Daniel's body only 100 metres or so, to where the clearing met thick bushland. An old sand-mining site was just behind the rows of macadamias that arranged themselves around the dilapidated demountable house. Brett had looked at it in the past as a possible place to run a sandblasting business from. Now he used it to dump the body of a child.

There was a lake, Brett said, through the trees. Down an embankment. It was thick scrub. Difficult to push through.

'Look, I'm not familiar with the area. Just draw us a little fuckin' map on that so that I, I know where you're talking about. Just like, from where the house was to where the, where the thing was,' Arnold said, handing Brett paper and pen.

Brett opened the back of his 4WD and carried Daniel out. He walked to the top of the embankment and threw him down. The slope was about a metre and a half. Brett jumped down after him and dragged him through trees, along the sand, until he figured he'd gone far enough. He told Arnold that that's when he stripped Daniel, bundling his clothes together to take with him. The little boy's naked body, he'd left under a tree, covered in a few branches and twigs that had littered the ground.

'His clothes I took back with me and threw them into the creek,' Brett said.

'Which creek?' Arnold asked.

'I'm not too sure.'

'Was the creek there?'

'No, no, it was on my way home ... it was still secluded and everything but, like an old logging bridge type thing. There's a creek there. It was fast-flowing and I threw his clothes in there.' Daniel's clothes had sunk as he watched. Nothing had ever been found, Brett said.

'You're lucky, aren't you?' Arnold said.

'Yep.'

'All right, so after you, after you've done all that ... I've heard something about a fucking watch, that you had a watch or some fucking thing.'

'Yep.'

'Did you have that?'

'All went in.'

'The whole lot went in. Everything? So you didn't keep anything?'

'There's nothing.'

'There's no chance anyone's gonna find anything?'

'Nah.'

'What have you done then?'

'I went home.'

He'd stopped in at his drug dealer's house on the way, Brett said. He was still insisting on it. He had no reason to continue with this lie after confessing to the murder. Even though he couldn't have spent half an hour sipping tea in Sandra Drummond's kitchen as he'd claimed.

He'd arrived home with the mulcher, waved to Tracey and continued on with his day as though nothing had happened. As he'd always done after attacking a child.

A week later, Brett loaded a shovel into his Pajero and drove back to the macadamia farm. He'd wanted to make sure nobody would find Daniel. The boy's picture had been all over the papers. All over the television. Police had been crawling the Sunshine

Coast — around the bus stop a good half-hour away. They were looking in the wrong place. Brett pulled his car in and crawled through trees and scrub down the embankment. He was shocked to find Daniel gone. Only a small fragment of bone was left. He crushed it into the ground with his shovel.

'I'll have to get you there with some of the ... we'll get a couple of the boys and sort all that shit out, right?'

They were taking him back. Arnold would send his own crew in. He needed to make sure no trace of Daniel was ever found. Brett would have to take them in, show them. Point out the exact place where he'd dumped a 13-year-old boy and left him for the animals.

It was a neat trap.

*

Fitzy was waiting when Arnold's minder walked Brett from the room. He would take Brett to lunch while Arnold made some calls. There was a lot to organise. Queensland detectives Brian Wilkins, John Carey and Grant Linwood hurriedly booked flights back home while arrangements were made for the next scenario. They were taking Brett back to the scene of his crime.

'What did he say about the big job?' Fitzy asked Brett.

It was on hold, Brett explained. Arnold had a few things he needed to sort out. Fitzy feigned surprise. He asked if it was still going ahead. Had Brett told Arnold about the surveillance he'd done at the airfield? Brett didn't know how much to say. He told his friend it hadn't been about that. Arnold had wanted to speak to him about the information Craig had discovered. The subpoena to the inquest. He'd be flying to Brisbane the next day, he confided.

'What's the deal?' Fitzy asked. Brett hesitated. 'You don't have to, mate,' Fitzy said. 'We all got a history, man.'

He'd murdered Daniel Morcombe, Brett confessed. But it

was OK. Arnold would sort it out. They were taking him back to Brisbane so he could help them do whatever it was that they needed to do. They were looking for a piece of bone — the only part of Daniel still there when Brett returned with a shovel a week later.

'I wish I was 10 minutes later getting that wood chipper,' Brett said.

'What do you mean?' Fitzy asked.

If he'd been 10 minutes later, Brett explained, he wouldn't have seen Daniel. Daniel would still be alive. It was a bizarre thing to say. He talked as they walked to Fitzy's car, Brett revealing the details of his darkest secret — now a secret no longer.

'You've got nothing to worry about,' Fitzy reassured him. 'Arnold will get it sorted.' They'd arrived at Fitzy's Commodore in the Hyatt's underground car park. Brett took the ticket and fed his cash into the machine.

Fitzy drove them to the Como Hotel. It had been a strenuous morning. It was time for a relaxing lunch and a beer or two. Brett was still coming to terms with his chat to Arnold. He'd promised himself he'd never tell anybody. Nobody had known until now. It had been his biggest secret. His safety net, he told Fitzy, had always been that nobody else knew what he'd done. It made him nervous.

They took a seat in the beer garden, Brett keeping one eye on the menu and the other on the waitress. 'Throw her in the air,' he told Fitzy, 'and she'd land on ya cock.'

They laughed and ordered a round of beers.

'Cheers!' they said in unison, bringing their drinks together. But not close enough to hear the chink of glass hitting glass. It was bad luck, Brett told his mate.

'We're into good luck,' Fitzy told him.

They talked about Brett's favourite topic as they waited for their food — sex. He liked kids, he told Fitzy, but he also liked men. He liked his girls big and his men small. That's why he liked Asians.

Fitzy didn't have much to say about that. 'I like chicks,' he told Brett.

He'd be in trouble if he ever made it to Indonesia or Thailand, Brett said. He'd have easy access to children.

Their meals arrived and Brett turned the conversation back to Daniel. The witnesses had been wrong. There was never any blue car. There hadn't been two men. It had just been him and Daniel. And he hadn't stopped his car under the overpass. As for the house where he'd killed Daniel, he knew the place well. In fact, if police ever found his DNA in the old demountable building, it wouldn't matter. That's where he'd taken men for sex. It's where he'd had his 'man fun', he said with a giggle.

The investigation team would read a lot into that statement. Was he expecting his DNA would be found one day? Was he preparing his excuses?

'It is probably ya deepest, darkest secret and I will not tell a living soul,' Fitzy said.

'It is my deepest darkest secret,' Brett agreed.

If he needed a release, Fitzy said, the group could look at sending him overseas. Somewhere like Thailand. It would keep him out of trouble. Brett liked that idea.

*

Brett was more than relaxed by the time they'd finished their lunch. He was still making plans to spend the money they'd be making from the ecstasy shipment that was now on hold. The big job. His $100000 payday. He told Fitzy he wanted a DVD player in his new car. He needed to be able to watch porn from the comfort of his FJ Cruiser. They headed to the pinball machines. Brett wanted to play Indiana Jones in the pub's front bar.

He'd need a death certificate and a new identity, he told Fitzy. It was the only solution. But he felt bad. If he had to disappear for a while, he'd be leaving Fitzy in the lurch. Fitzy would need to find someone else to work for him. Brett didn't want to let him down. But a new identity, a new life, was the only solution.

Maybe they'd make an Underbelly series about them, they laughed.

They were still at the pub when Fitzy's phone rang. They were wanted back at the Hyatt. Arnold had a plan.

*

There was a sports team milling in the lobby when Fitzy and Brett arrived back at the Hyatt. They took the lift to Arnold's floor and met him back in the Swan River Room.

The big boss got down to business. Brett was booked in to Perth's Mullaloo Beach Hotel. He'd stay there tonight. He wanted Fitzy to book plane tickets to Brisbane for three people. Fitzy, Brett and one of Arnold's men, Ian, would all be going to Queensland the next day. He pointed Fitzy towards his laptop and told him to book the flights as they talked.

Arnold took a wad of cash from his pocket — $5000 — and gave it to Fitzy. He'd be needing it for expenses over the next couple of days. They would fly to Brisbane on a Qantas flight at 7.30 a.m. the following day. It was all set.

'This time next week, we'll never talk about it ever again,' Fitzy told Brett as they left the Hyatt for the final time.

*

They watched the girls walking the beach path as they drove to Brett's hotel at Mullaloo Beach. A woman was walking beside a girl who could have been her daughter. She looked to be in her late 40s, the girl about 18.

'You can have the mum, I will have the daughter,' Fitzy joked.

'C'mon, mate,' answered Brett. 'You know I like 'em young.'

Brett's room was a three-bedroom suite overlooking the ocean.

They were impressed. There was even a washing machine. Brett had clothes that needed washing. Fitzy handed him $100 and told him to stick close to the hotel. He reached out to shake Brett's hand before pulling him into a hug.

'I'm proud of you,' he told Brett. He'd done the right thing. It was better that they knew. Now things could be sorted out, once and for all.

'I know the worst thing that can happen is that you just don't ring me any more,' Brett told the best friend he'd ever had.

CHAPTER THIRTY-ONE
I'M SORRY, DANIEL

THE TENSION THAT HAD plagued the covert operation throughout continued right till the end. Queensland had had a very experienced covert operative lined up to play the role of the group's 'cleaner' — much like Harvey Keitel's *Pulp Fiction* character Winston Wolfe, who had been called in to dispose of a body. Ian was the character written into the script to accompany Brett and Fitzy to the place where Daniel's body had been left. He was there on Arnold's orders to convince Brett they would 'clean up his mess' and prevent police from ever finding any trace of Daniel.

The West Australian police had few covert operatives left who hadn't already been used on the Mr Big sting. Given they were in Queensland, it would make sense to use a Queensland officer. But Western Australia disagreed, using one of its own to play the role of Ian.

*

It was a long flight for Brett Cowan and his restless legs. And he was nervous about being back on Queensland soil, where he figured police and their inquest subpoena could find him at any moment.

'I'm gonna actually take the battery outta my phone,' he said to Fitzy as they walked out of the airport.

'Why's that?' Fitzy asked.

'Oh just ... I don't know whether the police have got my phone number or nothing. They can suss out through towers and all that sort of shit.'

245

They were heading directly to the Sunshine Coast. No time like the present. Ian was collecting them from the airport.

'So how far is it?' Fitzy asked. 'Maybe about an hour away?'

'It's about an hour,' Brett agreed.

Ian was driving a Toyota Hilux. They needed Brett to direct them, so he took the front passenger seat.

'You're happy with us to do it, with what you spoke to Arnold about yesterday?' Ian asked Brett.

'Yeah, mate,' he replied.

Brett would take them to the house where he'd lived with Tracey, along the route he'd taken to collect the mulcher, past the abduction site and then to the place where he'd murdered and discarded a defenceless schoolboy. They'd see it all.

'Mate, whatever happens here ... by the end of the night, mate, it'll be done.'

*

Brett fell back to his usual routine of filling the silence with talk. The lychees that sell for five bucks a kilo. A road that was never finished and the 4WD track at its end. He directed them to the cottage on Alfs Pinch Road in Beerwah where he'd once lived with Tracey, Ian asking question after question about how that day had unfolded.

'Missus home?' he asked.

'Yep.'

'She know what's going on?'

'She doesn't. Nobody knew anything about what I actually did. This is the first word I've ever spoken about it.'

'Feel all right?' Ian asked him.

Brett was having a little trouble reliving his crime.

'Yeah, yeah and no,' he said.

Ian suggested they stop. Brett could have a break if he wanted?

But Brett was terrified of being seen. His old neighbours might recognise him.

'No, no, don't stop in the street though … cause I still know people that live here.'

'No dramas, mate,' Ian said.

Brett continued. 'Might be better if we don't stop at Beerwah at all.'

They drove on, Brett pointing out the house where his drug dealer lived.

'When does that come into it?' Ian asked.

'That comes into it on the way back.'

'OK. Do you stop long?'

'I didn't stop there. I waved to her,' Brett confessed. It had been another lie.

They drove past the Big Pineapple, where Brett and Tracey had had their wedding reception. Past the Suncoast Christian Church, where he'd listened to so many sermons.

'That's the church I was married in,' he said.

And then, casually, as if it had been another milestone in his past: 'That's where I parked my car, picked him up.'

'Did you see him?' Fitzy asked. 'Was he standing there when you went past there?'

'No.'

He took them to Frank Davis's house, where he'd collected the mulcher.

'How long were you there for?' Ian asked.

'Wouldn't be all that long because they were going out,' Brett said. From there, he'd driven home the same way he'd come. He couldn't remember whether he'd seen the broken-down bus on his way up or on his trip home, but he'd seen it, Brett told them.

'We're gonna be turning at the next left up here,' Brett instructed them. 'And I sorta … along here somewhere I spotted him.'

'So he was looking back towards town?' Ian asked.

247

'Yep, looking for the bus. The bus had broken down. It was late. He was a fucking cute little … and I parked right here.'

His choice of words showed how comfortable Brett was discussing his most important secret with his new 'brothers'. Fitzy didn't miss a beat.

'Right,' he said.

'And there was all big, all trees there,' Brett continued. 'So nobody could have spotted my 4WD.'

Brett had parked in the church car park and made his way down the embankment to where Daniel stood waiting.

'I sat back up against the wall. He was still close to the road and then the bus drove past and didn't stop. So I've gone and said, "Oh, fuck, I was expecting somebody to get off that bus, I'm going into town to see a … pick 'em up from in town, do you want a lift?" and he's gone, "Yes, please" and fuckin' walked back to the car, jumped in and fuckin' that was it. There was no struggle, no fuckin' screamin' and shoutin', nothing. He willingly got into my car.'

He'd sat in the front seat next to one of Australia's worst predators. That small, innocent boy had turned to the man giving him a lift and explained he was off to the Sunshine Plaza for a haircut.

'So I told him I'd give him a lift, but ahh, I had no intention of taking him to the shopping centre,' Brett said.

'What were you thinking, before that?' Ian asked.

'I don't … I really don't know what I was thinking. You know … I'm an opportunistic offender.'

'So he jumped in?' Ian prompted.

But Brett was uneasy. They were sitting outside the church where he knew so many people. His auntie and uncle had been pastors there.

'Can we move from here? I just don't want to sit here for too long.'

Brett hadn't driven to the Sunshine Plaza. He'd gone a different way.

'I just said, "I've just gotta duck home quickly and just let me missus know what was goin' on." And that's why we were goin' down the hill and not straight ahead. I said that to him and explained that to him. I had no intention of going anywhere near my wife.'

Brett had turned right at the roundabout instead of going straight. Long, slow minutes must have ticked by as Brett drove them in the wrong direction. Daniel had caught that bus many times before. He would have known the journey. The length of time it took for the blue bus to rumble between Woombye and the shopping centre. The drive from the Kiel Mountain Road overpass to the macadamia farm on Kings Road in the Glasshouse Mountains takes about 30 minutes.

At what point did Daniel question the quick trip home to see Brett's wife? At what point did he realise Brett could not be 'ducking home quickly'?

Had Brett turned to the small, polite child beside him and uttered the same words he'd used to terrify Clare? Had he locked the doors and told Daniel: 'You shouldn't trust who you get picked up by, should you?' Brett mentioned none of this to Fitzy and Ian.

'This ... is this a long way from the shops and shit?' Fitzy asked.

'Oh yeah, fuck yeah,' Brett said. 'Back where we came back from the highway, Sunshine Plaza's only, like 10 minutes, not even 10 minutes down the road.'

'So he didn't give a fuck ...?' Fitzy pressed.

'Yep.'

Brett directed them into the macadamia farm at the end of Kings Road. The demountable house where he'd killed Daniel was long gone. A row of sheds still stood. A giant mango tree threw its shade over the clearing where the house had been.

'This is private property here,' Brett explained. 'So there was a house, like a relocatable. That's where it happened. And then there was two old farmhouses, so they've all been taken out. So, as I said, the two old farmhouses were here two years ago. Two and a half years ago.' He didn't explain why he'd been back two and a half years earlier to know they were there.

'And that's where it happened,' he said casually. 'That's where he ... I thought he was going to run and my arm went around his neck and I choked him out. I actually felt that break in there ...'

'Did he say anything?' Ian asked. 'Did he make any noise, or ...?'

'Oh, when I started pulling his pants down, he went "Oh, no". I actually went into the house while he sat in the car. And then I said "Oh, me missus said come in and get a drink." You know, to make it look good I went in and then came back out.'

Some of the macadamia trees had only been saplings when Brett brought Daniel to the property. Now they were full-grown, dropping their hard-cased nuts onto the ground below.

'So, what, you put him back in the car or something?' Fitzy continued.

'Yeah,' Brett said. 'I put him in the back of the Pajero.'

'Like, breathing or nothing?' Fitzy said.

'Nah.' Brett moved them along. 'This used to be an old mobile timber mill factory down here. And I parked over there. Do you want to get out here?'

He'd driven just a short distance from the house, around the rows of macadamias to a large pond surrounded by thick stands of trees and shrubs. Brett knew the property because he'd thought about setting up a sandblasting business there. Now, on his return with Ian and Fitzy, he discovered someone else had done just that. He pointed at the ground where he'd driven in with Daniel's body in the back of his car. He'd used a tree branch, he explained, to sweep away his tyre treads.

'What, and you just carried him over here or something?' Fitzy asked, standing at the top of the embankment that led down to the pond.

'Yep. And I dropped him down there. And then got down there

myself and I dragged him over a, like it'd be covered by water by the looks of it cause that, the water wasn't there. I didn't bury him. I just put him under branches and shit. I've come back seven to 10 days later and found nothin'. Just one little bit of bone.'

'Can we go down there?' Fitzy asked.

'It's under water, where I did it,' Brett said.

'Can I have a shot?'

Brett took them a little closer.

'It's like being Bear fuckin' Grylls in there,' Fitzy said.

They looked for a way in. They could see wild pigs had been through.

'Is that why you put him there?' Fitzy asked.

'I didn't know that until after,' Brett said. 'I came back to, like, bury him.' There'd been nothing left. Animals had been through. Wild dogs and pigs were rife in the area.

'You feeling all right?' Ian asked him.

'Yeah, I'm nervous,' Brett said. 'Just wanna ... yeah. I don't really want to be here.'

He'd taken Daniel's clothes off down the bottom, he told them, and carried them back up the embankment.

'I didn't fuckin' check his wallet, pockets, or nothin',' Brett said. 'I just wanted to get out of here after ... I had no intention of knocking him, at all. I just wanted to have some fun with him then I was gonna take him back to the fucking shopping centre and drop him off. But when he ... not struggled, but fuckin' I thought he was gonna run and rah, rah, rah, and yeah, and grabbed him back in the house and choked him out.'

They struggled their way down the embankment to the wet ground below. Brett pointed out the place where he'd left Daniel's body and they turned to go back to the car.

Brett wasn't looking when Fitzy picked up a stick and placed it in the fork of the tree. It was a neat marker that would guide them back when the time came. Soon, this secluded spot at the end of a road of macadamias would be crawling with police.

*

He'd taken them to the wrong bridge at first. One looked much like the other and it had been many years since he'd stopped there to toss a little boy's clothes out the window. They stood on it, a wooden bridge wide enough for one car to cross the inconsequential Coochin Creek, and looked into the water, as though Daniel's red t-shirt might still be seen. They asked him again what Daniel had done when Brett had pulled down his pants. Had he tried to punch Brett? Pull out his hair? Brett was vague on the details.

'I'm not into 12-year-olds,' he mused. 'I was into seven- and eight-year-olds, so I don't know what attracted me to him. I'm not into big. Like, he was chubby but not overly chubby. I like my guys slim, not fat. I like my girls fat.'

'If he didn't struggle, I guess you would have dropped him off at the shops, eh?' Fitzy said, voicing a theory nobody believed.

'Yeah, well, I probably would have been caught in the end if I ... let him go,' Brett said.

They asked him if he'd noticed the memorial built in Daniel's memory. They'd passed it when they'd been to the overpass, next to the church. Did he get pissed off when he saw it?

'Not so much pissed me off,' he said. In fact, he'd felt guilty about what he'd done when they climbed the embankment to the place where he'd left Daniel's body.

'When I was down there, I was saying to myself, "Sorry, Daniel".' No, he said. He hadn't minded seeing the memorial. 'I'm glad it's there,' he told them.

*

They were back in the car, discussing the packs of wild dogs that roamed the area, when a group of the animals crossed the road ahead of them. They'd been discussing Daniel's body. How it had been gone when Brett had returned to bury it a week or so later. Fitzy had known Brett for months and had never seen him show any real emotion. So it came as a surprise to the entire covert team when Brett suddenly started shaking as they watched the dogs in the distance.

'I'm sorry, Daniel. I'm sorry, Daniel. I'm sorry, Daniel. I'm sorry, Daniel.'

He said it as though it were a chant. They'd remember it well — although the recording devices failed to pick it up properly. He shook as he repeated his mantra. And then he snapped himself back to the foolish, jovial psychopath they all knew too well.

*

'I got to ask ya, Paul,' he said, 'how can you not think of me as a fucking piece of shit?' Brett asked as they left the creek.

Fitzy was professional as ever. 'As you said,' he replied, 'ya haven't done it in fucking years.'

*

They drove past Sandra Drummond's house to complete the loop. He told them he had gone to visit his drug dealer. He'd shown Sandra's partner the mulcher in the back of the car. Kevin had a keen interest in anything with a motor. He'd stayed for about 15 minutes then continued on home, he recalled.

It had been a long day with a lot of driving. They dropped Brett at a hotel near the airport and left him with $100.

'It was good work today, mate,' Fitzy told him.

'No worries,' Brett said.

'Probably a hard thing to do, eh?'

'It has been my secret for near on eight years. That's why I have been so confident they can't get me on it.'

*

Surveillance teams had been recording Brett's every move ever since his plane landed on Queensland soil. They kept watch outside his hotel all night. But Brett was good at following instructions. Fitzy had told him to stay put. And he wouldn't let his mate Fitzy down.

*

Thursday, 11 August 2011: The investigation team had work to do. While surveillance crews watched Brett, Fitzy and Ian took a group of officers back to the macadamia farm in the Glass House Mountains. The stick Fitzy had left in the fork of a tree was an X marking the spot. He was filmed as he led them in, recounting Brett's confession as he went. They filmed the bridge where Brett had thrown Daniel's clothes into Coochin Creek. He took them to the bridge where Brett had first led them, before realising he was in the wrong place. And he also took them to the place where the demountable house had once stood in the shade of a giant mango tree.

*

Brett was staying in his room. At 12.40 p.m., the surveillance team spotted him as he emerged from the hotel. Wearing a black t-shirt and black jeans, Brett stood on the footpath and smoked a cigarette.

*

At 1 p.m. Brett and Fitzy headed to lunch. Detective Senior Constable John Carey had selected a pub at Redcliffe as a good place for one of the last scenarios he'd write. They wanted to keep

Brett talking. Get as much information as they could. They wanted Daniel's wallet and they wanted his fob watch.

'How ya going?' Brett greeted his mate.

'G'day, mate,' Fitzy replied. 'How are ya? What's going on, mate?'

They chatted away for a few minutes. Then Fitzy delicately steered the conversation.

'How you feelin', man? All good?' he asked.

'Yeah, good,' Brett said.

'Fuckin', the only thing, and I don't give a fuck if we don't even talk about it again, mate ... [Arnold] wants to know, fucking, what you were wearing on the day.'

'Burned it,' Brett replied.

'Burned the clothes?'

'Burnt that night.'

'Hundred per cent sure?'

'Hundred per cent, man.'

'Yeah.'

He'd burnt his shoes too, Brett continued.

'Where'd ya burn them?' Fitzy pressed.

'At home ... an old BBQ ... the ashes are fucking through my garden.'

'So, it's all gone ... you weren't wearing [a] hat, fucking nothing like that? You burnt everything?'

'Everything.'

Fitzy was full of praise. Brett could never get enough of it, they knew.

'That's gold, mate. That's good, man. Fucking covered yaself well then, hey? That's fucking sweet.'

'I thought I was gone, man,' Brett said. 'I really, I thought I was fucking gone, like, when they came and questioned me and asked me about it and I thought, that's it, I'm fucked. I just stuck to my story.'

'Yeah,' Fitzy said. 'How were ya sleeping that night, man? Were ya spinnin' out or what?'

'Yeah, I couldn't sleep.'

Fitzy told him not to worry. They were fixing things. Ian was fixing things. Paperwork was on the way. People were being contacted. It might take a bit of time but they were going to make it all go away. They would do that for him.

'Still gonna be subpoenaed to the inquest though, aren't I?' Brett said.

'Dunno. I don't know anything about that sort of shit, man.'

Maybe it was time for him to disappear, Brett mused. If police were fixed on him being Daniel's killer (and obviously he was, he joked to Fitzy), maybe the only solution was for Brett Cowan to 'die'. After all, they'd done that for Joe. He'd been given $10 000 and a plane trip to London. It sounded like a good deal to Brett.

'The only way I can see out of it … like Brett Shaddo dies … go overseas and come back with a new ID.'

'Well, Arnold will sort all that out, man,' Fitzy said. Ian was doing his job. Fitzy said Ian had been surprised just how big the Daniel Morcombe case was in Queensland.

Brett enthusiastically agreed.

'[He's] supposedly the only child that's gone missing but if you, if you read the paper last Saturday, yeah, like I read it online and then I read comments about it, there's like 25 detectives on this case — permanent,' he bragged. 'But what about all these other "misconducted" children … that have fucking been abducted and missing? Is there 25 fucking detectives on their case?'

Paul nodded. 'Why is this one so big then?' he asked.

'I don't know,' Brett said. 'Maybe his fuckin' mum and dad are fuckin' rich …' They drove on towards Redcliffe, Brett chatting away until they were interrupted by Fitzy's phone. Fitzy nodded along to the person on the other end — a carefully scripted conversation to get them what they needed.

'I'll ask him, yeah, no worries,' Fitzy said. He hung up and turned to Brett. 'He reckons, umm, the sticking point is this watch, man,' he said.

'I don't have it,' Brett replied.

'Never fucking seen it?'

'No, mate, nup.'

'Never fucking saw it or nothing. Can you remember feeling it in his pocket or nothing?'

'I didn't feel his pockets. I didn't go through his pockets or nothing.'

'Didn't ya feel his wallet in there though?'

'Yeah, that was just cause I was taking his pants off.'

'I don't care, but he's worried if that turns up — he couldn't have had it down his jocks or anything? You didn't see it in his jocks or anything like that?'

'No, I just went in, I paid no attention to his clothing whatsoever. I just took 'em off. Everything of his went in the creek.'

Fitzy applied a little more pressure. 'You gotta tell me the truth, man, cause he reckons that is the one thing that can undo us is the wallet and the fucking [watch].'

'I don't have any of it, whatsoever.'

Fitzy tried again. That fob watch would seal everything. It was ultimate proof. They'd had confessions before. They wanted more this time.

'You wouldn't fucking lie to me, brother, would ya?' he said.

'I stake my life on that one, Paul. I'll put my life up on that. Mateship too. My job, the whole fucking lot, man. I'll even put my kids' lives on it. I don't have it. I don't know where it is. I can guarantee I don't have it. And I don't give me kids' lives up at all. Other than me mum and dad … my kids and my family and that, that's it.'

Brett told Fitzy about dropping in to see his drug dealer on the way home. It seemed he had been there after all — although not for a half-hour chat and a cup of tea.

'I didn't know it was gonna happen … until it happened,' he said of murdering a small boy. 'It's just like …' he paused for a while, 'just how it's coming outta me mouth, you know? It's just so … it's like it's nothing.'

'Well, it doesn't worry you anyway, does it?' Fitzy said.

'Not now,' Brett said. And then: 'It does, but not really.'

'Yeah,' agreed Fitzy. They paused.

He hadn't meant to kill the boy, Brett insisted. He'd just wanted to have some fun.

'I would've like, I would've had, had a suck, made him suck me off, rah, rah, um, then takin' him, once I blow … that's it, I'm not interested any more. So I would've been, come on, let's go. Fuckin' takin' him to the shopping centre, let him out an' fuckin' driven off. But I wouldn't be sittin' here talkin' to you today if that had happened either.'

Fitzy was a professional. Covert operative 452 didn't miss a beat.

'Oh well, you don't know,' he said. 'You're telling us everything, mate — that's all we can ask, hey?' It was a gentle reminder. Make sure you tell us everything.

*

'What did it look like when you went back there, like a week later or whatever? Or couldn't you see him at all?' Fitzy asked.

'There was nothin',' Brett said. 'One little bit of bone an' it's just like, I'm looking for the whole skeleton. I walked past it a couple of times … what the fuck, where is it? It was just, like, two weeks an' there's nothing. I've never heard of that … there's always skeletal remains. There was just one bit of bone an', like that … just chop, chop, chop, chop, chop, chop, chop, chop until it was nothing in the ground, you couldn't see it.'

*

It was a shame, Brett told Fitzy, that he hadn't found himself one of those pedophile rings that you heard about in the media. Perhaps if he'd hooked up with an organised group of child sex offenders, he wouldn't have the two convictions. Pedophile rings 'pass kids around', Brett said. He wouldn't have had to abduct anyone if there were children being passed around.

'The kids do not know any different,' he insisted to Fitzy. They didn't know they were being abused. They didn't know it was wrong. He told his mate he'd be sure to let him know when the 'feelings' came back again.

'They reckon it goes in a six-year cycle,' Brett said. It had been six or seven years by the time he'd taken Daniel, he said. And it had been more than that since. When the time came, he told Fitzy, he'd let him know. He'd want the group to send him to Thailand so he could 'go and have some fun'.

'I am fucking proud to be a deviate,' Brett said. He loved pornography — particularly bestiality. It really got his blood boiling and his motor running. 'I don't mind looking at a bit of bestiality,' he said. 'I wouldn't go out of me way to fuck an animal though.'

*

Fitzy brought the conversation back to Daniel again. Why had he left him facing up, he asked.

'Just the way he lied when I had finished,' Brett said.

'What do you mean when ya finished?' Fitzy asked.

When he'd finished dragging him, Brett explained. He thought for a moment and corrected himself.

'Not that I dragged him,' he said. Probably carried him. He admitted the whole thing probably sounded bad. 'I can't believe I'm talking about it so matter-of-factly.'

Brett told Fitzy he'd like his new life to begin in Africa. The group could send him there for six months while they sorted out a death certificate and his new identity. He'd have to find a way to cover up the tattoos the police had photographed all those years ago.

In Africa, he said, he could be a 'hunter and collector'. He could find himself a child bride. About 12 years old would do. He'd watched documentaries on surviving in the wild. He'd seen Bear Grylls. He figured he'd get by just fine.

*

Brett took Fitzy to the metal recycling plant he'd spoken about so often. The place where he'd thought about disposing of a body by hiding it in the boot of a car. Fitzy said he'd assumed Brett must have got rid of a body there. He'd talked about it so much — even down to how to weld the boot shut.

'Nup, never done that,' Brett answered. 'Only done one [murder].'

He dropped Brett back at his hotel with $50 and instructions to 'lay low' while Ian continued his work.

*

The surveillance team continued on after Fitzy had driven away. They watched as Brett wandered into an antique store next to the hotel. A moment later, he walked into the hotel's foyer. They waited. At 6.30 p.m., he left the hotel and walked off down the street, his mobile phone to his ear. They watched as he walked into a bottle shop. Brett was spending his $50 on alcohol. After that, it was a convenience store. And then a public phone booth. He went back to the hotel, emerging at 9.30 p.m. to stand in the driveway and smoke a cigar.

He was back at 11 p.m. to smoke a cigarette as he talked to someone on his mobile phone. They followed him down the street to the Hamilton Hotel. At 2 a.m. he emerged and headed for home.

CHAPTER THIRTY-TWO
SHOCK VALUE

DETECTIVE SENIOR CONSTABLE GRANT Linwood, Queensland covert controller John Carey and Detective Superintendent Brian Wilkins were running on adrenaline. They'd spent the day doing paperwork, working out a plan, and caught a late flight back to Brisbane after Brett's conversation with the big boss, arriving well after dark.

On the night of 11 August 2011, Linwood fronted a room of around 30 detectives at Queensland Police HQ. They were in the crime operations conference room on level three and he delivered a briefing to the inner circle of the investigation. They were the people who would decide the next step. He'd given a similar briefing to Western Australia's covert unit. It was everything they needed to know about the schoolboy who left home to buy Christmas presents and never came back.

'This is Daniel,' he'd said, showing a picture of a beautiful boy with his mother's eyes. He was the reason they were all there. The little boy whose fate had gripped everyone.

Deputy Commissioner Ross Barnett was there. So was Assistant Commissioner Mike Condon and Chief Superintendent Gayle Hogan, and head of homicide, Detective Superintendent Brian Wilkins. There was the head of Queensland's covert unit, the head of the police legal unit and a collection of on-the-ground detectives. Stephen Blanchfield. Emma Macindoe. Ross Hutton and Gavin Pascoe.

Linwood knew his presentation back to front. 'Daniel is a fairly small, shy little kid,' he told them. 'He's not street-savvy.' He showed them maps and photographs of Sunshine Coast locations. Aerial views of Woombye. The Kiel Mountain Road overpass. The

Morcombe property. Pictures of thick, impenetrable bushland. The church Brett had once attended, so close to the bus stop. He showed them a time line of the day, 7 December 2003 — nearly eight years ago now. Pictures of the clothing Daniel had been wearing. The shoes he had been wearing. The fob watch he'd been carrying. The wallet.

'[Brett Cowan] was in the right place at the right time,' Linwood reminded them. 'One of the few people with form. Daniel Morcombe fits his MO.' Brett, he said, changed his appearance not long after Daniel disappeared. He looked like the comfit images, like the descriptions given by the bus passengers. He had the means. He had the opportunity.

He talked to them about Brett Cowan. About his upbringing. The stable family unit. The black sheep of a good family, the third of four brothers. His father's military background; his father was strict and believed in discipline. But there was no evidence Brett had ever been subjected to any abuse. Brett's brothers were successful. He was not.

Linwood talked about Brett's many jobs. Sandblasting. Welding. Tow truck driving. He'd recently been fired from his tow truck job. He'd crashed the vehicle and then lied about it. He talked about Tracey. Their children. Their marriage and separation. He talked about Brett's other relationships. His drug use. The adult match-making site he frequented. He watched the news. He read newspapers. He had an extensive criminal history. Theft. Dishonesty. He'd abused children in his youth. He'd been accused of sexually abusing many, many children. He'd admitted to abusing children at the army swimming pool. He was bisexual. He was a pedophile.

Linwood told them about the boy at the preschool in Brisbane. And then he told them about the other boy. The boy in Darwin.

*

The beautiful little boy lay on the stark white sheets of a hospital bed, his body a mess of injuries. The gentle hands of a nurse held his head in place. One on top, one under his chin. He had brown hair and big eyes. Just like Daniel Morcombe.

A police photographer took pictures as the nurse moved his head this way and that. On the back of the boy's head was a large, deep cut. Blood had seeped onto the pillow. His injuries had been cleaned, and most of the blood wiped away. But they were shocking.

Years later, when those photographs were shown to a room of seasoned police to make the most important of points, every one of those officers stared.

These injuries were not caused by a man who had used a child for sexual gratification. Every inch of the boy's body was bruised and bloodied. There where whip marks across his torso, as though he'd been struck with a belt or tree branch, over and over. Red marks could be seen around his throat, as though someone had squeezed until he'd stopped breathing. Bruises covered his face and body, as though an adult with a clenched fist had punched and punched until the tiny, defenceless boy's eye had swollen shut. There were large, sharp cut marks on his legs and body. Had it been the rusting, jagged car bodies that sliced through his skin and muscle?

And then there was the large, gaping wound at the boy's anus. Doctors had found dirt and ash in the wound. Brett had denied using a tree branch to assault the boy. But looking at those photographs, at the horrific number of injuries, it was impossible to see it any other way.

Brett Cowan had bashed the boy, whipped him, raped him with a tree branch and choked him until he passed out. Then he'd tossed his lifeless body away, into a rusting car body. No doubt he'd been sure the boy was dead. He'd been caught before after letting a child go. That boy had only told his mother, who'd told the police, who'd put him in prison. This time, he'd tried to make sure there'd be nobody to point the finger. It hadn't worked. What would he have done on the third try?

'This,' Linwood said, 'is what Brett Cowan is capable of.' He pointed at the photographs. At the boy in the hospital bed. 'In 15 minutes he's done that. Have a good look. This isn't about shock value. Have a look at the savagery. At the overkill.

'Could he have killed Daniel Morcombe? Have a look at what he's done.'

*

Assistant Commissioner Condon was playing devil's advocate. Cowan didn't have a blue car. A veritable crowd of witnesses had seen that blue car. They'd described it in detail. They'd selected photographs and talked about faded paint work. It couldn't be ignored.

At the back of the room, Deputy Commissioner Ross Barnett was taking furious notes. The final decision on an arrest would be down to him. After years of close liaison with the Morcombes, Police Commissioner Bob Atkinson wanted to be sure the final decision was made without any emotion. Without bias. Without prejudice. Barnett could make the call with a clearer head than he.

Barnett asked question after question. He flicked through the pages of his notebook, finding points he wanted clarified. He'd taken careful note of the boy in the photographs. Bloodied, bruised, whipped and choked. He looked like a younger version of Daniel.

It was time to make a decision.

*

Friday, 12 August 2011, 9.17 a.m.: 'Hey mate ... all good howz ya goin ... catch up with this arvo ...'

They came to collect him a little after 2 p.m. Brett had spent the morning sleeping off a hangover. The brown paper bag the surveillance crew had spotted him emerging from the bottle shop with had held a bottle of Johnny Walker Black Label. He'd had a big night. He'd won $200 on the pokies.

Brett gave directions as they made their way to a café strip on nearby Racecourse Road.

It was all looking good, Ian told him. They'd be on their way home to Perth the following day. Check-out from Brett's hotel was at 10.30 a.m. They'd be round to pick him up before then.

Brett noticed the dirt on the car when he got out of the Hilux. Ian had obviously been driving the back roads of the Glass House Mountains.

They ordered coffees and toasted sandwiches. The Ekka was in town — Brisbane's Royal Show. The investigation team had discussed their concerns the night before that Brett might turn up at the event. They didn't want this. The Ekka was too crowded. Too difficult to maintain surveillance. And there would be children everywhere. Fitzy had been briefed to tell Brett to stay away from the Ekka. Brett listened to his mate.

'You need to keep your head down,' Fitzy said. If Brett kept himself out of trouble, they would be good to leave the following day. And he had more news. The big job was back on. It would happen the following week. Brett should prepare himself for a massive pay cheque.

It was great news. Brett had big plans for that $100 000. It would be a new life, a far cry from the one he'd had when he'd stumbled across Joe and Fitzy. Back then he'd been homeless, staying with a woman he'd met on an adult dating site. He'd had no job and no money. He hadn't even been able to put credit on his mobile phone.

He was going to rent an apartment when the money came through, he told Fitzy. Something flash.

'It feels like we're on holiday,' Fitzy commented as they looked out onto Racecourse Road from their sidewalk table.

'We are, mate,' Brett said. Brett told them about his night. He'd been walking home and spotted police searching a car they'd pulled over. They'd been in an unmarked vehicle — a Toyota LandCruiser. He complained about dodgy police tactics. Police, he told them, used unmarked cars to bait drivers into driving badly. They wore civilian clothes, like undercover police, and sat at the lights revving their engines so the car next to them would take off at speed.

'Ya gotta watch for them undercover cunts, eh,' Fitzy said with a grin.

'It's entrapment,' Brett agreed. The conversation was relaxed. Brett was among friends and looking forward to the future. Fitzy told him to lie low that night. It was almost over. He gave Brett $50 for dinner and a hug.

'We're family now,' he told him.

They headed back to the car. It was 3.40 p.m. on 12 August when they left Brett at his hotel. They were close now. It was almost over.

*

Surveillance crews were in pursuit. They watched as Brett went into a service station to use the ATM. He walked back to the antiques store and went inside. Brett was a collector and he'd had his eye on an old-fashioned candle snuffer.

They watched as he walked back to the hotel, where he remained for about two hours. At 6.30 p.m. they spotted him again. He walked into the Woolworths store before ordering from a Chinese takeaway. By 7 p.m., he was walking in the doors of the Hamilton Hotel. He didn't stay long though. He was back out in under 15 minutes. He walked from the hotel towards the river, making his way through a large group of schoolchildren as he went. The surveillance crew held a collective breath and strained to see what he was doing. He seemed to be saying something to the kids as he walked among them. This was Brett Cowan. He could lure a child away in seconds. Kill them in minutes.

But Brett passed through and the group of kids continued on to where they were preparing to board a boat in the marina. He dropped back in to the Hamilton Hotel for a quick game on the poker machines. Then Brett made his way back to the hotel.

At 10 p.m. he was outside again. They watched him walk out the front and chat on his phone as he made his way back to the pub. The team moved inside the hotel. There was Brett, sitting at a table with a young couple. Later, he chatted to a man, aged about 30, at the bar. At 11.30 p.m., he was in front of the stage, dancing to the live band. By 1 a.m., he was on his way home. They watched him as he made his way, alone, to the hotel where he'd spend his last night of freedom.

*

Saturday, 13 August 2011, 6.55 a.m.: 'Mate ... pik ya up bout 945 ... c u then bro ...'

They picked Brett up from his hotel and hit the road for a second trip to the macadamia farm. He chatted with Ian and Fitzy as they drove north.

'Got a root last night,' he said. He told them he'd met a woman at the pub and taken her back to his hotel room. She worked for the Department of Child Services.

'That's a bit ironic, isn't it?' Brett laughed.

They laughed too. They knew he'd done no such thing.

Ian told Brett they would be flying out that afternoon. But first they needed to return to the macadamia farm. Ian wanted to do one last check for Daniel's fob watch. He wanted to be 100 per cent satisfied it wasn't there. It was fine with Brett. He hadn't liked being there on that first day but now he was feeling good about things. He'd told them his biggest secret and nothing terrible had happened. Soon he wouldn't ever have to think about it again.

Fitzy wanted to talk about the girl Brett had supposedly taken home. What was her name, he asked.

Brett paused. 'Courtney,' he said. Courtney lived in Windsor, a suburb in Brisbane's inner north.

'Did you punish her?' Fitzy asked.

'A little bit,' Brett said with a laugh.

*

In a service station toilet cubicle en route to the Sunshine Coast, Fitzy checked the recording devices he wore on his body to make sure they were working.

Then he pulled out his mobile phone to call his boss. They were nearly there.

*

Brett chatted away. He talked about the weather. He wasn't looking forward to a hot, dry Perth summer. He'd have to buy an air conditioner. He talked about putting in a bitumen driveway at Michelle's house. He talked about light planes and cars. He pointed out landmarks as they went. The Glass House Mountains, he said, were named by Captain James Cook, who'd spotted them as he sailed north up the coast and thought they looked like glass. (He was partly right. The mountains reminded Cook of the glass furnaces in his native Yorkshire.)

They turned onto Kings Road and made their way past rows of macadamia trees. They shake them, Brett explained, to get the nuts to fall off. Ian pulled the car in to a clearing and Brett got out. He took a cigarette out of his pocket and lit it up.

*

Detectives were already in place. They'd hidden in sheds. Among trees and behind the woodpile. An officer with a video camera stood behind a bush and police officers in camouflage gear, usually used to hunt out marijuana crops, were guarding the scene. They held their breath, silent as mice, as the sound of a car engine cut through the air. It had been nearly eight years. The car rolled in and Brett got out. He lit a cigarette and brought it to his mouth.

He barely flinched when they jumped out at him. They shouted at him to stay still. Don't move! Stay where you are! Police! He took another drag of his cigarette.

'Be cool,' Fitzy told him as police surround him too.

Brett stood smoking his cigarette as Detective Stephen Blanchfield stood in front of him, reading him his rights.

'Do you know who I am?' he asked.

'No,' Brett said.

Blanchfield told him he was under arrest for the murder of Daniel Morcombe.

'Yep,' Brett said.

He had the right to a lawyer. He didn't have to say anything but if he did, it could be used against him.

'Yep,' Brett replied. 'Yep. Yep. Yep.'

He repeated the same word over and over. He seemed calm. He kept smoking his cigarette, standing there in the clearing.

*

As Brett was being read his rights, dozens of detectives were conducting coordinated raids across Brisbane and the Sunshine Coast. They hit the old house at Alfs Pinch Road. Unsuspecting, long-suffering Peter and Marlene opened their door to officers armed with a warrant. His brothers were visited. The house of a former girlfriend, where Brett was known to have kept a shovel, was searched. They would leave nothing undone.

*

The investigative team gathered in an office at police headquarters. Brett had called a lawyer, picking one from a phone book plonked in front of him. He'd told police he wasn't talking. The detectives waited for the go-ahead to lay charges.

Assistant Commissioner Condon had always been a firm believer in Doug Jackway being their best suspect. The blue car. His lies. His tangled time line.

But it was up to Deputy Commissioner Ross Barnett to make the call.

He gave the order. Brett would be charged with murder.

*

Assistant Commissioner Mike Condon was already on the Sunshine Coast. With Brett safely at police headquarters, he stood at the front door of the Morcombe home to tell them the good news. It was about 5 p.m. when Condon knocked on the door. Bruce opened it up, holding a phone to his ear. Commissioner Bob Atkinson had beaten him to it.

'There's been a man arrested for killing Daniel,' he'd told Bruce.

The Morcombes were stunned. The covert operation had been a closely guarded secret. They'd had no idea anything had been happening about their son's case at all. Now, after eight years, they had an answer. Daniel was dead. Denise broke down.

PART FOUR
I DIDN'T DO IT

CHAPTER THIRTY-THREE
MURDERER

REPORTERS POURED INTO THE media room at police headquarters. Police Commissioner Bob Atkinson and his deputy, Ross Barnett, took their seats in front of a burgundy curtain, the QPS insignia hanging behind them: *With Honour We Serve.*

'Can I let you know at the outset . . .' the Commissioner began, 'that regrettably we're not going to be able to answer questions.' Cameras snapped as he handed over to Barnett.

'We wish to advise that a short time ago a 41-year-old man was charged with a number of offences relating to the disappearance of Daniel Morcombe at Woombye on the 7th of December, 2003,' he began. 'The charges proffered are murder, deprivation of liberty, child stealing, indecent treatment of a child under 16 and interfering with a corpse. The man will remain in custody and appear in the Brisbane Magistrates Court on Monday. This is obviously a very significant milestone in what has been a complex and protracted investigation.

'However, as the matter is now before the court, it would be inappropriate to discuss any aspect of the circumstances of . . . the arrest and the investigation leading to it. Today's arrest is underpinned by the dedication, tenacity and professionalism of every officer who has worked relentlessly on this investigation for nearly eight years. We have repeatedly affirmed our commitment to solving this disappearance and have never wavered in that resolve.' He shuffled the pages in front of him and turned to the Commissioner. Over to you.

'I'd just like to add to that by thanking and mentioning a number of people,' Commissioner Atkinson said. 'Firstly and most importantly, on behalf of the entire Queensland Police Service, we extend our thanks and appreciation to Bruce and Denise and the entire Morcombe family for their courage, their patience and their resolve over the last eight-year period.'

He thanked the Morcombes' supporters. The volunteers who had run and maintained the Daniel Morcombe Foundation. He thanked the public, particularly residents of the Sunshine Coast who had provided police with so much information over the years. The media, for keeping Daniel in the spotlight. Crime Stoppers.

'We also want to thank all of the police agencies across Australia and overseas who provided assistance to us in what is, without question, the largest missing person investigation in the history of the Queensland Police Service,' he said.

'And finally, but by no means of least importance, of course, I want to thank all of the detectives and all of the members of the Queensland Police Service, who worked with commitment, determination and continuous resolve in the investigation of this matter.

'Despite this breakthrough today, a significant amount of work remains to be done. And that includes the search of an area of bushland on the Sunshine Coast.'

Bruce and Denise had been told, he confirmed. Assistant Commissioner Condon had been to see them. The Commissioner had spoken to them as well. How they were faring was for them to reveal.

*

Bruce Morcombe stepped up to the microphones. There were more than a dozen on stands at the end of the driveway. They'd given so many press conferences over the years. They'd learnt what to say, how to keep their boy's smiling face on the television, in the papers. Bruce, normally so polished, faltered.

'Uhh, I'll, ahhh ... obviously yesterday's announcement of an arrest, umm, and a person being charged, was a significant step and it's a very difficult place Denise and I and the family find ourselves in,' he said. 'Which is somewhere where we've worked extremely hard over seven years and eight months to be in.

'And yet, when you're there ... umm ... it's a place where you don't want to be.' A day earlier Daniel had been missing. Now he was dead. Their son was dead. Their little boy had been murdered and now they stood in front of a dozen microphones.

'It's an extremely difficult time,' Bruce continued. 'It's not pleasant at all. We're really indebted to the police that have worked extremely hard over the full course of the journey to ensure that we are where we are today, which is a man being charged.'

They were limited in what they could say, he explained. The matter was now before the courts. He spoke quietly, stammering over words. He seemed in shock. The inquest, he said, had been crucial to achieving an arrest. It had been a review process that had put a suspect even more in the spotlight.

'Does it bring closure?' a journalist asked. Denise shook her head emphatically. What was closure? Were they supposed to feel better?

'Closure is not a word that we're very comfortable with,' Bruce said. 'And please consider that a man's been charged. Our priority as parents of Daniel is to find Daniel and that's what we're driven to do and we're reassured that the police service is very much hard-nosed in finding Daniel and returning his remains to the family.'

He thanked the media for their years of support. Full-page ads. Live television crosses. All around the country. They'd kept Daniel in the spotlight. And that had kept information filtering through to the investigation team.

'We'd never given up hope,' Bruce said. 'We've always said today's the day we find that information. And truly, little did we know, that yesterday was the day that we got up, that we did find some information. We still have a long way to go and really, our focus is not so much on the man that's been charged. What we want to do is find Danny. We've said right from day one, the person that's responsible picked on the wrong family and we said we'd never give up and we're true to our word.'

'Denise, are you angry?' a reporter asked.

She looked at them. Thought about it. Moved her weight from one foot to another.

'Not yet,' she said. 'Not yet.'

CHAPTER THIRTY-FOUR
DON'T SAY A WORD

TIM MEEHAN, A FIERY redhead with a textbook knowledge of the law, stood in his backyard among the chickens and dogs. He didn't answer his phone when it rang the first time. It was a private number and he was at home with his family. He let it ring out. When it beeped with a message a moment later, his curiosity got the better of him. He should check it. It might be a work call.

'Tim, you'll want to take this call,' the voice on the other end said. It was Detective Senior Constable Ross Hutton.

The phone rang again as soon as he hung up. This time Meehan answered. It was Brett Cowan. He needed a lawyer. They were charging him with Daniel Morcombe's murder.

'Sit tight,' Meehan said. 'Don't say a word.' It was standard advice from every lawyer to every client. Don't say anything. Wait for me.

Meehan arranged with detectives to visit Brett in the watch house that evening. It would take time to charge and process him. At 7.30 p.m., the lawyer was heading down Brisbane's Roma Street. Police headquarters, the watch house and the arrest court formed a tight little bundle in the city's northern corner. Meehan drove past a crowd of television cameras and journalists huddled on the pavement. He steeled himself for a barrage of questions. But nobody noticed him walk in the door. He grinned as the doors to the watch house closed behind him. He supposed he wouldn't be so lucky on the way out.

*

Tim Meehan had been working for Bosscher Lawyers since he'd graduated from law school. By 2011, he'd been with the firm more than a decade. Michael Bosscher and Meehan made quite a pair. Meehan was the consummate professional. A sharply dressed jiu jitsu enthusiast, he was passionate about the law. He believed in it. It wasn't for him to pick and choose his clients based on what crimes they'd committed. Justice had to be carried out and carried out correctly. And that meant that even the worst of the worst — Brett — should be represented by the most competent of lawyers. That way, if and when he was convicted, the entire process had been carried out properly.

Bosscher had begun practising law in 1993, when he was about 25. He'd spent his younger years travelling the world as a competitive downhill skier before deciding it was time to fulfil his dream — criminal law. He'd wanted to be a lawyer since he was a kid. Probably after watching too much television. He liked the idea of being able to help those at rock bottom. The people who couldn't help themselves.

Bosscher was smart and bolshy and he fought hard. He was good at running the business side of the practice. He made partner in a year. He taught himself never to judge the client. That was for the jury to do. He was there to help them through a process.

Bosscher and Meehan worked well together, despite the chasm between their personalities. While Meehan arrived in a neatly pressed suit, Bosscher rolled in to work each morning looking like he was about to rob the place. In fact, one morning he was essentially accused of doing just that. He'd pulled in to the work car park driving an old BMW. There was a boom gate that needed opening, so he hopped out of the car dressed in a pair of footy shorts and a singlet, tattoos on display. A cigarette hung from the corner of his mouth as he made his way to a small gate.

He turned to the sound of a car pulling in. Fast. Car doors slammed. It was the police.

'That's a nice car, sir,' one remarked. 'Is it yours?'

*

Brett Cowan was a skinny man with long hair. He sat quietly waiting for Meehan, as he'd been told to. There was something about a pedophile. They had a look about them. Brett didn't have it. He looked eerily normal. He didn't seem concerned about his predicament. The arrest. The murder charge. But there was one thing on his mind.

'Tim,' he said urgently. 'I need you to know I didn't do it. I didn't do it.'

CHAPTER THIRTY-FIVE
THE SEARCH

THE MACADAMIA FARM WAS kept under police guard for the night until the search for Daniel's remains could begin in earnest. It was arguably the most elaborate search in Queensland's history. They had to find Daniel. They had to find him for his parents. And they had to find him because without a body, Brett could claim he'd made it all up to keep his new friends happy.

The end of Kings Road was an overgrown swamp. It was virtually impenetrable. Spiders and snakes lurked among thick lantana. Muddy ground dropped away in steep banks to a sandy pond — the remnants of a sand-mining operation.

Police brought in a ladder to gain easier access to the area where Brett claimed to have dumped Daniel's body. To the tree where a little boy had lain, naked and covered in branches. They placed rows of sandbags and planks of wood to act as walkways. They called the State Emergency Services. They called in police recruits. Anyone they could spare. It was going to take a long time and a lot of people to do what they needed to do.

The Sunshine Coast's forensic coordinator, Inspector Arthur van Panhuis, arrived on scene on 13 August. He looked at their search site. The ground underfoot was very muddy and very wet. The ground was covered in pine needles and leaf litter. What would it have been like in 2003? Eight years had passed.

In August 2011, Queensland was still recovering from one of its greatest natural disasters. Just months earlier, a great wall of water had swept across the state, taking lives and homes as it went. The macadamia farm had gone under too. Would Daniel's remains have been washed away? Were they looking in the right place? How deep did they need to dig? What would the soil level have been eight years earlier?

Van Panhuis began making calls. Expert after expert was called in. Scientists, hydrologists, geologists. Griffith University Professor Jon Olley, a fluvial scientist, was asked to give his opinion on water movement through the site. Would Daniel's remains have been moved by floodwaters? Would his clothing have washed down the creek?

The news was good. Professor Olley told them that in all likelihood, the water would have risen through the macadamia farm and then dropped again. There would have been little movement. The creek had had no major flows in that time. And with the amount of debris — a spider's web of logs, branches and snags — any clothing tossed into the water would have become caught up relatively quickly.

The professor told them to dig between 30 centimetres and 60 centimetres around the embankment area. That should safely get them to the 2003 level. There was different advice for different sections of the farm. In some areas they'd only need to dig to a depth of around 10 centimetres. In others, they'd need to dig up to a metre. It was a diverse area of diverse challenges.

They brought in a senior hydrologist from the Sunshine Coast Council. He gave them advice on flows through Coochin Creek. They brought in cadaver dogs. Metal detectors. The Queensland Police dive unit arrived to search Coochin Creek for Daniel's clothing. They set up another search area by the mango tree, where the demountable house had been. They dug into the ground. Searched the sheds.

They'd tracked down the demountable building. It had been sold on and moved to a property in Landsborough. Van Panhuis went to inspect it. The once dilapidated building had been stripped and fully renovated. New walls. New floors. Everything was gone. They'd find no evidence here.

Orange-clad SES volunteers and police recruits arrived by the busload. They gathered in lines on their hands and knees. Mud and water seeped into their clothing as they inched, shoulders touching, along the ground. They held small gardening tools. Dirt and mud slid through dirty fingers.

At each end, a supervisor stood. If a searcher found something suspicious, they'd raise their hand. The supervisor would walk the line and assess the find. Bone experts, pathologists, police officers from the Scientific Unit — they were all on hand, ready to give an opinion. Hour after hour, inch by inch, they dug in the dirt. It was hard work. Harrowing work.

Detectives from the investigation team were keeping busy taking statements, preparing for court appearances. The rest waited with bated breath. What if they didn't find anything? Day after day they came back. SES volunteers skipped work. Spent days away from their children. For years, the people of Queensland had wanted to help bring Daniel home. Now, there was something they could do.

They found evidence of goannas. Wild dogs. A fox's den. Excavators were brought in. Backs ached and muscles grew tired. And still they dug. One day. Two days. Three days. Detectives began to worry. Brett sat in prison. What if they didn't find anything?

*

Bruce and Denise were not allowed into the search site. Police took them to higher ground, to look on from a distance.

Denise stood and stared. She'd thought that perhaps she'd sense something. Her son, so close, after being gone so long. She felt nothing. There was nothing.

They said a prayer for him and went home.

*

Monday, 15 August 2011: Brett sat in the dock for his first court appearance wearing jeans and a brown prison-issue jumper. If he was nervous or frightened by his predicament, he didn't show it. His hair was messy and matted and he kept his eyes down.

The room was packed to overflowing with reporters ready to record every word of the short hearing. Six police officers stood guarding the door. A national outpouring of anger had greeted the news that a man had been arrested for Daniel Morcombe's murder. Who was this monster? There was some concern a mob could turn up to confront the pedophile, now Australia's most hated man, as he fronted court. So far, Brett's name had been kept out of the media. A suppression order, put in place at the inquest, still stood. But not for long. Media outlets were already making application to have it lifted.

The hearing lasted just five minutes. Brett had been left in the cells until Magistrate Brendan Butler demanded he be brought into court. Meehan had argued Brett's appearance was unnecessary. The magistrate didn't care.

There would be no request for bail yet. In Queensland, a bail application on the charge of murder must be heard in the Supreme Court. Meehan used his time in court to request a lengthy adjournment. The case against his client was complex and they'd need the extra time, he said. Magistrate Butler gave him six weeks.

Outside court, the lawyer told the rabble of reporters that his client would strenuously defend the charges. He had instructions to apply for bail as soon as they were ready. Asked how his client was faring, Meehan told them: 'Under the circumstances, he's doing all right.'

*

Meehan had a little boy at kindergarten and another two children at school. There'd been frantic meetings after his face began appearing on television. Brett Cowan was so hated by the public that some of it was being directed at his legal team. The kindergarten and the schools Meehan's older children attended had concerns for their safety. What if someone tried to kidnap one of them in some sort of misguided revenge attack? They held talks about putting on extra security.

At family functions and BBQs, Meehan and his wife found themselves confronted by angry relatives. Why would Tim defend such an animal? The lawyer tried his best to explain his view of the justice system. But most people had made up their minds. His wife came to him in tears one day, begging him to drop Brett as a client. He told her he couldn't.

'This is not about me. It's not about you,' he told her. 'This is the legal system. It's about doing the right thing.' It was difficult to explain.

CHAPTER THIRTY-SIX
PROOF UNDENIABLE

WEDNESDAY, 17 AUGUST 2011: Somewhere on a secluded macadamia farm, among the pine trees and their fallen needles, SES volunteer Ross Tennesse sat back on his heels and raised his hand. He'd been searching an area they'd called 'the mud pit', a section of ground between the embankment and a pond. It was hard work. They were there in a line, on their hands and knees, in hats and sunglasses and full protective dress, inching forward. Inch after inch, digging in the dirt. Ross had seen it when he'd looked forward. There, just two feet ahead, was a shoe, sticking out of the ground. He put up his hand for the supervisor. Everybody froze. Ross moved back a little as a police officer walked the line to where he waited.

'Step back,' the officer said to the line of volunteers. They did. It was a solemn scene. Had they found him? Had they found a little boy who'd been dumped in the dirt? So loved by his family, discarded by his killer.

The forensic specialists came then. The shoe was photographed in place. Then they carefully removed some soil. And there it was: Globe. Daniel had been wearing his Globe shoes when he disappeared.

*

Denise had long ago given police the box that her son's new Globe shoes had come in. The shoe found at the Glass House Mountains was given to a forensic podiatrist, who would compare the wear on the sole with some of Daniel's other shoes.

'We need evidence,' Bruce told the *Courier-Mail*. 'We appreciate that's one thing this case has really struggled with. Evidence is going to be crucial and we'll just wait and see if the shoe may be the missing link. The shoe is significant but we'll wait for forensic tests.' The shoe, he said, hadn't changed anything.

'We're still looking for Daniel. You don't have a funeral for a shoe.'

*

Senior Constable Chae Rowland stood in Coochin Creek, his wetsuit soaked from the thigh-deep water he'd been wading through. It was 18 August and he was only 15 minutes into that day's search efforts, a laborious task for the police dive unit. The creek was a mess of tree branches and twigs, washed into intricate bird's nests of debris.

They were now about 15 metres from the bridge where Brett claimed he'd slowed his car to toss a bundle of Daniel's clothes out the window. It had looked like a spider web when he'd first spotted it. A thin, black thread. Nothing more. Rowland reached out his fingers to touch it. Cotton. He pinched the thread between his fingers and tugged, following its length to a bundle of twigs.

He followed it to its source. The faded, degraded waistband of a pair of underpants. Bonds. He could just make out the letters. It was the same brand Denise had bought for Daniel.

*

The shoe they'd found had belonged on someone's right foot. It had been worn by someone with child-sized feet. The same size shoe Daniel had worn. The same make. The same model.

It took them three days to find the other one. A scenes-of-crime officer on a line search had spotted it, nestled in among mud and leaf litter. They stopped. Called for a photographer. Ever so slowly excavated it from its bush grave. It was a Globe shoe for a left foot.

*

Later that same day, a volunteer on the search line stopped and raised their hand. There, in the dirt, was what appeared to be a bone. It was long and thin. There were experts on hand to give advice on whether an unusual object was bone or something else. Or if it was bone, whether it was to animal or human.

Sergeant Donna MacGregor from the police scientific unit walked the line to where the search team sat, unmoving. She looked at the object. It looked, to her expert eyes, just like a fibula. A human shin bone. She sent for the reference skeleton in her office. She wanted it brought to the search site. If they'd found one bone, they'd find more.

*

Walter Wood was a retired doctor, a forensic osteologist, an anatomist and an associate professor at Bond University. On 21 August 2011, he was at home waiting for a visit from the police. They'd phoned ahead. They needed his help. Could he take a look at some items found in bushland on the Sunshine Coast?

Detective Sergeant Graeme Farlow arrived with three packages in hand. Dr Wood opened the first with careful hands. A human left fibula, he declared. Belonging to a juvenile. He examined the contents of the next package. A left tibia. The third bone was a left humerus. Two leg bones and an arm bone. Slightly chewed, possibly by a dog or other carnivore. In the place where Brett Cowan claimed to have left Daniel's body, they were finding the scattered skeleton remains of a juvenile.

They'd find seventeen bones in all. Even as Dr Wood carefully assessed the three bones Farlow had brought to his house, SES volunteers were finding more.

Volunteer David Brushe had been raking through topsoil when

he hit something solid in the softness of the earth. It was a long bone. He stopped, raised his hand and waited.

It would later be identified as a human tibia.

*

Wetsuit-clad water police waded through Coochin Creek, searching through debris, through its muddy bed. Sergeant Gordon Thiry was somewhere between 15 and 20 metres from the bridge when he came across a pile of logs and debris caught in the creek bed. They pulled out a log and felt through the sand they'd exposed. There was hard sand and soft. And then Thiry's hands felt something foreign. A piece of material. It was a pair of shorts. Dark. Like those Daniel had been wearing. They found the belt a short time later. It wasn't far away. But it had been removed from the shorts.

Bruce Morcombe thought about what that meant when they told him of the discovery. He'd imagined so many terrible things over the years. He continued to imagine them now.

*

Queensland Health specialist forensic pathologist Professor Peter Ellis had visited the Glass House Mountains site several times. His first visit, on the afternoon of 15 August, before they'd found the first bone, had not gone unnoticed. Journalists recognised the seasoned pathologist and jumped to the conclusion a body had been found.

'Standard procedure,' a police spokesman told reporters. 'I wouldn't read anything into that.'

The professor toured the site. Watched overalled volunteers inch their way across the ground. Watched as bones and bone fragments were removed painstakingly from the earth.

When police were satisfied they'd found all there was to find,

Professor Ellis arranged the 17 bones into a sparse skeleton and conducted an autopsy.

There was a left humerus, a left scapula, a right humerus, a right radius, a part of the left pelvis, a part of the right pelvis, a left femur, a left fibula, a left tibia, a right femur, a right tibia, five vertebrae from the lower back, some pieces of bone that could have been ribs, and a small collection of bone fragments that couldn't be identified. He couldn't tell much from the very incomplete set. But the bones still told a story. For a start, they all came from the one person. There weren't two of any one bone. No duplicates, Professor Ellis told the police. He used an X-ray machine to examine the bones. He concluded they were from a child, aged somewhere between 10 and 15 years. He could be no more specific than that.

Some of the bones were marked. Small scratches on their surface. Professor Ellis believed these were the teeth marks of animals. Or, possibly, but less likely, from the garden implements volunteers had used to dig up the site. No gender. No cause of death. Neither of these important things could be determined. Later, the bones would be sent to different DNA experts. They'd need to be certain the bones were Daniel's.

*

A week after Brett's arrest, media reports began to emerge of an elaborate, covert investigation that police had carried out to bring him undone. Details of the sting had been so tightly controlled that it had become difficult for the covert team to do their jobs. Hour after hour they'd listened to Brett talk nonsensical rubbish. They'd listened to him talk at length about sadistic sex fetishes and child abuse and they'd laughed along at his wit. Aside from each other, there'd been nobody to talk to at the end of each day. Nobody to share a beer with, to laugh with. And the ongoing tension between the state police departments had made the situation even more difficult.

Despite their dedication to the secrecy surrounding the operation, the investigation team was surprised word had never got out. They raised eyebrows at one report, which claimed they'd lived in the same caravan park as Brett for months, watching him eat, work and interact with residents. They'd slept just metres away, the report claimed.

In reality, Brett hadn't even been living at the caravan park. He'd been living his usual parasitic lifestyle under Michelle's roof.

CHAPTER THIRTY-SEVEN

OUR SON, THE PEDOPHILE

AS SEARCH CREWS CONTINUED their laborious task, the investigation team was busy taking statements from those who knew Brett best. Over the coming days, detectives would track down Brett's auntie and uncle, Keith and Jenny Philbrook, his parents, his brothers and his many former girlfriends.

Detectives Grant Linwood and Emma Macindoe sat down with Peter and Marlene, the only people who had stood by Brett through the bad and the worst. For years they'd supported him. He'd lied to them, stolen from them, embarrassed them. And still they'd been there. They'd given him $5000 when he decided to move to Perth to start afresh. They'd bought him cars and found him places to live. They'd sent him clothing when he had nothing. They'd kept silent when he'd brought a series of women home. They'd trusted him to be honest with Tracey about his past.

'He has told us that he told Tracey everything about his past history,' Peter told the detectives. 'We have never questioned her about this, though. This is between them, husband and wife.' He described his son getting up to the 'usual mischief' as a boy. There'd been a few incidents where he'd stolen from them and his grandparents.

When Brett took up with Clare, Peter and Marlene had kept silent. They'd thought she was too young for him but he'd lied and told them he and Clare were just friends. He was just 'keeping an eye' on her. And then she fell pregnant. After the baby arrived, it became clear she was struggling. Brett called his ever-reliable mother and asked for her help.

'We went down and picked her up and brought her up here ... for about five weeks,' Peter said. 'Marlene sort of mothered her and showed her how to feed and bathe the baby, how to be a mother. We even went as far as buying her all new clothes and shoes. Brett came and picked them up and took them home. The house where they lived in Bundamba was a bloody shambles. A real pigsty. When we visited I wouldn't stay long. I just couldn't put up with it.'

Peter hadn't known anything about Brett abusing children when Brett was a child himself. He'd never heard any accusations. Nobody had approached him about Brett acting inappropriately.

'When Brett was growing up, he and I didn't have the best relationship because I was the one who had to kick his arse and things like that,' he said. 'I am not aware of Brett being the victim of childhood abuse or anything like that. He has never told me that.'

They were well aware that Brett had been a long-time suspect in the disappearance of Daniel Morcombe. Peter had even been with him to a formal interview with detectives.

'Dad, I don't know where this is going but I had nothing to do with it,' Brett had told him. Peter had thought his son seemed stressed when it was over.

'They gave you a fair hearing,' he'd said. 'They didn't terrorise you. If you didn't do it, then you've got nothing to worry about and Mum and I will support you.'

Peter told Linwood and Macindoe that Brett had always denied having anything to do with the schoolboy's disappearance.

'I'm his father and I have to believe him,' he said. 'If I knew he had done it, I'd be the first one knocking on the door. I didn't pursue the matter or sit down and cross-examine him or anything like that.'

*

Brett started getting into serious trouble some time after Year 10, Marlene told them. She couldn't even remember all the things he'd been in trouble over. Stealing. Drugs. Interfering with a child. She didn't think Brett had ever been sexually abused either. She'd asked him once. He'd told her definitely not. He'd written to her from prison and she'd written back.

'Brett never told me why he assaulted the boys,' she told Linwood and Macindoe. 'A lot of the things that he did wrong was because of his drug habit. Brett would lie to Peter and I about his drug use so I never knew what he was actually taking. I could tell by his eyes that he was taking drugs. I looked in his room on a number of occasions but could never find anything. Brett was a very easily led person. He always took the brunt of things that happened when he was growing up because he would not dob on anybody.

'Brett never really spoke to me about the things that he did wrong. Brett knew that Peter and I would always support him and try to get him back on the straight and narrow. He is my son and I will always love him. I know that Brett lied to Peter and I over the years to keep himself out of trouble and not to hurt us. He could look you in the eye and lie and you would believe what he was saying.'

*

Brett's eldest brother, Robert, a successful Sunshine Coast businessman, had nothing good to say about the black sheep of the family. Nothing at all.

'I was never close to Brett at any stage of our lives,' he told detectives. 'I don't ever really have any memory of even playing with Brett growing up.' Robert said Brett had been a 'defiant' child.

'In his teenage years, Mum and Dad told us that Brett had issues with food colourings and that was the reason for his behaviour,' he told them. 'If Mum or Dad ever left the house, I would be in charge. I don't recall anything being really out of the ordinary in our family during these times. I looked after the younger boys and apart from standard childish fights, didn't have any real problems.' They'd had little to no contact as adults. 'The only time we crossed paths was if we saw each other at Mum and Dad's house in passing.'

He'd seen Brett briefly when he was subpoenaed to appear at the inquest. The hearing had put Daniel's disappearance back on the news. Robert remembered seeing the artist's impression of the man spotted standing under the overpass.

'It was a long, gaunt face with a goatee and ponytail,' Robert said. 'I thought to myself that it looked exactly like Brett.'

His parents had always stood by his brother. Whenever Brett had done anything wrong, they'd been there to protect him.

*

Clare had put her strange and violent relationship with Brett behind her. Earlier that year, she'd married an American man she'd met over the internet.

On 11 August 2011 — the same day Brett was driven into a clearing and arrested by detectives who'd jumped from behind trees — she received a phone call. It was late, almost 9 p.m. Her husband had picked up her mobile and answered it for her.

'Hello?' he'd said.

'Tell Clare she's dead,' a man's voice said. Then the line went dead.

She was convinced it was Brett. It was a few days later she realised why he'd be calling.

*

Clare was watching the news when she saw it. The demountable building where Brett had murdered Daniel. The television station had shown it during a story about the search for the schoolboy's remains. She knew that building. She'd been there.

Detectives Emma Macindoe and Ross Hutton met her at a service station in Carseldine, north of Brisbane, with a video camera. They needed her to tell them everything. Take them through exactly what had happened.

It was when they were living at the caravan park on Bribie Island. Some time in 2009. Maybe August or September. Brett had suggested a drive. She'd agreed. It was late — but sometimes Brett did that. Sometimes he liked to go four-wheel-driving at night, taking her down well-worn bush tracks. He knew the area well. He didn't tell her where they were going that night. They sat in silence as Brett negotiated the bush trails. Clare had the window down, watching the trees go by. He pulled in to a clearing, where two buildings sat behind a massive tree.

'Are we getting out?' she asked him.

'Yeah,' he answered. 'Get out of the car.'

He had a mate, he told her, who did sandblasting around here somewhere. He sauntered away and she followed him, wondering what they were doing there in the middle of the night.

The first building was a mess of weeds and rotting timber. There was no front door, no front steps. They walked around the back and found some steps there. Inside were two rooms. Someone had used them to store collections of junk. Car parts. Wood. Glass. An upturned fridge, a broken counter and scrap metal. Brett found a bucket of shells and ran his hand through them. He picked one out and inspected it.

Clare walked out of the dilapidated building and into the one beside it. The door was falling off its hinges. There was more junk inside, rubbish on the floor. She nearly stepped on a piece of jagged glass. Brett had followed her inside. They poked around together before walking back to the first building. They didn't talk. They walked around, kicking things in the dirt. Clare wondered what they were doing there. Clearly nobody had been there in a long time.

Brett walked over to a row of sheds. Clare followed. She didn't like it there. The grass came right up her legs and she imagined snakes slithering around her feet. She decided she'd had enough and went back to the car. It was a long wait. Clare sat in the passenger seat as the minutes ticked by. What was he doing out there in the dark? She let 30 minutes go by before she got out to go and find him.

'What are you doing?' she said when she found him poking around by one of the sheds.

'Just looking around,' he said.

'I want to go home,' she said. It was midnight.

He came over to her. He wanted to stay a bit longer, he said.

'Fine,' she said. 'You can stay here but I don't want to stay here. It's dark.' Again, she went back to the car to wait. And again, she gave up waiting and went to find him.

Brett's jeans were undone and she could see that he was aroused. He directed her to the ledge of the shed and told her to sit up on the metal so they could have sex. She didn't want to. It was late and she didn't feel comfortable in this strange place with its crumbling, dirty buildings. She left him there and went back to the car. Five minutes later, he joined her. She had her ideas about what he'd been up to, out in the dark, alone.

She'd had no idea why he'd taken her there — until she'd seen one of those strange, dilapidated buildings on the news. He'd taken her to the same place he'd killed Daniel. And then, in the moonlight, he'd tried to have sex with her. Now she knew why he'd be calling. She could put him at the very place he'd killed Daniel.

CHAPTER THIRTY-EIGHT

FRONTING COURT

To: Bosscher Lawyers

> Ask Daniel if it was fair. Ask the other victims of this creature if it was fair for him to be out of jail. How can you sleep at night? Don't you have children? Don't you think the Morcombes have suffered enough? Shame on you. Use your talent, education and intelligence for some worthy cause.

To: Bosscher Lawyers

> I find you just as disgusting as the filthy maggot, Brett Cowan that you represent. What kind of a sub human are you to think that this murdering pedophile has been treated unfairly? How about poor Daniel Morcombe and his family? What is fair about what that family has gone through and will continue to go through for the rest of their lives? As a mother and caring member of society I am dumb founded as to how people of your calibre sleep at night and can only hope that you will one day be punished for your despicable part in these horrendous crimes.

To: Bosscher Lawyers

> Defending Brett Cowen you must be very hard up for work. How do you sleep at night defending such a pc of shit like this, how low can you go. He is not just a criminal heard murdered a CHILD, do you have kids ? obviously not i would think , shame on you .

297

To: Bosscher Lawyers

> How on Earth did you defend that evil cruel bastard? Money
> must have played a great part in doing so. I hope that you sleep
> well in knowing what you knew and still defending him.
> Lynne.

*

The committal hearing was set down for two weeks commencing at the end of November 2012 in the Brisbane Magistrates Court, more than a year after Brett's arrest. It would run for a week in November before adjourning to the following February for the second week of proceedings. The court schedule was tight. This hearing would determine whether there was enough evidence to proceed to trial. Dozens of witnesses would be called. Forensic experts, DNA experts, hydrologists and botanists. Detectives, eyewitnesses. People who'd seen and heard all kinds of things. Blue cars and white vans. A man by the side of the road.

If the case against Brett was weak, a magistrate could choose to throw it out. Nobody thought it was weak. Not even Brett's lawyers.

*

It was 11 a.m. on 29 November 2012. Michael Bosscher had just finished cross-examining the last of the DNA experts when he made an announcement that ended a battle the Morcombes had been fighting for years.

His client, he said, had signed a consent order releasing Daniel's bones. They had no intention of ordering any further tests on his remains.

Bruce and Denise hugged. They'd be asking for Daniel's remains ever since they'd been recovered from their bush grave.

The legal process meant they'd had to wait. Now they could bury their boy.

'Daniel's remains were discovered 467 days ago,' an emotional Bruce said outside court. 'He has been not in the family's unit for 3280 days. On anyone's perception, both of those are long numbers. We treat this as no joy, that announcement, but it is a step in the process to getting Daniel's remains released to the family and once they are released, obviously we can make plans for a funeral from there.'

On 7 February 2013, the last day of the committal hearing, Michael Bosscher agreed there was enough evidence against his client to proceed to trial.

'I can see that the prosecution have met the threshold test required,' he said.

Chief Magistrate Brendan Butler made it official.

*

It rained on 7 December 2012, the day of Daniel's funeral, and the ninth anniversary of his disappearance. It rained just as it had the day he'd died — that early-morning shower setting in motion a series of terribly unlucky events, delaying the start of the boys' shift picking passionfruit at the neighbour's farm, preventing them from going with their parents to the work Christmas party, leading to Daniel deciding to catch a bus to the Plaza to buy presents for his family instead.

Daniel's old school, Siena Catholic College, had agreed to host the funeral service. It was a sea of red. Boys in red socks. Men with red shirts or red ties. Women in red dresses. Girls with red ribbons in their hair. They came in waves of colour. Many had never met Daniel. But they felt close to him for so many reasons. The State Emergency Services volunteers who'd dug in the dirt to bring him home to his mum and dad. The police officers who'd searched for him, and then searched for his killer. The mums and dads who'd seen his face on television and looked at their own children with fear in their hearts.

Former prime minister Kevin Rudd took his seat in the school's chapel. Police Minister Jack Dempsey rose to shake his hand. Senior police sat behind the family. Deputy Commissioner Ross Barnett. Former Commissioner Bob Atkinson, who'd retired in 2012, refusing to step down until they'd made an arrest.

Marquees stood on the lawn outside the chapel for the hundreds who wouldn't fit inside. A large screen television gave those outside a view of what was happening in the chapel. The small white coffin covered in red roses sat in front of Bruce and Denise. Her hands shaking, Denise stared at her lap. Inside that casket was the little boy who'd been so like her. Shy and beautiful with those big, round, smiling eyes.

*

'A moment in time that will live with all of us forever occurred nine years ago today,' Bruce said, his voice projecting across a sea of red. 'Please do not be sad. Appreciate that the evil act which took Daniel happened a long time ago. Today is about embracing his return to family and being reflective of what might have been. Do we dwell on what we have lost or accept the space we are in and find some positives?

'I'm sure all who knew Daniel, including our family members, his friends, former teachers and classmates at Mountain Creek Primary School and Siena Catholic College, family friends among others, all agree the only way forward is to feel blessed to have known him. He may no longer be with us but Daniel's legacy lives on.

'The Daniel Morcombe Foundation is committed to doing all we can to ensure this never happens again by educating children on ways to keep safe and supporting young victims of crime. The national profile and media interest in Daniel's search has allowed

Denise and I to meet with many other family members of missing persons, murder victims and survivors of terrible crimes. Clearly the Morcombe family are not alone. We have been touched by each of your unique journeys and we will continue to do what we can to help.

'I pay tribute to the Queensland Police Service, SES volunteers, media outlets, government and business leaders, Crime Stoppers, the Queensland Homicide Victims Support Group, his former schools, parishioners and the broad community for never forgetting Daniel. I also acknowledge the efforts of West Australian Police and the Queensland Coroner for getting us to where we are today.

'I'm sure we have all discovered strengths we did not know we had. Australia is a better place because of this. Our children and grandchildren are safer because of Daniel's legacy. What is truly ironic about all the recognition, support, help and publicity his search has attracted is that he was such a quiet kid.

'He was not an attention seeker, yet because of his sparkling eyes and beaming smile, captured in photo after photo, he is someone everyone took into their hearts. That is what made him special.'

CHAPTER THIRTY-NINE
THE TRIAL

JUSTICE ROSLYN ATKINSON HANDLED a jury like a kindly grandmother and wayward witnesses like an incensed schoolteacher. And she had, in fact, taught. Her first job was in teaching before she turned her hand to acting. From there, she became a lecturer, teaching university students all about literature, drama, film and Australian studies. She was admitted to the bar in 1987. In 2002, she was appointed the chair of the Queensland Law Reform Commission, where she remained until 2013.

In 2014, she presided over the trial of Brett Peter Cowan.

*

All of Queensland had wanted justice served for Daniel, but few actually wanted to dole it out. On 10 February 2014, a crowd of potential jurors was ushered into the Queen Elizabeth II Law Court building's especially large Banco Court. Each one was given a number. In the courtroom where the trial would be heard, numbers were called at random. The person with that number was instructed to get up, enter the courtroom next door and walk towards the rows of chairs reserved for jurors.

A packed public gallery filled with journalists and curious onlookers watched as each person entered, waiting to see whether defence or prosecution would object to them serving on the jury. Twelve men and women would be selected, as well as three reserves. The trial was expected to take six weeks and jurors would be subjected to the horror of a little boy's murder. Some might not make it through. Illness or injury could force a juror to pull out. Three reserve jurors would ensure 12 made it to the end.

When 15 had taken their seats on the left-hand side of the courtroom, Justice Roslyn Atkinson began her spiel. Juries must be seen as being completely impartial, she said. Sometimes a juror might know a witness, or a family member of someone central to the case. Perhaps they know something about them. Perhaps they know the defendant or one of his friends or relatives. Maybe they feel that they can't be completely impartial for whatever reason. If that is the case, she needed to know.

'Could you please just raise your hand?' Justice Atkinson asked.

Most of them did. It was highly unusual. Normally one or two members of a jury might declare their inability to be impartial. Not the majority.

One by one, they filed up to whisper in Justice Atkinson's ear. With some, she nodded through their explanation before sending them on their way. Others she ruled should remain. Five more potential jurors were selected to replace the ones who had escaped. Two more of those claimed they could not serve impartially. And so the process went on. Eventually, after several false starts, six men, six women and three reserve jurors were empanelled to decide the fate of Brett Cowan.

Justice Atkinson thanked the crowd who'd arrived for jury duty without their numbers being called.

'It was important and necessary to have a large jury panel available,' she said. 'I thank you for your attendance.'

*

Brett Cowan's borrowed suit hung on his lanky frame. He was clean-shaven, his hair neatly trimmed. His lawyers would make sure he looked nothing like the grubby, long-haired, goateed man described by so many of the bus passengers. He looked entirely, shockingly, normal. He was friendly with his legal team. They were the only ones there to see him through the trial that would decide his fate. His parents, Peter and Marlene, would stay well away from the throng of cameras waiting at the main entrance to the court building. His few friends stayed away too. So did the many women he'd been with over the years. Nobody went to court to support Brett Cowan.

Bruce and Denise took their seats on the right-hand side of the public gallery.

Justice Atkinson read the charges against Brett. The jury, she said, on hearing all the evidence, would have to decide whether Brett was guilty of each offence. Murder. Unlawfully and indecently dealing with a child under the age of 16. Improperly dealing with a dead human body.

'I don't want you to read any media articles about this case,' Justice Atkinson told the jury. 'You mustn't tweet. Don't discuss it on Facebook. You can't blog. Do not attempt to investigate anything to do with this trial.'

Prosecutor Glen Cash rose to his feet. The friendly, often smiling prosecutor would work with Deputy Director of Prosecutions Michael Byrne. Byrne had successfully put triple murderer Max Sica behind bars. There were 158 people on the witness list. Cash read out every name. The jurors needed to be told in case they knew someone on it.

With the jury sorted, Justice Atkinson decided opening addresses would begin the following day. She sent the jurors home, informing the group they would be required Monday through Thursday each week until further notice.

*

Brett Cowan, Michael Byrne told the jury, had already confessed to these crimes. It had been a complete confession, made to undercover police. Byrne was first to address the jury when court convened for day two of the trial. A strange crowd had gathered in Court 11 on level five of the glass-walled District and Supreme Court building.

An elderly man with a peanut-eating habit noisily cracked open shells and ate as though at the cinema. Another in a pork-pie hat made snarky comments to reporters. The journalists sat in the front row, leaning forward to hear every word, furiously typing on iPads and laptops. They would arrive early each day to secure a seat. Others went up to a special media room where proceedings were shown on a television screen. A separate room had been put aside for the Morcombe family should they need time alone.

Daniel was 13, soon to turn 14, when he disappeared from his home on the Sunshine Coast, Byrne told the jury.

'It was out of character for him, he wasn't the sort of child who ran away and went missing,' he said. In fact, Byrne continued, they would come to learn that within an hour of his disappearance from that unofficial bus stop, Daniel was dead.

It would be eight years before police found 17 bones in a painstaking search of an area of Sunshine Coast bushland. They found them, he said, because Brett Cowan told there where to look. They should ignore the blue car. It had nothing to do with Daniel's abduction.

'Let me make it perfectly clear,' he intoned, 'the Crown case is that the defendant had nothing to do with that blue car.' Brett, he continued, had come undone because of a 'highly sophisticated, elaborate undercover police operation'. He'd willingly admitted to the crime after becoming convinced he was on the cusp of joining a criminal gang.

'You will see the defendant tell Arnold "Yeah, OK, yeah … I did it",' Mr Byrne said. '"I never got to molest him or anything like that, he panicked and I panicked and I grabbed him around the throat and before I knew it, he was dead".' Byrne read the words Brett had used. '"Yeah, like, sort of, when he started to struggle, like, I was starting to pull his pants down … and he said 'Oh no' and he started to struggle. I was standing … squatting and yeah, I grabbed him".'

The crown case rested on the confessions Brett had made to

undercover police officers. And the jury needed to be convinced that, for once, Brett was being truthful when he made them.

*

Angus Edwards was the barrister Bosscher and Meehan had chosen to work with them on Brett's defence. There'd been no discussion. As far as they were concerned, Edwards was the best. The former DPP prosecutor wore his red hair long, like he'd stepped offstage with the Bee Gees into a courtroom. He never wore a tie under his robes.

Edwards had been viewed as a major talent in prosecution. As a defence lawyer, he was even better. No matter how detestable the client, a jury couldn't help but be charmed by the red-haired barrister.

*

'Who dunnit?' barrister Angus Edwards began. 'There is no dispute he confessed … but does that mean he did it?' Brett, Edwards said, had a $100 000 reason to make it up. To falsely confess. He'd had plenty of motive to do so. If he hadn't confessed, he would have lost his mates, the money and the new life he'd discovered. He would have been called back to the inquest — maybe even arrested.

Edwards urged the jury to pay particular attention to evidence given by another man: Douglas Jackway. Jackway was a convicted pedophile who fitted with many aspects of the investigation. He drove a blue car, just like the one described by many witnesses.

'After having served eight years in jail for driving up, grabbing and abducting a boy off the side of the road and taking him away to rape him, you will hear how even though Jackway was caught in the act by the father of the boy, he still denied he had done it,' Edwards told the jury. 'You'll hear evidence about how Jackway changed his appearance. About how he dyed his hair around the time of Daniel Morcombe's disappearance.'

He said there were some aspects of Brett's confession that had not proved to be true. Daniel's shoes had been found in bushland, when Brett had claimed he'd thrown them in the creek. Daniel's remains had been found 60 metres from where Brett had taken the undercover officers that day.

It was close enough, the defence would suggest, that perhaps someone had told Brett where Daniel's body had been dumped. He'd known roughly. But not exactly.

'It is not even in dispute that Mr Cowan confessed to abducting, molesting and causing Daniel Morcombe's death and dumping his body,' Edwards said. 'The key issue in all of this is whether you think Mr Cowan was telling the truth when he confessed or whether he was not telling the truth, whether he was making it all up. That, ladies and gentlemen, I expect, will be the central issue in this trial.'

*

Bruce and Denise were the first to give evidence. Witnesses who hadn't yet testified were not allowed inside the courtroom in case their testimony was influenced by what they'd heard. Bruce and Denise getting the first slot meant they were free to sit in on the rest of the trial.

'He was a very shy boy,' Bruce said of his son. Not the type to go off with a stranger. Daniel had caught the Sunbus alone about 15 times before that day. He used to catch the bus to school, too.

He told the court how he and Denise had gone off to their work Christmas party, returning home in the afternoon to a near-empty house. He told how they'd searched for him, how they'd eventually gone to the police.

'Have you ever heard from Daniel since that day?' Byrne asked.

'Not in any way, shape or form, no,' Bruce said.

Denise took the stand next. Shy and softly spoken, just like her missing son, Denise gave her own account of the day she'd never forget. She'd looked for him as she took the rubbish to the end of the driveway. She thought he might have caught the early bus home. She might catch sight of him walking down the road, towards the house.

'I didn't see Daniel or anyone,' she told the prosecutor.

*

Forensic coordinator Inspector Arthur van Panhuis was next. He showed the jury a map of the Glass House Mountains macadamia farm. He pointed out the steep embankment leading down to where Daniel's body had been dumped. The map was marked where search teams had found each of the 17 bone fragments, as well as the Globe shoes.

Justice Atkinson sent the jury home at 4.30 p.m. It had been their first full day of evidence and already they'd seen the raw grief of a mother and father who had lived through a nightmare. Who were still living it.

*

The first of the DNA experts took the stand on day three. Dr Jeremy Austin was a research scientist from the University of Adelaide. His specialty was mitochondrial DNA. Humans have two kinds of DNA — mitochondrial and nuclear. Mitochondrial DNA could only be inherited from the mother. Nuclear could be inherited from both parents, Dr Austin explained. He told the jury he could do a mitochondrial DNA comparison with himself and a sample from his own mother and get a match. He could do the same with his brothers, because they would have inherited the same genetic information from their mother.

'One of the advantages of mitochondrial DNA is it tends to

survive for a much longer time in degraded samples,' he told the court. On 23 August 2011, Dr Austin was given one of the bones found at the Glass House Mountains site — a humerus.

'The mitochondrial DNA profile from the bone sample was a 100 per cent match to Denise Morcombe and to the sons, Dean and Bradley Morcombe,' he said.

Dr Dadna Hartman also ran tests on the humerus. The chief molecular biologist at the Victorian Institute of Forensic Medicine told the court she was an expert in the extraction of mitochondrial DNA. She compared the bone sample with reference samples from Denise and Bradley Morcombe.

'The profiles were identical,' she said.

Queensland Health forensic pathologist Peter Ellis, who'd caused such a media stir when he arrived at the Glass House Mountains site, took the stand just before the lunchtime break. He listed the bones and bone fragments found by the volunteers who'd dug through the dirt. Arm bones. Leg bones. They'd never found the skull. He hadn't had enough information to determine a cause of death. But, in his opinion, the bones had come from a young, growing human, aged 10 to 15.

A string of State Emergency Services volunteers took the stand. The evidence from the scientific experts had been smooth. Relaxed. The volunteers were nervous as they tried their best to recount a day three years earlier when they'd dug up the bush grave of a little boy.

The jury was shown photograph after photograph of Daniel's remains. The day before, they'd seen pictures of his smiling face. A little boy with big, expressive eyes and a smile to match. Now they looked at pictures of bones. Small bones. Long bones. They were black and coated in dirt. They were told some had small scratches on their surface that were probably teeth marks from animals.

'I'm just wondering if I should offer them a five-minute break if we're going to be showing them photo after photo of the bones,' Justice Atkinson said after a while.

She looked at the jury to see how they were faring. One was nodding.

'Yes? I've got one yes.'

Five hours later they trailed out for the day. The little boy who'd once smiled for the camera was now a series of broken, blackened bones.

*

A long line of scientists filed in and out of Court 11. Dr Paul Bennett was a podiatrist who looked at the Globe shoes found at the Glass House Mountains site and compared them with Daniel's school shoes. The wear patterns were consistent, he told the court.

They heard from a botanist and a hydrologist. An environmental officer who'd conducted water sampling. And then the animal experts took the stand.

Denise Morcombe had left the courtroom when pictures of Daniel's bones were flashed across wall-mounted television screens. She left the room again now.

Lee Allen, a zoologist with Biosecurity Queensland, had visited the Glass House Mountains site in September 2011, to provide investigators with advice on animal activity in the area. It was an area he'd expect to find wild dogs, pigs and foxes — although he'd only found tracks from dogs during his inspection. He told the jury wild dogs were certainly capable of making off with human remains.

'Wild dogs could smell a carcass or food like that probably half a kilometre or even further in a forest situation,' he said. 'Normally what you find is the carcass is pulled apart and limbs would be carted off in different directions. Usually what you see with a carcass that has been scattered by wild dogs is the main carcass stays together and limbs and bits and pieces get dragged off. Once a lot of the weight has decayed away they could drag a fair quantity, a fair weight.'

Dr Allen was passionate about his area of expertise. He was simply a scientist describing the feeding behaviour of wild animals. But in front of him, a courtroom of people was imagining the body of a little boy, torn limb from limb by hungry dogs.

There was more of the same from the next witness. Mark Goullet, a pest controller with a company called Ferals Out, had much experience with the Sunshine Coast's wild animal population.

'I was contracted to remove dingoes and other wild dogs right there at the Big Pineapple and across the road at Woombye State School and at a pineapple plantation which is now a development site,' he said. In 2003, when Daniel disappeared, dingoes in the Glass House Mountains would have numbered in their hundreds. 'It didn't really matter what time of the day you drove around a property on the Sunshine Coast ... there were dingoes walking the streets,' he said.

He was sure wild dogs and pigs would be capable of moving off with human bones. He'd even seen birds of prey carrying large bones.

'There's plenty of pigs and plenty of foxes, as there are dingoes, still there at the moment,' he said.

*

The bus passengers told their stories. The little boy in the red t-shirt who'd tried to wave them down. The shady man who'd stood behind. Passing drivers who had seen much the same.

Ross Edmonds, the driver of the Sunbus that had failed to stop, told the court in a quiet voice how he'd been told not to pick up passengers. A second bus, travelling a couple of minutes behind, would do that. He'd seen Daniel as he tried to wave the bus down.

'A young chap in the red shirt and black trousers and another chap sitting up on the side of the bank,' he said.

The court heard from Kevin Fitzgerald, the partner of Brett's drug dealer, Sandra Drummond.

'Sometimes he'd drop in for a cuppa and a chat, other times he'd drop in to score some marijuana,' he said.

Did he remember Brett coming by on the afternoon of 7 December 2003?

'He might of, he might not, but I don't remember it,' Kevin said.

Sandra Drummond was also called to take the stand. Did she recall Brett stopping by with a mulcher in the back?

'No, I don't remember that,' she said.

The court listened as the people who'd seen a blue, box-shaped car took the stand. It had been an older model with faded paintwork. A man and a boy stood beside it.

*

Douglas Jackway, a small stout man who looked as rough as he spoke, gave his evidence via video link on 25 February. He sat in a room not much more than a closet, facing a camera. A large maroon door was behind him. He wore a prison-issue green singlet revealing the large tattoo across his throat. This man was a criminal. There was no mistaking it. The jury knew they were hearing the words of someone not fit for society.

The defence team had wanted him in the courtroom. They'd wanted the jury to see him, in person, this man who was entirely capable of abducting a boy. But Justice Atkinson had not been willing to take the risk. The jury was not allowed to know about Brett's past. It would be disastrous. They, like many of the investigating officers, would take one look at his history and know, without doubt, that this was the man who'd taken Daniel.

Jackway had been in the prison system a long time. He knew Brett's past. Justice Atkinson worried Jackway might blurt it out. She'd be forced to declare a mistrial. So Jackway appeared on television screens around the court. They had set up a kill switch. Justice Atkinson told defence barrister Angus Edwards he was to hit it should he get any sense Jackway was about to shout out what he knew.

Edwards told her he wasn't the only person in the room responsible for pushing that button. She relented. They should all be on alert, she said.

The charismatic barrister faced off against the man on the screen.

'On Sunday, the 7th of December,' he began, 'were you on the Sunshine Coast?'

'No, I was not.'

'Did you abduct Daniel Morcombe?'

'No, I did not.'

'Were you in any way involved in the abduction of Daniel Morcombe?'

'No.'

Edwards began delving into Jackway's criminal past. Then technical issues with the sound began. For a while, the court could hear Jackway, but Jackway could not hear the barrister.

'Fucking hell, mate,' Jackway swore.

They cut the link.

It was an exasperated witness they returned to when the video link was running again. He was losing patience already.

Edwards began what would be a lengthy and detailed list of questions about the abduction and rape of a young boy. He asked Jackway to agree that he'd taken a young boy as he rode his bike with friends. That he'd sped off with the boy in his car. That he'd crashed into the bridge and dragged the boy out, leading him into mangroves. That he'd raped the child, even as the police and the boy's father approached.

'As the people approached, you threatened to cut the boy's throat with a knife,' Edwards put to him. 'You didn't have a knife, did you? And the boy yelled out that you didn't have a knife and you were restrained.'

Edwards told Jackway he'd threatened to kill the boy's family as he was led away. And then he denied that he'd ever touched the boy.

'You never, ever said that you did that. You always said, no, I wasn't responsible. You said, it wasn't me, even when you were caught with him.'

'Yeah, that's right,' Jackway piped up. 'I thought I didn't cause I was all fucking drugged out. I didn't believe I did do it because of the drugs.'

Edwards told him he'd never shown any desire to change his behaviour. He'd refused to participate in the sex offenders course. He'd assaulted another prisoner. Smashed two televisions. He'd made no attempt to rehabilitate at all.

'Do you agree with that?' Edwards pushed.

'No, not really.'

He asked Jackway whether he knew of an inmate named Les McLean. Jackway wouldn't admit to knowing him. He was a prisoner who'd served time at the same facility as Jackway. He'd been taking medication as part of a sex-change procedure. He also went by the names Billy Jo, Bobby Jo and Melissa McNicol. It seemed like a left-field question but it was important. McLean was the link. There was no proof Brett and Jackway had ever crossed paths. But McLean was a friend of Brett's. McLean had been calling Brett's phone as Brett was being arrested. He'd continued to call throughout that afternoon.

It was likely McLean and Jackway had crossed paths in prison. Perhaps, the defence was suggesting, Jackway had abducted and killed Daniel Morcombe. Perhaps he had told McLean about it. And perhaps McLean had told Brett.

Jackway, the barrister said, had been released from prison on 7 November 2003. But just as he was about to be released, he was already bragging of his next crime.

'You told an inmate you would abduct, rape and bury a child and bury the child in an area where the child could not be found,' Edwards said.

Jackway had disagreed with everything the lawyer said. He disagreed with this too. He shifted constantly in his seat, his temper flaring as Edwards continued his interrogation. He got up to leave during one burst of anger, declaring he'd had enough.

'Sit down, Mr Jackway!' Justice Atkinson commanded in her best schoolteacher voice.

And like a scolded child, he took his seat, his eyes down, mumbling an apology.

'Can I just ask a question?' he said at one point. 'Who's on trial here? Am I on trial? What's this got to do with this court case?'

Edwards was unmoved.

'You just focus on the questions and answer them and we'll get through it a lot more quickly, Mr Jackway, all right?'

'How about you go and fuck yourself, you fuckwit?'

Edwards didn't blink. 'All right,' he said. 'Now how about I ask you a question?'

Jackway had asked friends to provide him with an alibi, should police come calling about Daniel Morcombe, Edwards insisted. He'd been driving a blue car. He'd had two $50 notes on him that day — the same amount of cash Daniel was believed to have been carrying.

'I had nothing to do with Daniel Morcombe,' Jackway insisted.

*

Detective Senior Constable Ross Hutton was next to give evidence. Yes, he said, Douglas Jackway had given varying versions of his movements on 7 December. Yes, he said, Les McLean had tried to call Brett twice the day he'd been arrested. He'd sent a text message as well. Yes, the blue car had been a major focus of the investigation.

Whether or not a person had a blue car, Hutton continued, had been a consideration in whether or not they continued to be pursued by police.

*

Angus Edwards made sure the jury knew all about Les McLean. McLean suffered from multiple personality disorder. In 1997, he'd gone to jail for assisting in a suicide. Now he was here in Court 11 as a witness at Brett Cowan's trial for murder.

'Sometimes you're one person and sometimes you're another person?' Edwards said.

McLean agreed.

'And sometimes you can't remember what the other person has done or said?'

McLean agreed with that too. Edwards showed him a photograph of Jackway. McLean might know him as 'Rat', he said. They'd taken heroin together.

McLean agreed he'd seen Jackway once since leaving prison. He knew Brett much better. Brett had visited McLean's parents' home. They'd gone to church together.

Had Brett ever taken McLean to a sand-mining site?

McLean said he didn't remember anything like that.

'I suggest you did go to a demountable building near the Glass House Mountains, do you remember that?' Edwards pressed.

'I don't remember going to any demountable building.'

On 14 September 2006, Edwards continued, Brett had been at McLean's home where they'd discussed Daniel Morcombe's disappearance.

'I do remember Brett coming to me and telling me he'd been interviewed.'

They'd talked about more that day, Edwards said. McLean had had information on the case. Information from the person who'd killed Daniel and hidden his body. McLean had told Brett what he knew.

'No,' McLean said.

'I suggest to you, that you told him it [Daniel's body] was near the demountable building at the sand-mining site?'

'Never.'

He'd told Brett in some detail where Daniel's body lay — down a gully on the sand-mining site, Edwards persisted.

'Never.'

He'd told Brett that Daniel's clothes had been thrown from a bridge into a creek with running water.

'Never.'

He'd told Brett not to tell anyone. McLean was scared of getting beaten up by Jackway.

'Never.'

He'd called Brett when he'd discovered Brett had been arrested, Edwards suggested. He'd called more than once.

'I don't believe I recall ringing several times. I don't recall,' McLean said.

*

There was a collective gasp when the covert officer who'd played Paul 'Fitzy' Fitzsimmons took the stand. The jury had seen him in footage played on the court's television screens. Fitzy had a blond ponytail, loose-fitting jeans. He walked and talked with a surfie swagger. But the man who walked into court was completely different. The real Fitzy looked at home in a detective's suit. He had close-cropped dark hair. He spoke with the clipped professionalism of an experienced police officer.

Journalists in the front row elbowed each other and stared in shock at the man who'd taken the stand, revealing for the first time the elaborate lengths of one of Australia's most sensational undercover operations. He took the jury through the scenarios they'd played out. The brothels. The guns. The diamonds.

'It was a large criminal organisation … and I was, I guess, a mid-level member of that organisation,' Fitzy said.

Brett kept his head down. It was the first time he'd seen the man he'd thought was his best mate since the day he was arrested.

*

'Arnold' was the 115th witness to take the stand. The jury was now into its twelfth day of evidence.

Until now, it had seemed almost plausible, almost possible, that Jackway could be the killer. The blue car. The dodgy alibi. His history of abducting a boy. Bragging to inmates that he was going to kill a child and leave the body where it would never be found.

Perhaps he had bragged to someone else. And perhaps that person had confided in Brett. And then Brett, who'd had so much to lose, confessed, to hold on to his new life. Edwards was charismatic and compelling.

But then the confession video was played to the court. At 12.35 p.m., the television screens in Court 11 came alive with an image of a burly man in a suit. And Brett, lanky in jeans and a leather jacket. Brett was on the couch, his arms hanging loosely over his knees. Hands clasped.

'Yeah, OK. You know ... yeah. I did it,' Brett said. He went through the horrible details like he was recounting a trip to the supermarket. It was entirely convincing.

The jury listened as Brett described the boy he'd killed as 'cute'. Discussed, with matter-of-fact casualness, pulling down the terrified boy's pants.

'He tried to get away,' Brett said, as though it was something unfortunate that had happened. 'I knew if he got away I was fucked. Panicked. No, no, no. This was all at the end. I could've been a lot longer, like, if he, if I didn't panic. I could've been there for an hour doing stuff. It was 10 to 15 minutes and I was back in the car and driving back home.'

*

318

After 16 days of evidence — fewer than expected — the witnesses had all been heard. Justice Atkinson looked down at Brett, still in the same suit he'd worn that first day, and asked him if he wished to give evidence on his own behalf. Would he take the stand?

Edwards got to his feet. His client would like to decline.

*

Michael Byrne QC was first to deliver his closing address. Brett had been drawn in to what he thought was a criminal gang, he said. But at no time was he led to believe it was a violent gang. It was not a gang where murders or killings were carried out for financial gain. It was a world of corrupt police. Of brothels and blood diamonds. Of high-paying drug deals. They'd told him over and over that their outfit was professional. Violence wasn't necessary.

'Do not for one moment think he must have thought ... he had to admit to a homicide to prove himself,' Byrne said. It was incredibly significant that Brett had taken them to the place where Daniel's bones were found. He'd even realised they'd first gone to the wrong bridge, later taking them to the place where they did find Daniel's clothes.

There was no evidence at all, Byrne said, that Brett had been told about Daniel's abduction and murder by someone else. No evidence at all that someone had told him where Daniel's body could be found.

'You might think he could only have known that from his personal involvement in those events because he killed Daniel, he dumped his body and threw away his clothing,' Byrne said. Brett Cowan was finally being honest when he said 'Yeah ... I did it.'

*

Edwards began his closing remarks with an important point. If the prosecution had not proved there was no possibility either

Jackway — or the blue sedan — was involved in Daniel's disappearance, they had to find Brett not guilty.

'The real question in this trial is, who did it? Cowan? Jackway? People in a blue sedan?' the barrister asked. 'Now of course I suggest to you the evidence strongly suggests Jackway and a blue car … because Jackway was driving a blue car. You would not be doing anyone any favours in closing this chapter by convicting the wrong man.'

While there was no direct evidence Jackway and Brett's friend Les McLean had spoken about Daniel's murder, the jury could draw a 'rational, logical inference'.

'Do you think it is all just some bizarre set of coincidences that the man with the blue car, Jackway, disappeared for hours on the day of the abduction? A man with a terrible criminal history for doing something very similar?' he said.

'McLean knew him in prison and you know they were in the same prison together. That McLean was with him when he took heroin after Jackway was released from prison, that McLean repeatedly tried to telephone Cowan on the day of his arrest, that Mr Cowan asked but was denied an opportunity to speak to Mr McLean.' Nobody, he said, had ever come forward to say they'd been the driver of the blue sedan.

Brett, Edwards continued, had been manipulated for months. He'd been slowly drawn in to the gang. He'd been paid money. He'd been promised the world. Their mantra, as they'd told him again and again, was trust, honesty and loyalty. But that wasn't Brett's mantra.

'His mantra was money,' Edwards said. He'd even offered to fake his own death to stay with the gang. He was willing to do anything. 'You might think it would be easier for him to confess to something he didn't do than fake his own death,' Edwards said. 'If you cross a national crime gang, what's going to happen? If you know too much, what's going to happen?'

Brett, he said, stood to make millions working for the crime gang. The big job, about to take place, would see him take home a $100 000 pay packet. It was more money than he'd ever dreamed of making. He'd made friends, too. His new mates had become his family. He'd never fitted in before. It was, as he told Fitzy, the stuff dreams were made of.

'In the end he was a man with nothing who was being offered everything.' Brett, Edwards continued, could never produce or describe Daniel's fob watch because he never saw it. He couldn't claim to be in a blue car because he didn't have one.

'The reason his confession doesn't match the objective facts is because he's not guilty,' he said.

*

Justice Atkinson turned to face the jury. She'd prepared a PowerPoint presentation for her final address.

'You are not to indulge in intuition or guessing,' she told them. 'You must approach your duty dispassionately, deciding the facts upon the whole of the evidence.'

In order to find Brett guilty, they had to be sure of four things — that Daniel Morcombe was dead, that Brett Cowan had caused his death, that the killing was unlawful and that Brett had intended to cause his death or grievous bodily harm.

If they weren't satisfied beyond reasonable doubt of Brett's intent, or unlawful purpose, they could find him guilty of the alternative charge of manslaughter.

It had been a long journey for the men and women of the jury. And for three of them, it was time to go home.

'I want to thank you very much for your careful and close attention during this trial and the dedication with which the three of you have approached your task,' she told the reserve jurors.

'You may feel disappointed. You may feel relieved that you have no further part to play in this trial.'

Then, at 12.13 p.m. on 12 March 2014, six men and six women

walked in single file from Court 11 to decide whether a man had murdered a little boy.

*

Channel Seven's Carly Waters had arrived early to court each day of the five-week trial to secure a seat in the packed courtroom. The feisty blonde had held court in the front row, telling rowdy members of the public to stop talking when it seemed as though they'd forgotten where they were.

'It's not a cinema,' she'd hissed in the peanut-munching man's direction on day one. When the jury filed out, Waters was determined to stay in her seat until they came back. She sat there, with a small group of reporters, for the rest of the day.

Justice Atkinson sent the jury home at 4.30 p.m., telling them to be back for a 9.30 a.m. start the following day. The waiting resumed. Then, after seven and a half hours of deliberation, journalists sitting in the front row got the news everyone had been waiting for.

'We have a decision on Mr Cowan,' the bailiff announced.

The court filled with the detectives who'd worked so hard for so long. Many had spent weeks milling about in the foyer, unable to come in to court until they'd given evidence. Now, suit-clad, they spread across the back row. Bruce and Denise took their seats on the right-hand side, their sons, Bradley and Dean, beside them. The Morcombe family wore red. All eyes were on the jurors as they filed in.

'Have you agreed upon your verdicts?' the judge's associate asked.

'We have.'

'Do you find the accused, Brett Peter Cowan, or Shaddo N-unyah Hunter, guilty or not guilty of murder?'

A tiny pause. A room full of people leaned forward. Journalists on Twitter had fingers poised over iPads.

'Guilty.'

Denise sobbed. 'Yes!' she cried out. The family hugged and cried in each other's arms. Journalists typed furiously. Detectives grinned. It was over.

Brett didn't react at all.

*

Justice Atkinson adjourned for lunch. Court would reconvene at 2.30 p.m. for sentencing submissions. Outside the Queen Elizabeth II Law Courts, a mass of media circled the front entrance. Dozens of cameras lined the pavement in an arc. A scattering of television journalists were providing live, rolling commentary.

Seven's Kay McGrath, a close friend of the Morcombes and a patron of the foundation, had sobbed on air as she'd announced the jury's verdict.

Bruce and Denise shook hands with Michael Byrne QC and his team and thanked the detectives who'd worked on the case. They'd given a special thanks to the undercover team.

At 2.30 p.m., court resumed. The jury had been sent home but eight of the twelve returned to hear the Morcombes read their victim impact statements. But first they listened in horror as Michael Byrne QC read aloud from Brett's history. The time he'd raped a little boy in a toilet block. And the time he'd almost killed a child in a Darwin caravan park. They glared at him, some shaking their heads in disgust.

*

Bruce Morcombe stood up and walked to the witness box. Finally, after so many years without his boy, Bruce was allowed to confront the man who'd taken him away.

'Ten years ago you made a choice that ripped our family apart. Your decision to pull over and abduct Daniel for your own evil pleasure ultimately caused a level of personal pain to each of us that has made it hard to go on.

'Over the years, we have made a pledge to [the] media with determined self-control on the outside while on many occasions, particularly in the first few months, I was physically ill each morning with the unbearable images of what may have happened to my son Daniel.

'Even today I'm haunted by thoughts of how long he was actually held captive and what unspeakable things you did to him in those sheds at the end of Kings Road at Beerwah. Why was he really dumped without clothes? Why was his belt loose and not still looped through his pants? It makes me nauseous thinking about your total lack of respect for a child's life.

'Listening to you describe and watching a smirk grow on your face, how you threw Daniel's lifeless body down an embankment and a week later you returned and crushed his skull with a shovel — "Chop, chop, chop, chop, chop," you coldly explained in an emotionless, matter-of-fact way.

'We now have to live out our days with the unimaginable images of wild dogs devouring our much loved son's remains. Daniel did not deserve that. He was a great kid and would not hurt a fly. You have robbed him of 70 years of life. Our family's sleepless first night without Daniel on the 7th of December, 2003, haunts me even today. That feeling of helplessness and unimaginable pain never leaves you. The next day I recall picking up Dean after work on the afternoon on Monday the 8th of December. He asked me, "Have they found Daniel?" These are four small words that torture me even today because I had to answer no.

'I listen to Denise's broken sleep punctuated by frequent night-mares, and look into the face of my younger twin boy who has lost his soulmate, are all the images often relived which have had a profound effect on how I function. Nothing about my life today resembles how we enjoyed life as a family before that day. Our friends from 2003 are different because we are no longer the same people. We can be short-tempered and have a streak of bitterness and carry anger caused by your deliberate, selfish actions.

'We were forced to move away from our unique garden paradise, the much-loved family home. We were running a successful small business and were forced to sell it. We could not return to regular employment because we were constantly distracted with disturbing thoughts. We were forced to sell all our hard-earned investments just to survive. But survive we did, because you made one monumental mistake that day. You picked on the wrong family. Our collective determination to find Daniel and expose a child-killer was always going to win.

'Perhaps the greatest impact that your heinous crime has had on me has been witness to the impact it has had on the other people that I love. You have caused immeasurable mental stress and anxiety to not only me but to Daniel's mother, Denise, Daniel's brother Dean and Daniel's twin, Bradley ...

'A cunning plan by police and your greed has brought you undone. You have been exposed as an opportunistic, perverted, cold-blooded, child-killing pedophile. Central to the facts are not whodunnit but youdunnit and may Daniel's soul rest in peace.'

*

Denise Morcombe could not bring herself to read her statement aloud. It had been difficult listening to Bruce voice their nightmare to the man who'd brought it to them. Brett had sat unmoving, his head down, as Bruce had rained down years of grief and torment. Predator. Pervert. Revolting. Michael Byrne took his copy of Denise's victim impact statement and announced he would read it for her.

'The first second after Daniel was born eight weeks premature I knew he was special. His big eyes stared at me and we bonded immediately. Nobody will ever know the love I felt for Daniel. At 4 p.m. Sunday, 7 December 2003, while getting Daniel's clothes off the line, I knew something was wrong. Daniel wasn't due to return to the bus stop until 5.30 but for some unknown reason I was anxious. Hence I went to see if he was there at 4.30.

'I don't know what it was but I knew that when Bruce returned home soon after 5.30 from the bus stop without him, I knew I would never see him again. I have made a vow to Daniel I would find out where he is and that justice will be done. For years I haven't slept more than three hours at a time. I have lived and breathed each day to find the answers. I have bad nightmares every couple of weeks, screaming at night, "No, no I won't go with you".

'I see my son lying by himself in that dark eerie bushland being destroyed by wild animals. You, Mr Cowan, left him there. You have no respect for a human life. He was an innocent boy, starting to grow up and learning about life. He was gentle, he loved animals and wanted to be a vet. He would never hurt a soul. He was scared of the dark and often slept on the floor next to me.

'Mr Cowan, only you know how petrified he was as you drove down Kings Road with him but I can only imagine. Mr Cowan, only you know Daniel's last look in his eyes as you choked him to death but I can only imagine.

'My life is not the same as 10 years ago. A different house, a different job, different friends. My family has also been destroyed. Not only has your deliberate calculated actions affected me, Bruce, Dean and Bradley, but it has destroyed my parents, my brothers and extended family.

'Gone are happy family functions we all enjoyed, you took that away from us. We all know one person is not there and we will never recover from that.

'Mr Cowan, I saw you smiling with your son Peter and former wife in a photo taken on Boxing Day 2003. You had a smirk like nothing had happened. A happy family snap. Meanwhile, my family was living in hell searching for our son who you knew was dead. I hope you have a life of loneliness and unloved for your entire life.

'I hope you are never released as you have no remorse for any of your past horrific crimes against innocent children. This day hasn't brought closure but the streets are safer without you walking them, and looking for your next target to destroy ...

'I hope your jail time is difficult and you are never released. For me, I have a purpose. As thanks to all who have searched for Daniel I wish to explain his tragic story. I will continue my work with the Daniel Morcombe Foundation teaching children to be aware of people like you. By doing this, I hope there will never be another child who goes through what Daniel did from a sexual freak like you.

'I have accepted I will never see Daniel again and I have no control over what your sentence is. But if there is a God and he knows the love that a mother has for her son, you will pay for your actions, you will pay big.'

*

Dean crossed the court to stand in the witness box, his statement in his hands. Daniel's brothers had rarely spoken publicly. Bruce and Denise had always shouldered that burden.

'Brett Cowan, what you did on December 7, 2003, has impacted hundreds of people. Daniel was my brother and you have robbed him of a life he would have loved to have lived, robbed Bradley of a twin and lifelong best friend, robbed my parents of a son they loved, robbed us of being a normal family ever again ...

'Not finding a body for all those years definitely took its toll on me. Simply throwing him off an embankment, dragging him along the ground, leaving him unburied, naked then going back to chop up his skull with a shovel — these are the acts of a psychopath who cannot be rehabilitated. I'm glad you have been exposed for the murdering, sexual predator that you are.

'Rest in peace, Daniel.'

*

Michael Byrne rose to his feet again. He would also be reading the statement prepared by Daniel's twin, Bradley.

'In December 2003, Daniel and I had just finished Grade 9. We shared hobbies and interests and a bond that was special, a bond only twins can experience.

'Twelve days after you abducted and murdered my brother, it was our fourteenth birthday. Teenage birthdays are supposed to be something you look forward to. This was not a fun day, it was torture. Another week would pass and that was Christmas Day — another painful day for me and all of the family. Daniel and I also had a trip to Melbourne booked in January to visit our grandparents. I ended up flying down alone.

'Time after time, day after day, special event after special event, none would ever be the same again. Ten years have passed and milestones are never celebrated like they should have been. My eighteenth and twenty-first birthdays have come and gone without a double celebration. That hurts me.

'I lost my way academically. My grades suffered and I lacked concentration at school. This caused me to not return after Grade 11. I could no longer handle the attention of being Daniel's brother at school, at home and anywhere I went. I have become very withdrawn.

'I had ambitions of going on to university and becoming a pilot but all these dreams fell apart. I am not the person I could have been. I am consistently angry and battle mood swings. But life goes on. Thanks to family support, I have held a steady job since I left school. I am getting married in August of this year. I have, with my fiancée, purchased a home. But it never leaves you. Brett Cowan, your selfish actions have hurt me in ways no one can imagine.'

It had been an emotional day. Justice Atkinson told the court she would sentence Brett the following morning. To the Morcombes, she passed on her deepest respects.

'Your strength and the way you've conducted yourselves has been one of the main factors that's brought us to the outcome we have today,' she said. 'The police — your determination to bring this investigation to conclusion and to ensure there was evidence that Cowan could properly be convicted is to be commended. It sends a message not just to Cowan, but to anyone who conducts a terrible crime and thinks they are smart enough to get away with it that you won't. And [that] you will use whatever you have available to make sure that person is brought to trial.

'The covert police officers ... they are truly amazing. The officer who played the crime boss particularly and the men known as Paul Fitzsimmons and Joseph Emery. They were required to perform their role week in, week out, day and month out. They did and they performed it extremely well. We all owe them a great deal of gratitude in the way they conducted themselves.'

She praised the State Emergency Services volunteers — members of the community from all walks of life who'd dug in the dirt until they found Daniel. It was thanks to them that the Morcombes had been able to bury their son.

'For the defence team, this is a difficult job, defending someone who the community has a right to hate and has the right to regard his offences as the gravest and most horrible offences that can be committed. So it takes a lot of courage and perseverance to appear for such a man and you all did extremely well.'

Outside, jurors were waiting to hug Bruce and Denise.

CHAPTER FORTY
LIFE FOR A LIFE

JUSTICE ATKINSON HAD NOT wanted to begin without the Morcombes. The court was packed. Detectives and journalists who'd been unable to get a seat crammed into the doorway. She asked the detectives if they'd heard from Daniel's family. Everyone looked at each other. Detective Senior Constable Ross Hutton grabbed his phone and walked outside to call them.

They wouldn't be coming, he told the judge. They wouldn't waste a minute longer on Brett Cowan. Justice Atkinson nodded and turned to her notes.

'Brett Peter Cowan, also known as Shaddo N-unyah Hunter, stand up,' she ordered. 'You have been convicted by the jury on one count of murder, one count of indecent treatment of a child under 16 and one count of interfering with a corpse. Circumstances of your offending were described by you in chilling detail to undercover police. On your account, which the jury accepted as true and accurate, as do I, you saw Daniel Morcombe standing and waiting for a bus under the Kiel Mountain Road overpass. You knew, but he did not, that the bus he was waiting for had broken down.

'You saw an opportunity. You got out of your car, you stood behind him. You waited. You were, in your own words, an opportunistic offender. You were waiting for an opportunity. When the bus went past him, it had been arranged that another bus following afterwards would pick him up. He did not know that. He wondered what he would do.

'You offered a plausible story. You'd been waiting, you said, for a friend. You would now have to drive to Maroochydore to pick up your friend, would he like a lift? You didn't look like a monster. You didn't look like a pedophile. You looked like a normal person. You persuaded him that that would be the safe thing for him to do. He walked with you to your car and he got in your car ...

'This is not just a murder but a terrible murder. It has had widespread and shocking impacts. And of course primarily on his family — his parents and of course his two brothers, particularly his twin brother.

'But you gave no thought to them and it's not apparent to me that you've ever given a thought ... to them. I've seen no evidence in the months that you've been in this court and in the times where I've heard you talk about this offence, that you ever felt any remorse for what you did apart from feeling sorry for yourself, that you might get caught.

'And of course it's had an impact on the wider community. The kidnapping and abducting of a child, the abduction of a child in broad daylight, by a stranger, is very unusual. And for that we can all be extremely grateful.

'The fear of the stranger drives fear into the hearts of everyone in our community that vulnerable children might be taken by people like you and dealt with in this way. And the reaction to this case over the many years since it happened has shown the fear and revulsion caused to ordinary members of the community by your behaviour. So these are chilling and disgraceful crimes.

'You are a convincing and adaptable liar and you're prepared to lie in order to advantage yourself. Whenever anyone is considering the prospect of granting you parole, many years in the future, they should mark my words that you are a convincing, forceful and adaptable liar and prepared to lie to advance your own interests. Any profession of being rehabilitated by you will have to be seen in that light.

'I have had before me, in the sentencing hearing, the victim impact statements from various members of the Morcombe family whose statements were moderate, dignified but expressed the deep pain that your actions have imposed upon their lives. A pain that can never go away.

'You have tragically and pointlessly snuffed out a young life. It is Daniel Morcombe of course who is the victim of this offence, in circumstances where he would have felt a great fear.

'Another insight into your personality comes from your demeanour after you told what you did. As I said in the pre-trial hearing, you appeared very happy with yourself and unconcerned about the enormity of the crime to which you had just confessed. Indeed, you expressed your confidence about not being prosecuted because you couldn't be pinned for it. Of course you thought you were very smart but you weren't as smart as the police ... and while you were saying that, you were being tape-recorded and video-recorded ... which just shows you were not quite as smart as you thought you were.

'I am able to set a non-parole period for an eligibility date longer than 15 years which is the statutory minimum. In view of your criminal history, and the enormity of crimes you have committed, it is appropriate in my opinion to set parole eligibility date after you have served 20 years of your sentence. But let me make it clear, that does not mean that I am of the view that you should be released in 20 years' time. That is not under my control; that's a matter for the parole authorities.

'But as I've said, they should take into account that you are a plausible and opportunistic liar before they consider any view you might have about whether you've been rehabilitated.'

In other words, Justice Atkinson had sentenced Brett to life in prison. In 20 years, he would be eligible to apply for parole. The parole board, while considering whether Brett should be released, would be handed a copy of Justice Atkinson's sentencing remarks. They'd see her warning.

Brett was a liar. He could not be rehabilitated. Don't let him convince you otherwise.

EPILOGUE
DANIEL'S LEGACY

ON 21 MARCH 2015, more than 600 people gathered in a room full of red in Brisbane's iconic City Hall. The women wore red dresses; the men, red ties. They sat around tables draped in red velvet and decorated with the specially created Daniel Morcombe red rose. Red lights shone from the building's glass dome.

It was the tenth Dance for Daniel — a fundraising event put on by Bruce and Denise each year to promote their foundation and keep up the fight to protect vulnerable children. It was Daniel's legacy. Bruce and Denise would spend their whole lives trying to prevent other children suffering the fate of their beautiful boy. They'd spend every day ensuring he wasn't forgotten.

Community leaders, politicians and senior police sat among the crowd of diners. The now retired police commissioner Bob Atkinson was there. So was Assistant Commissioner Mike Condon and the current Police Commissioner Ian Stewart. The evening was hosted by respected journalist and television identity Andrew Denton. The Queensland Police band would play for the tenth year running.

Entrees were served as Prime Minister Tony Abbott took the stage. 'It is great to be here to support one of the most important causes of all — keeping our children safe,' he said.

'Now, I have to say as a parent myself that the loss of a child is every parent's worst nightmare. I think all of us owe an enormous debt to Bruce and Denise Morcombe. They could have nursed their grief. They could have retreated once more into private life. But they confronted the most awful tragedy any parent could face and turned this into a chance to help all children find a safer world — and in so doing, they have ensured Daniel has not died in vain.

'For 10 years now, the Daniel Morcombe Foundation has been working to keep our children safe. And schoolchildren across our country now have access to resources, to materials, to techniques to keep them safe in the face of the potential hazards that too many of our children face ...

'But I want to pay tribute above all else to Bruce and Denise Morcombe. Nothing much happens unless someone makes it so — and Bruce and Denise Morcombe have dedicated a decade of their life to keeping children safe. It is a wonderful cause. They are wonderful Australians and we all are in their debt.'

It had only been a few short weeks since Labor's Annastacia Palaszczuk was sworn in as the new premier of Queensland, her party beating the Liberal National Party in a historic victory. That evening at the Dance for Daniel she pledged her government's commitment to protecting Queensland children.

'My government wants to make sure that our children are safe and also that this state is a safe place to raise our children,' she told the audience. 'For a decade, that's exactly what Denise and Bruce have been doing — dedicating themselves to the safety of young Queenslanders, more recently to children right across Australia.

'Four years ago, Denise and Bruce were appointed as Queensland child safety ambassadors. In that role, the Morcombes have delivered their important child safety message to tens of thousands of students, parents and educators. They really mean it when they say no school is too small or too far away ... they have presented at 340 schools, from small schools in rural and remote communities to large regional metropolitan schools. Daniel's legacy now reaches well beyond his home state of Queensland ...

'Your strength and courage have inspired a nation. I hope that what you are achieving gives you some joy to add to the memories you have of your beautiful boy.'

They replicated the set of Andrew Denton's show *Enough Rope* on stage, couches arranged so Bruce and Denise were facing their interviewer. It was one of thousands of occasions when they'd answer questions publicly about their murdered son.

Bruce had used the night to announce Daniel's story would be made into a feature film. *Where is Daniel?* was already in pre-production. He talked about the early days when they'd first started speaking to schoolchildren about keeping safe.

'We just learned as we went along,' he told Denton. 'And certainly, those early [school presentations], we were putting ourselves, putting the children, in Daniel's position at the side of the road. Why was he vulnerable? Where can we improve to make sure another child in his circumstances can be safe? And the very simple things were, where possible, don't travel alone. Tell somebody where you're going, what time you're going to be home — those really simple core messages that have been around a long time.

'But it's only when you link those safety messages — and there's a dozen others — back to Daniel's very real story... because too often the kids think bad stuff only happens on the news, it happens on the other side of the world, it will never happen to me. We quickly say, well, Daniel probably thought exactly like you're thinking right now...

'Please listen to these messages, grab hold of these skills because they may well hold you in good stead some time down the track.

'[With] the advent of iPhones and iPads ... the world [is] potentially a more dangerous place because predators all lurk online. And that's a really dangerous place these days.'

*

Nobody visits Brett Cowan but his lawyers. They go to him at Wolston Correctional Centre, where he spends his days in protective custody, to discuss his appeal. When that is over, even those visits will stop.

It is a lonely existence for a man who was convinced he was

about to embark on a new life of parties, mates and money. A man who'd shopped for a new car and a jetski. Who'd planned for cruises and real estate and boats.

After a jury found Brett guilty of Daniel's murder, newspapers and television stations revelled in every detail of his criminal background. His past victims told of lives ruined. They sobbed on television as they talked about the man who'd raped them and left them broken.

Peter and Marlene Cowan had always stuck by their son.

'Brett knew that Peter and I would always support him and try to get him back on the straight and narrow,' Marlene told the police in 2011. 'He is my son and I will always love him.'

They had stuck by him for so long. They'd found him a home after he was released from prison after raping the boy in Darwin. They'd bought him a car. They'd given him $5000 to start a new life in Perth. They'd sent him clothing and called him regularly.

They went to visit him just once after he was convicted of murder. The revelations in the media had told them the truth their son had glossed over. They saw him that once — and then they didn't come back. For Brett, it was a sad realisation. His mother and father had been the only ones to stand by him, no matter what. And now he'd lost even them.

When Queensland correctional facilities banned smoking in prisons in 2014, Brett posted his remaining cigarettes to his lawyers. He didn't want them to go to waste and his legal team were the only ones still speaking to him.

His lawyers believe he will live out the rest of his days in protective custody. There is a 'bash on sight' order among inmates for anyone able to access Queensland's most hated prisoner. Anyone who fails to do so faces a beating themselves. There are few, if any, who would feel sorry for him.

Denise Morcombe's words are coming true.

'I hope,' she said in her victim impact statement, 'you have a life of loneliness, unloved for your entire life.'

List of Covert Operatives

DOZENS OF COVERT OPERATIVES from Queensland, Western Australia and Victoria worked together to form a fake organised crime gang with the oft-repeated mantra 'trust, loyalty, respect'. Together they convinced Brett he was part of a glitzy, underground world of prostitutes, paid police and protection money. Below are the operatives and the roles they played.

Joe Emery — The first operative to make contact with Brett. Joe sat next to him on the plane back to Perth after Brett testified at the inquest in Queensland. Introduced Brett to the criminal organisation.

Jeff — The crime gang's West Australian boss. Gang members would hand in protection money to Jeff after each job.

Paul 'Fitzy' Fitzsimmons — A West Australian lieutenant, answering to Jeff. Fitzy played a major role in befriending Brett and gaining his trust.

Cassie — A Perth brothel madam who they often visited to collect a portion of her takings.

Dean — A gambling addict who borrowed money from the gang.

Brooke — A prostitute who was working on the side and had to be reeled in by the gang.

Jake — One of Brooke's customers.

Carlos — An illegal crayfish diver.

Eddie — An Asian restaurant owner with Chinatown connections.

Henry — A corrupt immigration official able to obtain fake passports.

Dave — A crooked bank manager.

Con — A fruiterer with a gambling habit.

Kristen — Cassie's 'stand in' madam.

Bayden — A customs officer who gave the gang access to a warehouse so they could steal cigarettes.

Jason — A driver and member of Fitzy's crew.

Dougie — A Harley-riding member of an outlaw motorcycle gang.

Doug — A Perth-based gun supplier.

Unnamed court official — A court staffer who was 'pretty high up but not a judge'.

Ali — A bank employee from Albany who helped the gang get fraudulent credit cards.

Simon — A corrupt and paranoid port manager from Albany.

Ronnie — The crime gang's Victorian lieutenant, equal in rank to Fitzy.

Kostya — Con's Victorian equivalent. A fruiterer who paid the gang protection money.

Kim — A Victorian prostitute who handed over earnings and protection money.

Kaz — A Victorian prostitute who handed over earnings and protection money.

Robbo — A Crown Casino gaming manager who is able to 'clean' money.

Arnold — The crime gang's national boss. Arnold was used to pressure Brett into confessing.

Victor — Arnold's Melbourne-based bodyguard.

Gary — A corrupt Melbourne-based detective who conducted background checks and brought information to Arnold.

Tom — A Melbourne-based diamond dealer.

Craig — A corrupt West Australian police officer who delivered information to the gang. He discovered a subpoena from the coroner's court was about to be served on Brett.

Baz — An SAS soldier who acquired guns for the gang.

LIST OF COVERT OPERATIVES

Adam — Arnold's Western Australia-based bodyguard.
Chrissy — Arnold's 'lady friend'.
Ian — The 'fixer' or 'cleaner' sent with Brett to the place where
    he'd left Daniel Morcombe's body.

Acknowledgements

There are many people who selflessly gave their time, efforts and energy to help me tell this story. My thanks firstly go to those who have asked not to be named. Thank you for your insights and passion. I am grateful for the endless support from my employers and colleagues at the *Courier-Mail* and the *Sunday Mail*, particularly David Murray, whose encouragement and advice were invaluable. Thanks to Michael Bosscher and Tim Meehan for the legal expertise. You have a difficult and thankless job that few understand. Thanks also to the team at Echo Publishing and The Five Mile Press. This was my first book and your help along the way was greatly appreciated. And finally, to my friends, family and especially my partner, Dan, who steered me firmly back in the direction of my computer when I'd decided I couldn't possibly write another word.

Immersing yourself in the world of a sadistic pedophile is not easy. It's difficult to accept what some people are capable of. It's hard to imagine what it must have been like for the covert team who spent hour after hour, day after day, in Brett Cowan's company, weaving their delicate trap. I hope this book goes some way in recognising the important work they did.

Bruce and Denise Morcombe have dedicated their lives to arming children against such predators. Their work is equally important. If you would like to donate to the Daniel Morcombe Foundation, more information can be found at www.danielmorcombe.com.au.